L.B. FOOTE   PHOTOGRAPHER
WPG.

TAKING A BIRDS-EYE VIEW OF THE CITY

HOISTED ON A DERRICK FROM THE TOP OF McARTHUR BLDG. PORTAGE AVE.

AN ELEVATION OF 278 FEET.

The History of Canadian Cities

WINNIPEG
An Illustrated History

Alan Artibise

19768

James Lorimer & Company, Publishers
and
National Museum of Man,
National Museums of Canada

Toronto 1977

ISBN 0-88862-150-7 cloth
      0-88862-151-5 paper

Design: Don Fernley

Cartography: Geoffrey J. Matthews

Printed and bound in Canada

Canadian Cataloguing in Publication Data

Artibise, Alan F.J., 1946-
  Winnipeg

(The History of Canadian cities)
ISBN 0-88862-150-7 bd.   ISBN 0-88862-151-5 pa.

1. Winnipeg, Man. — History.   I. National Museum of
Man.   II. Title.   III. Series.

FC3396.4.A78   971.27'4   C77-001529-8
F1064.5.W7A78

James Lorimer & Company, Publishers
35 Britain Street
Toronto

Credits

Manitoba Archives: 10, 15, 19, 21, 31, 33, 35, 37, 39, 48, 53, 60, 61, 67, 71, 72, 73, 77, 79, 81, 101, 107, 117, 121, 124, 125, 127, 140, 141, 145, 149, 150, 151, 160, 162, 164, 165, 168, 171, 183, 187, 189, 191, 195

L.B. Foote Collection, Manitoba Archives: 41, 45, 49, 51, 59, 63, 69, 83, 85, 89, 90, 91, 92, 93, 94, 95, 96, 97, 103, 108, 112, 113, 115, 118, 119, 120, 123, 129, 131, 132, 134, 135, 136, 147, 153, 154, 155, 157, 159, 161, 167

Manitoba Government Photograph: 196

Public Archives of Canada: 3, 25, 27, 47, 65, 82, 137, 138

The United Church of Canada Archives: 43

Table of Contents

List of Maps   6

List of Tables   6

Foreword: The History of Canadian Cities Series   7

Acknowledgements   8

Introduction: The Origins and Incorporation of Winnipeg   11

Chapter One: The Formative and Boom Years, 1874-1913   23

Chapter Two: Crisis and Decline, 1914-1945   109

Chapter Three: Transformation and Challenge, 1946-1970   163

Appendix: Statistical Tables   199

Notes   208

Suggestions for Further Reading   216

Index   220

List of Maps

1 Red River Settlement in 1836

2 Winnipeg in 1872

3 Winnipeg in 1875

4 Boundary Extensions 1873-1913

5 Winnipeg in 1907

6 Ward Boundaries 1882-1919

7 Winnipeg in 1913

8 Ward Boundaries 1920-1971

9 Boundary Extensions 1914-1963

10 Winnipeg's Geographic Position

11 Land Use in Winnipeg 1955

12 Metropolitan Winnipeg 1963

13 Land Use and Spatial Growth 1966

14 Unicity 1972

Appendix
List of Tables

I The Growth of Manufacturing in Winnipeg, 1881-1971

II Number of Males Per 1,000 Females in Winnipeg, 1881-1971

III Urban Population Growth and Distribution in Manitoba, 1871-1971

IV Population Growth in Major Western Cities, 1901-1971

V Population Growth in Winnipeg, 1871-1971

VI Birthplace of Winnipeg's Canadian-Born Population, 1881-1961

VII Birthplace of Winnipeg's Foreign-Born Population, 1881-1971

VIII Ethnic Origins of Winnipeg's Population, 1881-1971

IX Major Religious Affiliations of Winnipeg's Population, 1881-1971

X Age Composition of Winnipeg's Population, 1886-1971

XI Population Growth in Winnipeg and Suburbs, 1901-1971

XII Value of Building Permits Issued in Winnipeg, 1900-1970

XIII The Labour Force of Winnipeg by Industry, 1881-1961

XIV Ethnic Origins of the Metropolitan Winnipeg Population,1901-1971

XV Class Politics in Winnipeg: Citizens' Groups

Foreword
The History of Canadian Cities Series

The History of Canadian Cities Series is a project of the History Division, National Museum of Man (National Museums of Canada). The project was begun in response to a continuing demand for more popular publications to complement the already well-established scholarly publication programs of the Museum. The purpose of this series is to offer the general public in Canada a stimulating insight into the country's urban past. Over the next several years, the Museum plans to publish a number of individual volumes dealing with such varied communities as Montreal and Vancouver, Chicoutimi and Saskatoon, Toronto and Saint John.

It is the hope of the National Museum of Man that the publication of these books will provide the public with information on Canadian cities in an attractive, stimulating and readable form. At the same time, the plan of the series is to have authors follow a standard format and the result, it is anticipated, will be a systematic, interpretative, and comprehensive account of the urban experience in many Canadian cities. Eventually, as new volumes are completed, *The History of Canadian Cities Series* will be a major step along the path to a general and comparative history of Canadian cities.

The form chosen for this series — the individual urban biography — is based on the assumption that a community's life has meaning not discernible by a study of fragmentary portions only; that the totality of the urban experience is usually not present in thematic studies. Since the distinguishing feature of a good urban biography is the attempt to see the community as a whole and to relate the parts to a larger context, it was felt that the study of individual cities was at this time the best approach to an understanding of the Canadian urban experience.

In this volume, Alan F.J. Artibise tells the story of the evolution of the City of Winnipeg from a tiny settlement in 1812 to a major Canadian metropolis in 1970. Dr. Artibise is an Associate Professor at the University of Victoria. He was educated in Winnipeg at the University of Manitoba, where he received his B.A. in 1967. He did his graduate work at the University of British Columbia, completing his Ph.D. in 1972. Since then he has taught at Cariboo College in Kamloops, B.C., and has worked for the National Museum of Man as Western Canadian Historian. He is the author of two books and numerous articles on Winnipeg's history.

Alan F.J. Artibise
D. A. Muise
General Editors

Acknowledgements

In the course of my work on the history of Winnipeg I have incurred vast debts to many individuals and institutions. I received the time and the resources necessary for research and writing from the Canada Council, the National Museum of Man, and the University of Victoria. I also received considerable assistance from the friendly and helpful staff of the City Clerk's Office, City of Winnipeg, and from the librarians and archivists of the Provincial Library and Archives of Manitoba and the Public Archives of Canada.

For many stylistic and substantive suggestions on an earlier draft of this study I wish to thank three friends and fellow historians: J.M.S. Careless of the University of Toronto, J.E. Rea of the University of Manitoba, and G.A. Stelter of the University of Guelph. Ann Cowan, James Lorimer, John Deverell and Anne McKee also read the manuscript at various stages in its production and gave me helpful commentaries. I am grateful as well to June Belton of the University of Victoria whose secretarial skills and patience made this project, particularly in its later stages, more enjoyable than it might otherwise have been.

I must also acknowledge my debt to Hugh Kennedy of the Planning Division of the City of Winnipeg and to Hans Hossé of the University of Western Ontario from whose work several of the maps included in this volume were drawn.

Portions of this study, in quite different form, have appeared in other books and periodicals. I must first thank McGill-Queen's University Press for permission to use material which originally appeared in my book *Winnipeg: A Social History of Urban Growth, 1874-1914*. I must also thank the editors of the following journals for use of portions of articles published previously: Canadian Historical Association, *Historical Papers 1972*; Historical and Scientific Society of Manitoba, *Transactions*; *Histoire sociale/Social History*; *Manitoba Pageant*; and *Prairie Forum*.

The most valuable of a writer's materials is uninterrupted time in which to work, and I am grateful beyond measure to my wife, Irene, and my son, Henri Yuri, for their gifts of time and their cheerful protection of it against incursions.

Finally, I must add the caveat that while everyone mentioned above made the task of researching and writing this book easier and is partly responsible for whatever merit it may possess, none of them bears any responsibility for the book's shortcomings.

Alan F. J. Artibise
University of Victoria
July, 1977

For Irene and Henri Yuri

The steamship Dakota is shown here located at the Hudson's Bay Company post of Upper Fort Garry (May 1873). The Dakota later became famous as the ship which carried the first railway locomotive to Winnipeg in 1877.

Introduction
The Origins and Incorporation of Winnipeg

The most important event of [1862] was the actual beginning of the village of Winnipeg. Just where the fur-runners' trail coming down the Assiniboine to Fort Garry crossed the trail running down the Red River — in present-day Winnipeg the corner of Main Street and Portage Avenue — Henry McKenney, a half-brother and partner of Dr. Schultz, built a store. With much amusement and even with jeers, the people from the Fort and the settlers from Point Douglas and points farther down the Red watched this building go up. It was much too far from the river, they said, and in the spring the land was so low, it was nothing but a swamp. Further cause for ridicule was found in the shape of the building, which being long and high — a second storey was to serve as a stopping place — had to be shored up with timbers against the prairie winds. Noah's Ark was the name given to it, and it was predicted that its owner would have need for the boat which usually accompanied the toy ark of the day. But Henry McKenney had caught his own glimpse of the future and was not to be laughed out of his plans. Before long he was followed by others and the first land boom of Winnipeg was on.

M. McWilliams,
Manitoba Milestones, 1928

The origins of the first permanent, agricultural settlement in Manitoba were not strictly connected with the fur trade. Indeed, the fur traders of the Northwest would undoubtedly have been content if no settlers had ever decided to found a permanent colony in their domain. And, for nearly half a century, this outlook on the part of both the North West Company and the Hudson's Bay Company seriously hindered the growth of a settled community in the Northwest. Yet, ironically, it was the fur trade — or rather the economic prosperity it engendered — that was to give birth to a city on the banks of the Red and Assiniboine Rivers.[1]

Between 1610 — when the area that was to become Manitoba was first reached by sea by Henry Hudson — and 1812, the future province remained the exclusive domain of the fur trader and Indian. The first indication that this would not forever continue to be the destiny of the Northwest came in 1811. Lord Selkirk, a philanthropist who had already tried to plant colonies of distressed Highland crofters and Irish cotters in Prince Edward Island and Upper Canada, acquired from the Hudson's Bay Company title to some 120,000 square miles of land along the Red River. The following year his newly chosen Governor of "Assiniboia," Miles Macdonnell, selected as the best location for a new colony Point Douglas, a mile below the Northwest fur trading post of Fort Gilbraltar at the confluence of the Red and Assiniboine Rivers. And, in September 1812, Macdonnell and thirty-six Scottish and Irish labourers set to work to found a new settlement.

In the days when the only highways through miles of wilderness were the waterways, the site chosen for the colony was a logical one, situated as it was at the intersection of two major river arteries. One, the Assiniboine, flows east some three hundred miles from central Saskatchewan. The other, the Red River, starts its journey in the United States and flows north to empty into an inland sea, the mighty Lake Winnipeg. And it was here where the turbid waters of the two rivers meet that the Red River Colony had its beginnings.

The terrible cold of winter, the recurring floods in the spring, pitiful inexperience, and the hostility of the North West Company agents in the area combined to make the early years of the colony trying ones. The company seemed determined to destroy the settlement which stood across its east-west lines of communication. Relations between the Selkirk colonists and the North West Company were strained and culminated in a sudden and deadly burst of passion at Seven Oaks on June 19, 1816. A group of seventy armed and mounted North West Company servants, some of them Métis, clashed with twenty-eight Selkirk colonists in what became known as the Seven Oaks Massacre. As a result, twenty-two men were killed, only one of them from the North West Company side. What was most tragic, however, was the butchering of the bodies of the wounded and dead following the skirmish. The leaders of the North West Company contingent, Cuthbert Grant and Peter Prangman, were unable to restrain their men. The dead were stripped of clothing, many of them were disembowelled and scalped, and several skulls were smashed with rifle butts. The mutilated corpses were then left on the plain where wolves preyed on them.[2]

The violent struggle between the Hudson's Bay Company and the North West Company finally came to an end in 1821 when the British and Canadian fur companies united. But even with this major problem removed, it was painfully evident in the years after 1821 that the colonists' attempt at agriculture in the midst of a vast wilderness — unbroken, undrained, and uncontrolled — was at best a gamble. The fact was that between 1812 and 1849 the colony remained largely dependent on the buffalo hunt for its major supply of food. Moreover, the provisions of the hunt were traded to the Hudson's Bay Company and it was only this exchange of goods that enabled the colony to survive these difficult years.

The Red River settlement was a far more pleasant place after 1821 than it had been before the union. In 1822, ten years after the first Selkirk settlers arrived, the crops were good enough to provide food for all. Then, just as the colony seemed to be thriving, natural disaster struck. The great flood of 1826 was neither the first nor the last that occurred at the confluence of the Red and Assiniboine Riv-

ers. It was preceded by other floods in 1776, 1790, 1809, and 1815 and would be succeeded by still others in 1852, 1882, 1892, 1904, 1916, 1948, and 1950. But the 1826 inundation was one of the worst ever recorded. On May 2, 1826, the Red River rose nine feet. By May 7, there was a lake three miles across where the city of Winnipeg now stands.[3] One witness to the events in May 1826 gave this account:

> Terror was depicted on every countenance; so level was the country and so rapid the rise of the water, that on the 5th [of May] all the settlers abandoned their homes and sought refuge on higher ground. Every description of property became a secondary consideration, and was involved in one common wreck, or abandoned in despair. The people fled from their homes for dear life, some of them saving only their clothes on their backs. The shrieks of children, lowing of cattle, and the howling of dogs added terror to the scene. . . . Hardly a house or building of any kind was left standing in the colony. Many of the buildings drifted along whole and entire, and in some dogs were howling dismally, cats jumping frantically from side to side; but the most singular spectacle was a house in flames, drifting along in the night, one half immersed in water, the remainder burning furiously. . . . During this heavy trial only one man lost his life, but many were hairbreadth escapes.[4]

As might be expected under these conditions, the population growth of the settlement was slow. From 419 inhabitants in 1821 (of whom only 154 were female), the colony grew to only 5,000 by 1849, including the French-speaking Métis.[5] Yet there was a bright side to life in the colony in the years following the flood of 1826. By 1830 the colony had recovered from both the violent struggle between the North West Company and the Hudson's Bay Company and the flood and, for a few years in the 1830s, enjoyed a period of peace. The colonists' lives were regulated by the seasons, the church, the Hudson's Bay Company and the family. By the early 1840s the settlers were split into several recognizable communities along the banks of the Red and Assiniboine Rivers. This wide dispersal indicated that the original plan of establishing a settled and secure community had not yet been achieved (see Map 1). Apart

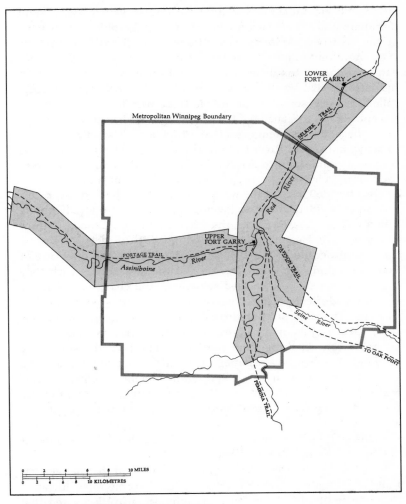

1 Red River Settlement in 1836

from natural disasters such as floods, prairie fires and grasshopper plagues, a major reason why the Red River colony did not develop beyond an uneasy balance between river lot farming and the buffalo hunt was that the Hudson's Bay Company remained unconvinced of the feasibility of combining colonization and the fur trade, whatever the necessity of lowering the costs of provisions. Accordingly, the Company did not encourage the independent government of the colony, for it felt that a well-organized colonial government would be an inducement to settlers and a challenge to its authority. On the other hand, company officials realized that a weak government could result in chaos. As a compromise the Hudson's Bay Company allowed the settlers the responsibility, without legal authorization, to manage their affairs in an orderly fashion. But the Company's local officials were ever watchful that its trading privileges were not breached and until 1849 they retained control of the colony.

There were, however, other more important reasons for the colony's failure to prosper during these years. These resulted from the isolation of the settlement from the settled regions of the continent. After the merger of 1821 and the severing of ties with eastern Canada, the only commercial outlet was through Hudson Bay, and even this was limited to the commerce of the fur trade, carried in one or two ships annually. This unquestioned dominance of the fur trade, under the monopoly of the Hudson's Bay Company, meant that there was but a limited market for the infrequent surplus farm produce of the river lots or the provisions of the buffalo hunt.

Between 1821 and 1844 the Company was able to enforce its monopoly with a minimum of effort. In 1844, however, Norman W. Kittson opened a post for the American Fur Company at Pembina and adventurous young men in the colony were soon carrying their catch to this establishment.[6] For the next five years a continual struggle was waged by the Hudson's Bay Company against these free traders. The matter finally came to a head in 1849 when Pierre G. Sayer, a free-trading Métis, was brought to trial for engaging in illicit trade. Sayer was found guilty but was not sentenced and the company's monopoly was effectively, if not legally, broken. Henceforth the Hudson's Bay Company made no attempt to support its claims by appeal to its legal status; instead it relied on its competitive strength. And in most cases, notwithstanding the existence of

American traders, the free-traders in the colony were for some time forced to rely on the Hudson's Bay Company since goods were still transported to Red River far more cheaply by way of Hudson Bay than by any other route.[7]

Although there was little initial change in the fortunes of Red River following the Sayer trial, the establishment of free trade and the opening of new lines of communication with the south signified the beginning of the end of the old order in the Northwest. One of the chief results of the opening up of trade in the colony was that between 1849 and 1859 the ever increasing numbers of free traders rapidly trapped out the land of the Winnipeg basin and by 1859 the Company had few agents left in the area. Their withdrawal left a vacuum in the colony that was quickly filled by the competing interests of American and Canadian companies.

Increasingly after 1849 external forces began to work major changes in the life of the community. On the one hand, the advancing American agricultural frontier up the Mississippi Valley had been marked by the formation of the Territory of Minnesota in 1849, and by the rapid growth of St. Paul as the centre of commerce for the upper Mississippi and Red River Valleys. By 1860 the colony's business relations were almost exclusively with the United States and the only regular mail communication the people of Red River had with the outside world had been established through the American republic. Economic ties then seemed to indicate eventual annexation to the United States. Moreover, there appeared in the colony after 1860 an American Party, closely allied with St. Paul merchants, which continually stressed the economic advantages of annexation. They pointed out that union would be speedily followed by organization as a territory and the beginning of rail construction. To a people so long isolated and unprosperous, such developments looked promising.

But as a balance to this southern pull there was a similar resurgence of interest by eastern Canada in the Red River region. A Select Committee of the House of Commons of Great Britain, set up in 1857 to report on the Hudson's Bay Company's exclusive license to trade in the Northwest, had recommended that in the southern region the way should be left open for eventual acquisition of the valleys of the Red and Saskatchewan by Canada. Besides the importance of this recommendation, the Committee's hearings aroused considerable interest in the Northwest. When it was found that there was a great lack of climatic and geographical knowledge of the area two exploring expeditions were dispatched. Perhaps even more important than these events was the pervasive propaganda campaign conducted by George Brown in Canada West. In his influential Toronto newspaper *The Globe*, Brown eloquently called for the resumption of the old trade with the Northwest and the annexation to Canada of the entire region. The combined result of all these developments was that a trickle of "Canadians" began to arrive in the Red River Colony after 1857 and by 1860 they had formed a counterpart to the American Party. And, to give voice to their views, a newspaper, the *Nor'Wester*, was established in 1859.[8]

Thus by 1860 most of the white inhabitants of the Red River Colony were divided into two incompatible groups; one advocating union with the United States, the other union with Canada. A third group, the Métis, were also faced with a difficult decision during the crucial decade of the 1860s. The Métis were the offspring of French-speaking white fur traders and Indians, and as such they found adjustment to increased settlement and changing economic conditions difficult. Neither white nor Indian, they were rebuffed by both.[9] The attempt by all three of these groups to establish a new society, each in its own pattern, generated forces that caused considerable conflict throughout the 1860s. The final decision came only in 1870 when, as a result of the Red River Rebellion, Manitoba entered Confederation. It was in this atmosphere of political uncertainty that the settlement of Winnipeg sprang up; a settlement founded by a group of crass, hard-nosed Upper Canadians who, in a few short years, swept aside the efforts and hopes of several generations of Red River residents and replaced them with visions of creating a thriving prairie metropolis.

By 1859 the Hudson's Bay Company had found that the general trade of its store at Upper Fort Garry had become more lucrative than the fur trade. Other business interests also discovered that with the increasing population of the area a demand had arisen for goods and services that could not be fully met by the Company and by 1865 there were more than a dozen business establishments surrounding the Fort.[10] One of these was the Royal Hotel run by Henry McKenney. Born in Upper Canada of Irish parents, McKenney had operated a frontier trading store in the Minnesota Territory before

In the pre-railway age, the people of the small settlement of Winnipeg received their supplies either by steamboat or Red River cart. This primitive, two-wheeled vehicle, held together by rawhide and wooden pegs, was a boon to early settlers and freighters. It carried nearly a half ton of freight over almost any kind of terrain, including the muddy streets of early Winnipeg, c. 1875.

coming to Red River in 1859. On his arrival in the colony McKenney opened a cozy and home-like inn that, in addition to providing accommodation, also included a small general store. By the spring of 1862 McKenney had prospered to such an extent that he decided to get out of the hotel trade and build a larger general store at a new location. His new establishment was to be the nucleus of the future city of Winnipeg.[11]

McKenney's store was built where the fur-runners' trail coming down the Assiniboine to Fort Garry crossed the trail running down the Red River — in present-day Winnipeg the corner of Portage Avenue and Main Street. This choice of a site caused much amusement and even jeers from the people at the Fort and the settlers at Point Douglas and points further down the Red. The store was a considerable distance from the Red River and was situated on land so low that it often flooded in spring. But McKenney held to his vision of the future and before long others followed; in a short ten years these few buildings grew in number to swallow up both Point Douglas and Upper Fort Garry.[12]

Despite the future prospects for growth the infant settlement of Winnipeg remained between 1863 and 1870 a relatively unimportant part of the larger Red River Colony.[13] At this time there were three distinct groups of buildings within the borders of present-day Winnipeg. Besides McKenney's store and the other structures that soon were built around it, there were the homes and farms of a few original Selkirk settlers located on Point Douglas. To the south, at the confluence of the Red and Assiniboine Rivers, was located the Hudson's Bay Company post of Upper Fort Garry. These groupings of buildings, however, made up only a part of the larger Red River Colony for up and down the Red River and along the banks of the Assiniboine were located the river lot farms of Scottish, French and Métis settlers.

Moreover, during the 1860s the designation Winnipeg was not even commonly used to distinguish the buildings surrounding McKenney's store from the other parts of the colony. The name Winnipeg was first used in 1866 on the masthead of the *Nor'Wester*. The previous issues of this newspaper, which began publication as the first newspaper in the Northwest in December 1859, carried the designation Red River Settlement, Assiniboia. The name Winnipeg originated in the Indian name given to the lake forty miles north,

win meaning muddy and *nipee* meaning water. The designation stuck and by 1870 maps of the area showed the Town of Winnipeg, even though this was erroneous in that it had not yet been incorporated either as a village or town. Despite the usage of the name Winnipeg within the area, the nascent city was for some time known to the outside world as Fort Garry and it was not until 1876 that the post office had its name changed to Winnipeg.[14]

Winnipeg's modest development prior to 1870 is also revealed in a contemporary description. When Reverend George Young arrived in 1868 to begin the ministry of the Methodist Church, he suggested that it took great foresight to imagine that from such crude beginnings an important city would grow.

> What a sorry sight was presented by that long-thought-of town of Winnipeg on the day we entered it! What a mass of soft, black, slippery and sticky Red River mud was everywhere spread out before us! Streets with neither sidewalks nor crossings, with now and again a good sized pit of mire for the traveller to avoid or flounder through as best he could; a few small stores with poor goods and high prices; one little tavern where 'Dutch George' was "monarch of all his survey"; a few passable dwellings with no "rooms to let," nor space for boarders; neither church nor school in sight or in prospect; population about one hundred instead of one thousand as we expected — such was Winnipeg on July 4th, 1868.[15]

The growth of Winnipeg as a distinct community really began with the entry of Manitoba into Confederation in 1870. From a population of only 100 in December 1870 the community grew to 215 in 1871; 1,467 in 1872; and 3,700 by 1874.[16] In these years the leading element in Winnipeg was a fusion of private free-traders with newcomers, many of them volunteers who had come west to put down the Riel uprising. They were for the most part British and Ontarians by origin but by virtue of their common interest in creating a new western city they rapidly became passionate Winnipeggers. A careful enumeration of the population by the newly established *Manitoba Free Press* in November 1872 indicated that the population of 1,467 was made up of 1,019 males and only 448 females. This disparity, the paper noted, was commonly "noticeable in most Western towns, and is here explained by the fact that

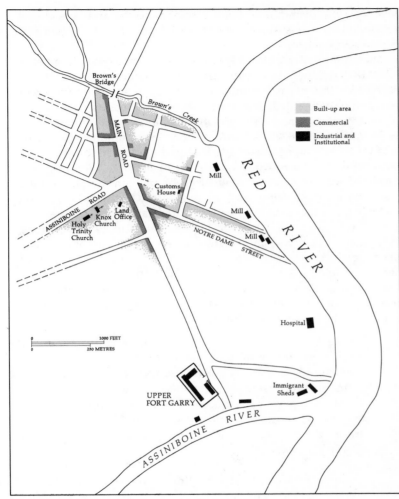

2 Winnipeg in 1872

Built-up area

Commercial

Industrial and
Institutional

few immigrants are accompanied by their families, for whom they first secure a home, and then return or send, as well as because so large a proportion is made up of young men, who left the crowded family homestead to take part in the vast lottery of this territory, where the great cities and Provinces of the future furnish the field for competition."

Why the unattractive village of Winnipeg and not Point Douglas or St. Andrews should have attracted the new arrivals after 1870 is explained by many factors. Perhaps the most significant of these was the proximity of the village to Upper Fort Garry. Following the proclamation of the Manitoba Act in July 1870 the Hudson's Bay Company establishment became the seat of the government not only for the new province but for the Northwest Territories as well. And the government agencies, small though they were, greatly exceeded in volume and importance the petty business of the former District of Assiniboia. Located here too was the first Dominion Lands Office in the west, which was to handle the large and vexatious business of adjusting the titles of old inhabitants, to administer the Métis reserves, and to register the claims of new settlers. Also, the Canadian garrison was partially stationed at the Upper Fort until, in 1872, the Fort Osborne Barracks were built in Winnipeg. Expenditures by the military on food, supplies, and entertainment greatly boosted local trade. Even more important in the long run was the fact that many soldiers elected to take their discharge on the spot in order to take up farms near the settlement of Winnipeg. Glowing reports sent home or carried home by those soldiers who returned were a powerful stimulus that induced waves of Ontario settlers to migrate west. By 1872 the two previously distinct settlements of Winnipeg and Fort Garry were beginning to merge (see Map 2). Significantly, it was Winnipeg that swallowed up the Fort, for the city's rapid rise as a commercial centre exceeded and overshadowed the old role of the Hudson's Bay Company in the Northwest.[17]

It is true, of course, that the old dependence on the fur trade was not completely or suddenly replaced by other types of commerce. Indeed, the fur trade remained the chief business of the city until at least 1875 and along with the Hudson's Bay Company many private entrepreneurs maintained a vigorous business in furs. But none of the firms — not even the Hudson's Bay Company — confined itself any longer to fur. The opening up of the region after 1870 meant that there would soon be a great demand for merchandise, lumber, agricultural implements and land. Winnipeg's growth in the years 1870-1874 was a result of that settlement's businessmen aggressively stepping forward to fill these needs. Increasingly after 1870 fur traders became retailers and wholesalers, as businessmen turned to supplying not only Winnipeg's needs but those of the merchants of the new settlements which rapidly sprang up across the province.

Two examples of local business expansion may be taken as fairly typical.[18] A.G.B. Bannatyne had established himself in the Red River colony in 1848. At first, "His business house was confined to meeting the wants of the red man, but as civilization advanced the demands of the public changed and the class of goods carried also." By 1881 Bannatyne and Company held a prominent position among the wholesale and retail dealers of Winnipeg, dealing in "fancy and staple groceries, provisions, wines, liquors and cigars." Even more successful was James H. Ashdown. He arrived in Winnipeg in 1868 and began business in a small way as a tinsmith with his whole enterprise valued at $1,000. By 1875 Ashdown had begun to do some large contract work and his wholesale trade had so increased that he operated two separate establishments, one retail and one wholesale. By 1881 he was worth over $150,000 and had established branch stores at Portage la Prairie and Emerson. In his united manufacturing, retail, and wholesale business, both in Winnipeg and branches, Ashdown employed over seventy-five people. The versatility of Bannatyne and Ashdown was characteristic of many other businessmen in Winnipeg. It was a quality that was appropriate to a period of transition from a fur to an agricultural economy and was to reach a climax when several firms further diversified by becoming the first grain-buyers in Winnipeg. [19]

Winnipeg's growth in the years after 1870 was also marked by a thriving business in real estate and finance. By 1880 there were no fewer than fifty-nine separate financial and real estate interests in the city and "There was a lively business in advertising the qualities of Manitoba land, in informing and directing land seekers, in arranging sales of land and scrip, and in buying on speculation both town lots and farm lands." Between 1871 and 1873 there was a mild boom — the first of many — in Winnipeg lots. Indeed, despite Winnipeg's growing importance as a commercial and agricultural centre, it was in real estate that the great fortunes of its leading citizens would be made.[20]

The rapid growth of Winnipeg during the tumultuous months of 1871-1873 should have left little time for residents to concern themselves with the future. Yet early in 1872 a popular movement began to incorporate the fledgling settlement of Winnipeg as a city. There were several reasons for the growth of an incorporation movement in Winnipeg in 1872 and 1873. Before incorporation, municipal affairs in Winnipeg were administered under an arrangement established by the provincial government in 1871. Winnipeg was provided with an assessor, road surveyor and constables, but little else.[21] Residents of Winnipeg were thus forced to attempt a solution of their municipal problems on a private basis. In 1871, for example, it was suggested that local merchants supply fire-fighting equipment. But it was immediately apparent that without a broad tax base and a set of recognized bylaws the burden of municipal services would be shared unequally and unfairly.

Early in January 1872, Alexander Begg, a local merchant, published the first number of the *Manitoba Trade Review* and in it he expressed the following sentiments:

> On the 16th of next month the Legislature will sit, and it is well for us to take into consideration the propriety of incorporating our town. If we let this chance slip, who knows but others more enterprising may get ahead of us, and thus change the whole aspect of the place in a few years. Our Province is bound to grow rapidly and we must not sleep, lest others, alive to the importance thereof, may incorporate a town just outside, or not very far from our present limits. There are many benefits to be derived from an Act of Incorporation; why not, therefore, hold a meeting of the older heads to discuss the matter freely. . . .[22]

Subsequent articles by Begg stressed the benefits to be gained by incorporation. Corporate powers, he felt, would allow for fire protection, municipal works such as sidewalks and streets, and the preparation and enforcement of bylaws "to regulate matters generally, so as to answer to the public good and not the ideas of individual parties."[23]

Northwestern Transportation Co. Stage Coach office at the corner of Rorie and Post Office Streets, 1880.

Begg's call for a public meeting was acted upon in February when at a mass gathering a series of resolutions were passed calling for incorporation. These were then forwarded to the legislature with every expectation that they would be promptly acted upon. To the citizens' dismay, however, the legislature adjourned with no mention of incorporation.[24] Whatever the reasons for the legislature's refusal to act immediately on behalf of Winnipeg's residents, the citizens quickly decided that it was because "certain interests" were opposed to incorporation.[25] These interests were the Hudson's Bay Company, which at the time owned approximately one-third of the taxable property in the proposed city limits, and four other property owners who were said to own twenty-five percent of the remainder. It was generally believed that the Hudson's Bay Company delayed passage of the desired legislation in an attempt to avert paying taxes on its large holdings.[26] This belief was encouraged by the opposition to incorporation of a local newspaper, The Manitoban, which was felt to be "intimately associated with the Hudson's Bay Company influence."[27]

Following this first rebuff, "indignation meetings" were held throughout the summer and fall of 1872, culminating in a mass meeting in December. At this latter gathering unanimous support was expressed in favour of incorporation and a citizens' committee was formed and entrusted with the responsibility of drafting a suitable bill to present to the legislature early in 1873. A report on a draft bill was presented to the citizens at another meeting in February 1873. It called for a council of a mayor and eight aldermen; a fixed, four-ward system; and laid out a host of corporate powers including taxation. When the measure was quickly ratified by the citizens it was then sent to the legislature for approval.

Legislative action was taken this time but it was soon apparent that the citizens' bill would not be left intact. Revisions proposed by the legislature were drastic. The possible rate of taxation on improved property was reduced by half while that on unimproved property was cut to one-twentieth of one percent of the assessed value. Moreover, the corporation was prevented from borrowing money, while fees collected for licenses were to be turned over to the province. Finally, to add to the residents' consternation, the name Winnipeg was changed to Assiniboine.[28]

The reaction to these revisions was predictable. At a mass meet-ing early in March the populace protested bitterly and appointed a committee which subsequently interviewed the Legislative Council and vigorously urged the restoration of the original bill. The bill was eventually restored to its original form but some people remembered that the Speaker of the House, Dr. C. J. Bird, had at one time ruled it out of order.[29] In retaliation for his action he was lured from his house in the small hours of night on the pretext of seeing a dying patient, driven some distance and given a treatment of warm tar and bruises. A reward for information leading to the apprehension of the instigators of the escapade was offered but never claimed.[30]

Perhaps chastened by this show of political indomitability and by several subsequent stormy invasions of the House when it was in session, a redrafted bill was considered and passed at the next session of the legislature. On November 8, 1873, royal assent was given and the fur trade station known as The Forks and a part of the Red River Colony merged to form the new City of Winnipeg.[31]

One of the more noteworthy facts about the Act of Incorporation was that it was based entirely on the Ontario system.[32] The provision for a ward system, property qualifications for aldermen and mayor, and the dates for nominations, elections and meetings were all identical to Ontario statutes. The slate of elective and appointive officials and the powers of the mayor were also based on Ontario examples. Likewise Winnipeg possessed all the bylaw-making powers of an Ontario city. In short, the remaking of Manitoba in the image of Ontario was begun most markedly in Winnipeg.[33]

The legislation incorporating Winnipeg as a city was quite elaborate and the act itself comprised some 128 sections and ran over forty pages.[34] Corporate authority was vested in a council composed of a mayor and twelve aldermen, three for each ward. Council members, including the mayor, possessed judicial as well as administrative powers, although they could not impose penalties involving hard labour. Some of the numerous specific powers of the civic corporation included the passage of bylaws concerning nuisances, safety, sanitation, fire, police and markets. And to administer their enactments council was empowered to appoint a clerk, assessors, collectors, city engineer, health officers, constables and a host of other civic employees.

Civic revenue was to be raised in a number of ways. Taxation

FROM POST OFFICE LOOKING NORTH.

Main Street, 1882.

could be imposed upon real and personal property while various license fees could be collected. Only liquor levies had to be shared with the province. Enterprises such as auction rooms, liveries, and peddling were among those requiring licenses.

Application of the new legislation was not long in coming, for the city's first civic election was held in January 1874. It was preceded by a fairly lively campaign with the main issue being the extent of each candidate's connection with large property interests such as the Hudson's Bay Company. The winner of the mayoralty contest, Francis Evans Cornish, called the first meeting of council for January 19th, 1874, at 12:00 noon. It was held on the second floor of a new building near the corner of Portage Avenue and Main Street. Quite naturally council's first activities involved the establishment of a framework in which it could operate. Accordingly, aldermen were selected to strike standing committees for the year. These included finance, assessment, local works, fire and water, police and licensing. The mayor was an *ex officio* member of each committee. City council also adopted such parliamentary procedures as committee of the whole, notice of motion, three readings for bylaws, and adjournment through lack of a quorum. In February an assessor, chief of police, and city engineer were chosen while previous appointments of city clerk and chamberlain were confirmed.[35]

Financial activities served to bridge these purely structural efforts. Procedures, committees and appointments only became purposeful when they achieved concrete results. Some of the first expenditures of council were on sidewalks — $8,246; roads — $3,204; and bridges — $621.[36] During this first year all funds were provided from current income. The Hudson's Bay Company's opposition to incorporation is easily understood when it is noted that its property, assessed at $273,000, provided a major portion of the property taxes collected in 1874. Liquor fees comprised the largest part of the license revenue, while fines, often as low as twenty-five cents, were a negligible factor.

As could be expected in a new city like Winnipeg in 1874, there were many obvious and expensive local works projects that needed to be carried out. For this reason and also because of low current income city council in 1875 gained popular approval of its first money bylaw. This measure called for the expenditure of $250,000 on civic improvements such as sewers, fire equipment, waterworks, civic buildings and streets. Some interest was also shown in health matters when council established a special committee to participate in the management of the Winnipeg General Hospital and granted a sum of $500 to that institution.[37]

By virtue of these and other activities city council established itself by the end of 1874 as a functioning local government. Many activities essential to the establishment of a community which had previously been poorly performed or neglected were attempted and, with some glaring exceptions (such as provision for adequate sewage and water facilities), were successfully completed. Yet even before the first flush of pride in the new city had faded, Winnipeg's characteristic optimism was severely tested on several fronts. The prospect that Winnipeg would be bypassed by the great transcontinental railway promised by the Prime Minister, Sir John A. Macdonald, loomed large, but other problems, such as the vulnerability of the community to flooding, were also ever present. This early and continuing necessity to concentrate so much of its capital and energy on counterbalancing the effects of Winnipeg's poor geographic location was an important element in the city's early development. It meant that many of the benefits that other communities received as a matter of course could be had in Winnipeg only at great cost. But whatever the cost, such problems were never once considered to be too high a price to bear by Winnipeg's civic and business leaders. What is perhaps even more noteworthy is that the economic priorities they set out and slavishly adhered to were seldom questioned. Thus Winnipeg's motto, "Commerce, Prudence, Industry," was representative of the city's material aspirations, although the middle adjective would have been more descriptive had it been "Optimism."

Chapter One

The Formative and Boom Years 1874-1913

All roads lead to Winnipeg. It is the focal point of the three transcontinental lines of Canada, and nobody, neither manufacturer, capitalist, farmer, mechanic, lawyer, doctor, merchant, priest, nor labourer, can pass from one part of Canada to another without going through Winnipeg. It is a gateway through which all the commerce of the east and the west, and the north and the south must flow. No city, in America at least, has such absolute and complete command over the wholesale trade of so vast an area. It is destined to become one of the greatest distributing commercial centres of the continent as well as a manufacturing community of great importance.

William. E. Curtis,
Chicago Record Herald, 1911.

ECONOMIC GROWTH AND METROPOLITAN DEVELOPMENT

By the time Winnipeg was incorporated in November 1873 it had enjoyed several years of growth and prosperity. Comprising only some thirty structures in 1870 — many of them "rickety-looking shanties that looked for all the world as if they had been dropped promiscuously on the verge of a boundless prairie"[1] — Winnipeg had well over nine hundred buildings by the end of 1873. Over four hundred of these were houses, twenty-seven were occupied by manufacturers, over one hundred by merchants, and the balance were offices, hotels, boarding houses and saloons. By the fall of 1874 the population of the community had grown to three thousand and the assessed value of the city property amounted to over $2,000,000 (see Map 3).

In spite of this initial spurt of growth, the newly incorporated city of Winnipeg was not much more than a wooden shack village standing aloof from Upper Fort Garry. An observer examining the community's future would not have found much reason for encouragement. If Winnipeg and its hinterland were to grow, the growth would have to be achieved from two main channels: natural increase and the influx of immigrants. Natural increase was bound to have only a minimal effect in these early years in a community where men outnumbered women almost two to one. Nor did the immigrant factor appear very promising. Winnipeg was at this time not only little known in other parts of Canada, but it was also completely isolated from the settled portions of the country. The lack of transportation facilities made the approach to the colony difficult, to say the least. Immigrants had the choice of overland routes by the Lake of the Woods; the Hudson Bay route through Lake Winnipeg; or the route by rail to St. Paul, Minnesota, and then by oxcart or flat boat to Winnipeg. All were long, tiresome journeys, and discouraged prospective settlers. The Wolseley expedition, for example, which was sent out in 1870 to keep the peace in the Red River Colony, required ninety-six gruelling days to reach Fort Garry from Toronto via the Dawson Route and Lake of the Woods. It was not surprising with these conditions that westward bound Canadian settlers emigrated in large numbers to the relatively accessible American frontier.[2]

Winnipeggers took frequent note of these poor conditions and petitioned the federal government to improve facilities. But as important as the issue of transportation was to the residents of the young community, there was still room for some pointed humour. In July 1874, for example, the *Manitoba Free Press* carried a story describing conditions on the Dawson Route. The story told of a point along the route where a group of travellers observed a pole about ten feet high stuck in the ground. Attached to the pole were a tin of butter, a piece of pork, and a slip of paper with the following words written on it:

> Stay, weary traveller, thank your God
> You're safely o'er the Dawson Road
> I'm sure it will do you some good
> To take a little rest and food
> 'Gainst mercies small do not mutter
> You're welcome to this pork and butter.

It is understandable, then, that Winnipeggers took a strong interest in railways. Without railways the agricultural exploitation of the west was impossible. The exportation of the staple products of the west and the importation of commodities from the east and abroad depended on cheap and efficient transportation. Furthermore, unlike settled communities in the east, such as Toronto and Montreal, Winnipeg could not fall back on water transportation for its commercial needs. Thus the selection of the route for a Pacific railway, the great undertaking that was to complete the transcontinental federation of British North America, overshadowed all other interests in the period before 1886. The *Manitoba Free Press* stated the issue bluntly in December 1873: "The two great wants of this country are railroads and settlers. The former is necessary to secure the latter." The selection of the route would also affect the direction and increase the speculative element in settlement. In the early 1870s one thing was certain — the railway had to cross the new Province of Manitoba. The question was where.

At first the federal government adopted a route south of Lake Manitoba and the prospect attracted settlers to Winnipeg and its hinterland. Then came delay and uncertainty with the Pacific Scandal of 1873 and the fall of the Macdonald government, followed by the December 1874 announcement of the new Prime Minister, Alexander Mackenzie, that the railway would cross the Red River

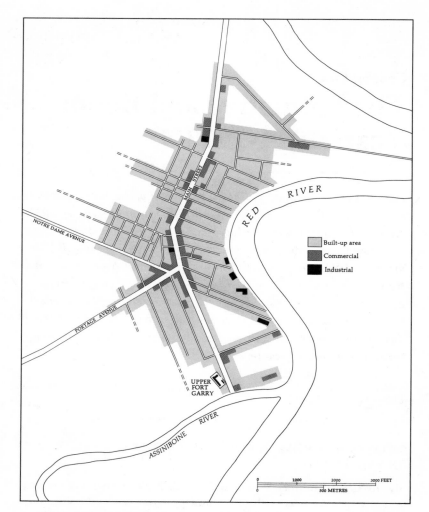

3 Winnipeg in 1875

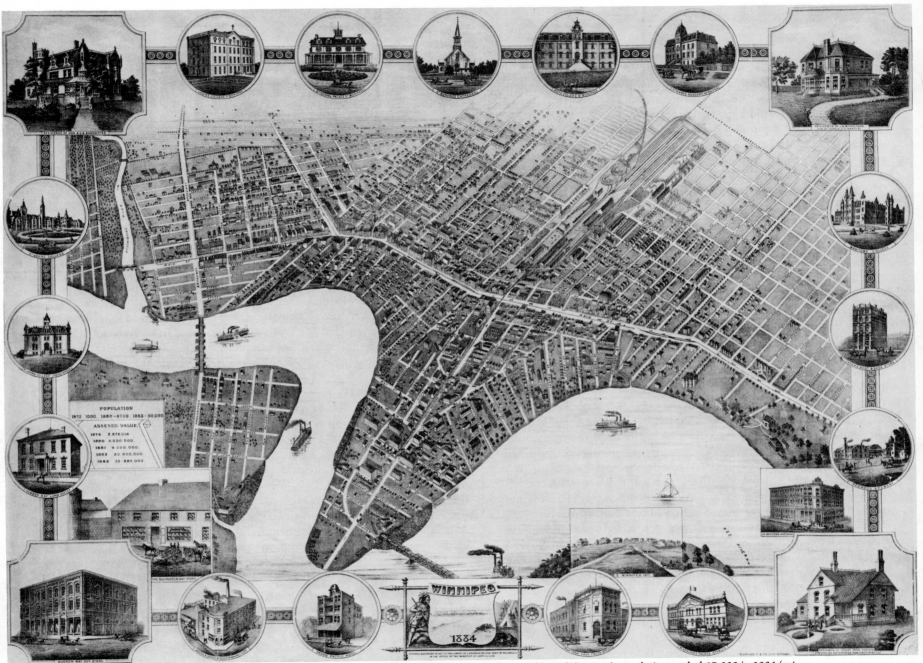

Bird's-eye view, 1884. The dramatic impact of the coming of the railroad to Winnipeg is illustrated here. Winnipeg's population reached 17,000 in 1884 (not the 30,000 indicated on this map) and the extent of the built-up area expanded rapidly. New districts were opened up across the Assiniboine River in Fort Rouge and west of Main Street north of the CPR tracks. The most evident change, however, resulted from the construction of two bridges across the Red River and the considerable industrial development represented by the railroad yards, shops and roundhouses of the CPR. Practically overnight Winnipeg became a major railway centre.

not at Winnipeg but at Selkirk, and would run northwestward from that point toward Edmonton. This decision was potentially deadly for Winnipeg: it meant that railways in the Red River Valley would be mere branch lines and the main thrust of settlement, and its implicit benefits, would bypass Winnipeg.

Winnipeggers, vigorously represented by the Board of Trade, at first fought this decision. Mass meetings were held, a Citizens' Railway Committee was formed, petitions and memorials were drawn up and forwarded to Ottawa, and delegations including the mayor and prominent businessmen were sent off to the capital to plead Winnipeg's case. But when Prime Minister Mackenzie met all these efforts with stubborn inaction, the determined citizens of Winnipeg tried to make the best of a bad situation by insuring that Winnipeg would at least have a direct link with the main line, as well as a "colonization" railway to the southwest. These negotiations continued slowly between 1875 and 1878 without much success. After years of effort the community's struggle to make Winnipeg the Gateway to the West appeared fruitless.[3]

The closing months of 1878 were brightened, however, by the completion of the Pembina branch and the inauguration of direct rail service between St. Paul, Minnesota, and Winnipeg. The city at last had an effective outlet for the wheat crops of its surrounding hinterland and good times once more seemed in store for the young community. This prediction was supported by Macdonald's and the Conservatives' return to office in September. During the campaign they had hinted that, if elected, they would redirect the transcontinental line through the city. Winnipeg voted heavily for the Conservative candidate, Alexander Morris, in the election.[4] Following the election, the Citizens' Railway Committee and city council hoped to persuade the new government to change the main line route by quick and determined action. Thus a mass meeting was hurriedly called for November 8, 1878. A memorial was drawn up, sponsored by the Board of Trade and endorsed by city council, that described the injustice under which Winnipeg felt it suffered. The most important part of the memorial, however, was the offer of a bonus of $300,000 to aid in the construction of a bridge across the Red River at Winnipeg. Following further extensive negotiations, the city was victorious and in 1881 a main route through Winnipeg was confirmed.

The decision that the main line of the Canadian Pacific Railway would pass through Winnipeg seemed to guarantee that the city would become the hub of commercial activity in the Northwest. In the years following 1881 this prospect was more than fulfilled as Winnipeg rapidly became the most populous and prosperous community in western Canada. If economic and population growth were the city's primary goals, then the according of exemption from taxation forever to all Canadian Pacific Railway property, the grant of free land for a passenger station and $200,000 in cash, as well as the construction of a $300,000 bridge over the Red River, were justified. Yet the high cost of obtaining the railroad involved much more than these inducements. The upsurge in Winnipeg's fortunes that followed the coming of the CPR reaffirmed the conviction that railways were the key to rapid and sustained growth. Thereafter city council did everything to encourage railway development and nothing to control it. This attitude had serious long-range consequences for Winnipeg's physical appearance and social fabric.

The prospect of Winnipeg's glowing economic future raised land values as businessmen vied for commercial locations in the developing metropolitan centre, and home builders for residential sites. Out of such anticipation the Winnipeg real estate boom of 1881-1882 developed.[5]

During the boom, Winnipeg experienced the wildest sixteen months of its history. The excitement began with speculation in Winnipeg lots and in other Manitoba townsites and continued deliriously until lots in Edmonton, Prince Albert and even Port Moody, British Columbia, were bought and sold in a gambling fervour. Speculation became rife and Winnipeg soon had over three hundred real estate offices, while real estate agents became "as numerous as the sand on the seashore. The educated and refined as well as the illiterate took part in all manner of land transactions."[6]

Winnipeg's hotels, some of which had only canvas roofs, were jammed. Speculators packed the numerous bars which sprang up overnight, and they held property auctions day and night anywhere and everywhere, even the backs of buckboards. Canvas-topped sleighs, painted with pictures of golden cities, patrolled the streets, with bells ringing and barkers touting the auctions. Lots were brazenly advertised in non-existent towns, even in swamps.[7]

Jim Coolican, known as the "Real Estate King," whose place of

The land boom which Winnipeg experienced in 1881-1882 succeeded in gaining the interest of eastern Canadians, as this illustration from Grip magazine of March 1882 indicates. During the boom the price of land on Main Street rose as high as $2,000 a front foot for choice locations; a price that surpassed those of Chicago! Similar prices for land in Winnipeg were not reached again until the 1970s.

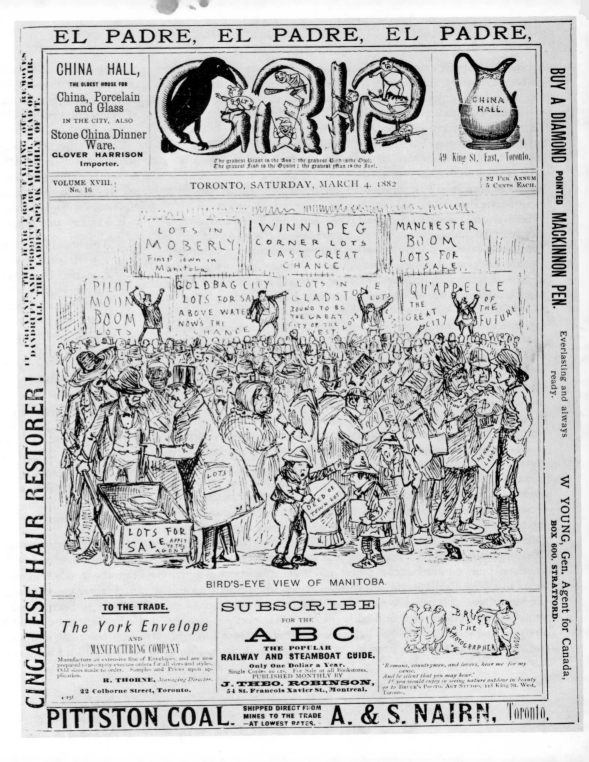

business, near the corner of Portage and Main, was the scene of daily and nightly auction sales, was one of the outstanding town characters. A plump, red-cheeked man, with a flowing black moustache and eyes that twinkled like the diamonds he sported, Coolican wore a sealskin coat reputed to be worth $5,000. He sold so many lots on unpaved Main Street that he earned the title "Marquis de Mud." His auction mart in a ramshackle building was like a Barnum and Bailey circus; in two weeks he sold a million dollars' worth of lots. He was reputed to celebrate a lucrative sale in a champagne bath.[8]

Such frantic speculation could not last, however; and after a frenzy of excitement the boom collapsed late in 1882. Nevertheless, an immense volume of construction activity continued in Winnipeg and the west and this supported a local building materials industry of considerable proportions. The most thriving industry in Winnipeg throughout the 1870s and 1880s was housebuilding. Houses were often built in twenty-four hours, but there were so many prospective occupants that the city was dotted with hundreds of tents. More imposing structures were also built during this period. Financial firms from eastern Canada and Britain erected western headquarters in the city, while a continuing accumulation of substantial fortunes by Winnipeggers supported the organization of locally owned financial institutions. In short, Winnipeg was in these formative years beginning to assume the role of the great metropolitan centre of western Canada, housing the leading economic, administrative, educational, and entertainment institutions of the region.

As Winnipeg grew and prospered in these years there sprang up among the business and professional group — the commercial elite — an unshakeable optimism that was to be of great significance for the future of the city. Of Anglo-Saxon background, Protestant religion and relatively humble origin, this elite shared the firm belief that the future of their community was boundless. A place where there had been no one but fur traders and Indians before, but which today numbered a thousand, might be expected to number tens and even hundreds of thousands tomorrow. From the outset Winnipeggers were aggressive, determined to protect their position against any town which appeared to challenge it. Whether from Ontario, the Maritimes, or England, prosperous merchant or labourer, young

or old, most Winnipeggers rapidly became and steadfastly remained avid city boosters who measured the city's progress in quantitative terms — numbers of rail lines, miles of streets, dollars of assessment, value of manufacturing output, or wholesale trade, and so on.

One of the best examples of this mentality is contained in a volume published in Winnipeg in 1886. Written by W. T. Thompson and E. E. Boyer, the booster tract was entitled *The City of Winnipeg, The Capital of Manitoba, and the Commercial, Railway & Financial Metropolis of the Northwest: Past and Present Development and Future Prospects.* The first paragraph of the book reads as follows:

> The history of Winnipeg, with its wonderful growth and marvellous progress, reads like a chapter from some work of romance. It seems almost miraculous that in the short space of fifteen years there has arisen here the city of to-day. Fifteen years ago no city, no railroad, no street, no church, no schoolhouse, no home — nothing but a small post of the Hudson's Bay Co., where the native Indians gathered to dispose of their furs — to-day, the thirty thousand people, the twenty-five millions of business, massive mercantile blocks, railways connecting with the Atlantic and Pacific and stretching to the great cities of the United States, church edifices of magnificent structure and proportions, elegant school-houses, miles of street railway, the mansion and residence, the electric light, the comforts and refinements of the highest type of civilized life. It is indeed one of the marvels of the age — a growth unprecedented, a progress unsurpassed in the history of the world. Nowhere on either hemisphere has there been a parallel case. Winnipeg stands alone in her onward march of development.

Winnipeggers were obviously not parochial. The rapid growth of large wholesale and real estate companies, for example, gave many Winnipeggers a regional, and at times even a national, outlook that often transcended local and provincial interests. Thus while Winnipeg was to become and remain Manitoba's chief urban centre, it always thought of itself as more than that. Indeed, the metropolitan ambitions of Winnipeg were far more sophisticated than those of other western towns and cities. The large number of Ontario-born

Main Street in the late 1880s.

businessmen in Winnipeg were concerned with the progress of the whole Dominion, not just Manitoba or the west. They realized their fortunes were closely connected with the economic growth and political stability of all provinces. In short, Winnipeg was a "Canadian" as well as a "Western" city, and this attitude is perhaps best shown by the nickname often used for Winnipeg, "Bull's Eye of the Dominion."

Measuring progress in material terms, Winnipeg's businessmen directed their efforts toward achieving rapid and sustained growth at the expense of any and all other considerations. Regarding Winnipeg as a community of private money makers, they were little concerned with creating a humane environment for all citizens. Accordingly, habits of community life, an attention to the sharing of resources, and a willingness to care for all men were not much in evidence in Winnipeg's struggle to become the "Chicago of the North." Instead, the most noteworthy aspect of Winnipeg's history in this period was the systematic, organized, and expensive promotion of economic enterprise by public and private groups within the city.

The growth ethic of Winnipeg's commercial elite meant also that little thought was given to the consequences of growth. As one perceptive observer noted:

> The fact is that Winnipeg in her feverish desire to grow, only to grow, was not in the least concerned to grow properly and healthfully, to develop sanely. Her mad passion for evidences of her expansion, her insistent demand for figures to prove growth, and only growth, be it by building permits, or by bank clearances, or by customer receipts, or by pavement mileage, or peradventure by the price of vacant land, any process of growth demonstration, have blinded her to the fact that cities cannot live by growth alone.[9]

But Winnipeg's leaders had little time for thoughts like these. They saw themselves unchallenged as community builders in a mushrooming city, where personal and public growth, personal and public prosperity intermingled. There was simply no room for skeptics or, as they were often called, "knockers."

It was, then, with these commonly shared attitudes and beliefs, and with the distinct economic advantage of being on the main line of the Canadian Pacific Railway, that Winnipeg entered into the greatest boom in the city's hundred-year history. During these years, from 1886 to 1913, the sub-metropolitan centre of Winnipeg evolved into a full-fledged metropolis as it established the complex and delicate network that enabled it to control a hinterland stretching from northwestern Ontario to British Columbia.

For almost three decades following the completion of the transcontinental railway, the city of Winnipeg enjoyed a level of growth and prosperity that is unequalled in the history of Canadian urban development. The completion of the railway in 1885 opened western Canada to large-scale settlement and development. Strategically located at the point where the barren Laurentian Shield gave way to rich prairie farmland, Winnipeg was the logical focus for branch lines feeding the main transcontinental railway. Deliberate policy, in the form of tariffs which discouraged trade with the United States, ensured the west would be a hinterland of the east and that Winnipeg would be the key city in east-west trade.

The tempo of development in the west rose to a crescendo in the years after 1886, with the greatest expansion taking place in the first decade of the twentieth century. The boom was due to a propitious combination of factors: the price of wheat remained high; capital to finance development was readily available; interest rates were at their lowest point for two hundred years; appropriate dry-land farming technology was understood; a basic transportation system was in place; and the final completion of the colonization process in the United States brought an intensification of interest in the "Last Best West."[10] Also, large-scale agricultural development required investment on a corresponding scale in the construction of railways and urban distribution centres. In short, the agricultural development of the west produced a demand for skills and services that only a large metropolitan centre could fulfill.[11]

With a keen sense of the growth potential of the city, Winnipeg businessmen, in particular those who were involved in the Winnipeg Board of Trade, encouraged competitive railway building. The revoking of the CPR monopoly clause, which prevented competition and resulted in high freight rates, came about in 1888 as a result of considerable agitation on the part of Winnipeggers.[12] The end of the monopoly meant the immediate construction of branch lines and the eventual construction of other transcontinental rail-

This view of Main Street, 1910, shows Ashdown's Hardware Company, one of the first businesses in Winnipeg. James H. Ashdown came to the city in 1868 and started his wholesaling business in 1869. His business prospered and Ashdown became a millionaire and the city's best known ''merchant prince.'' He was mayor in 1907 and 1908.

JAS. H. ASHDOWN

James H. Ashdown, 1909.

ways through Winnipeg.[13] Freight rates dropped, new markets developed, and employment opportunities increased, further enhancing Winnipeg's status as a western metropolis.

The Board of Trade was also instrumental in bargaining for special freight concessions and in 1886 was granted a fifteen per cent discount on goods shipped west from the city by local companies. In 1890 the same concessions were granted on goods brought from the east.[14] These concessions favoured only wholesalers in Winnipeg and prevented the growth of competing large-scale wholesale functions in other prairie towns. They also prompted eastern wholesalers to open branches in Winnipeg. These concessions, combined with others made in 1897 and 1901, and with the fact that Winnipeg was closer to the market and could fill orders more quickly than eastern firms, gave Winnipeg a most favourable position in the wholesale trade. By 1913, the wholesalers of Winnipeg ruled an empire of vast dimensions, extending fifteen hundred miles west to the Pacific Coast, four hundred miles east to the Great Lakes, and hundreds of miles north.[15]

Long before 1913, however, there was feverish activity in the Winnipeg wholesale district. The *Manitoba Free Press*, for example, gave this description in November 1901. "Lights shining from the windows of wholesale warehouses and offices with rows of clerks bending over ledgers at 9 or 10 o'clock in the evening are indications of the immense business done by the wholesalers of Winnipeg. . . . Never in years has the wholesale trade been as heavy as it [is now]. Firms have sold out their lines completely. Clerks in the wholesale houses have been working overtime for the last two months and in some cases midnight still finds the staff at work."

The railways also made Winnipeg the administrative centre of the agricultural production of the prairies. By 1890 Winnipeg was the undisputed headquarters of the Canadian grain trade. This function required that grading and sorting of grain from country elevators be undertaken in the city prior to shipment to terminal elevators at the Lakehead. Large-scale grain marketing facilities located in the city, and in 1890, a Board of Arbitration was established to hear disputes concerning the grain trade. After early failures a Grain and Produce Exchange was established in 1887 and in a few years was to have an important influence on the international grain market. In 1897 a futures market was established for wheat

and telegraphic communication ties were made with other world markets. The grain trade furthermore spawned the growth of ancillary consultants, agents, brokers and shippers within the city.[16]

The rapid expansion of Winnipeg's function as a grain trading centre attracted experienced grain dealers from eastern Canada and the United States. Members of the Richardson family came to Winnipeg in 1880 from Kingston, where they had long been prominent in the Ontario grain trade. The family did very well in the prairie city; in a few short decades the Richardsons rose to a position of dominance in both Winnipeg's and Manitoba's power structure.[17] Messrs. Searle and Peavy, both Minnesota grain dealers, established in Winnipeg during this period branches which ultimately rivalled in size and importance the original offices in Minneapolis. Local men also shared in and contributed to Winnipeg's expansion in the grain trade, including Nicolas Bawlf, who had come to Winnipeg in 1877 and established a flourishing flour, seed and grain business. The giant United Grain Growers firm was organized by western farmers on a cooperative basis, with members receiving patronage dividends out of profits earned by the company.[18]

Winnipeg was also developing complex financial institutions during this period. As the centre of the Canadian grain trade, Winnipeg developed financial institutions to serve that activity. Numerous bank branches, brokerage houses, transportation and insurance agencies were created specifically for the grain transactions. Revenue from grain trading was channeled through the city, thus encouraging the growth of numerous wholesaling and service functions for the expanding prairie region, financing real estate activities in Winnipeg and the west, and generally providing an important source of capital for western Canadian development.

The growth of financial institutions in Winnipeg extended well beyond these direct relationships with the grain trade, however. Real estate, insurance and banking developed important linkages over an extensive western hinterland. By 1900, with the growing maturity of the prairie economy and the growth of the city itself, Winnipeg possessed a number of substantial financial institutions developed initially to serve western interests, though sufficiently competitive to break into national markets. In 1904, for example, the Northern Trust Company was organized and in 1905 two city businessmen established a private bank, Alloway and Champion,

Cart and oxen, 1899. Until the post-1920 period, when Winnipeg and other Canadian cities witnessed the takeover of their streets by automobiles, trucks and buses, scenes such as these were common. In the earlier period Winnipeg ran on animal-power, particularly horses and oxen. All the large stores in the city and many of the smaller ones used light horses and wagons for deliveries. The railway companies operated both express and baggage transfers. The bread and milk companies all had horse-drawn vehicles. The ice companies made their daily deliveries with fleets of heavy wagons, each drawn by two horses. Coal and wood deliveries and the collection of trash were also conducted by horse-power.

T. W. Taylor and Company Limited, Printers.

Paving St. Mary's Road, 1912.

destined to become the largest private banking business ever known in Canada. In 1911 this institution sold out to the Canadian Imperial Bank of Commerce. By 1906 the Winnipeg-based Great West Life Assurance Company was operating nationally. Similarly, the Canadian Fire Insurance Company soon established a national reputation. In 1907, a Stock Exchange was operating and trading in all aspects of development from northern Ontario to the Pacific coast was taking place.[19]

The huge increase in western demand for manufactured products during this period spurred the growth of Winnipeg's manufacturing sector (Appendix, Table 1). With only some thousand persons employed in 1881, there were over fifteen thousand working in manufacturing establishments by 1913, with the value of production jumping from $1,700,000 in 1881, to almost $50,000,000 by 1913. Firms which processed western produce, such as flour mills and packing plants, and firms producing construction materials, such as paint, lumber, and bricks, were in the forefront of this expansion.

The tempo of growth in the city was also affected by the fact that city council offered special inducements, including low property taxes, to industrial firms considering the establishment of plants in Winnipeg.[20] The Winnipeg Development and Industrial Bureau was organized in 1906 to boost local industry, and in the next few years received thousands of inquiries from firms interested in establishing branches in the city. In the period 1907-1910, for example, the Bureau commissioner reported that he had handled 58,000 enquiries for information and had in that time sent out as many letters in reply. He went on to say that "We have distributed over two million pieces of printed matter including every size from a four-page leaflet up to a hundred-page, highly illustrated booklet. In our press service department we have supplied over one million lines of news matter about Winnipeg to magazines, newspapers, and other publications in the British Isles, Eastern Canada and the United States and with these we have furnished over two thousand photographs for illustrations."[21]

The Development and Industrial Bureau was active in other areas. One of its proudest achievements was the building of a permanent Exposition Building in 1912. The idea behind the project was to have a centre where businessmen who visited the city could come "to be informed of the industrial conditions and circumstances of our capital, and . . . definitely plan out the founding of new enterprises in our midst." In 1911 the Bureau began a program "for assisting worthy British workmen to bring their families to Winnipeg." The objects of the Imperial Home Reunion Movement were described by the Bureau: "Apart from promoting better conditions and surrounding men with family life, the plan works out to the betterment of the business community as a whole in as much as it gives the workmen a greater degree of stability and contentment; it brings no inconsiderable number of new people to our city as residents and as consumers, where otherwise money for their support was largely sent out of the city."[22] Other work carried out by the Bureau included the opening of the first civic art gallery in Canada in December 1912; preparation of illustrated lecture material for use in England, eastern Canada, and the United States; the production of moving pictures; and the promotion of an "Annual Business Men's Tour of the West to promote closer business relations with Winnipeg."[23]

As the undisputed metropolis of the West, Winnipeg was the main repository of entrepreneurial capacity, skilled and unskilled labour. Winnipeg contractors obtained a large share of the construction contracts let by the Canadian Northern and Grand Trunk Pacific railways. Due to its size and location, Winnipeg was the central clearing house for western labour. Private employment agencies, located in shacks near the CPR station, received the demands for labour from farmers, railway contractors, bush camp operators, building contractors, and so on, and through crude wall posters obtained the required hands from the great throngs of immigrants newly arrived to the city. Winnipeg's metropolitan status in the labour market benefited local manufacturers as well, since they were generally able to obtain help without difficulty from among local workers and their families.

By 1913, Winnipeg had eighteen private employment offices, located mainly in the immigrant section near the CPR station. These agencies recruited men from recently arrived immigrants and the casuals of a frontier city. Railways and bush contractors were their chief clients and the employment shacks were always plastered with such notices as "100 Men Wanted", "2 Teamsters Wanted", "1 Cook Wanted." Men would step into the agencies,

Winnipeg was the great labour market of western Canada, containing numerous placement offices. In 1913, for example, Winnipeg had 18 private employment offices, located chiefly in rough shacks in the poor foreign section near the CPR depot. These recruited their men from recent immigrants, those precariously established in the city and the many transients of a frontier community. Railway and bush contractors were their chief clients and the shacks were always plastered with signs. Men would step in, inquire the details and if the job were satisfactory, sign a contract agreeing to work. The agent charged the contractor a fee, usually a dollar, and some charged the man also.

check on the advertised position, and sign a contract agreeing to work. The agent made his profit by charging the employer a fee.[24]

The importance of railways in Winnipeg's economic structure assured the growth of organized labour in the city since railway workers were among the first to seek collective protection. Several local unions were organized in the 1880s, and the American-based Knights of Labor was established during these years. But it wasn't until the 1890s that the trade union movement really expanded. During this decade a Trades and Labour Council was organized to give greater strength to the growing number of unions, the first shop craft lodges were established by CPR maintenance workers, and *The People's Voice* (later *The Voice*), a newspaper dedicated to the cause of labour and progressive reform, was founded under the editorship of Arthur W. Puttee.[25]

By 1900, conflicts between workers and employers began to break out with increasing regularity. Several strikes were fought in the railway system but the major strikes occurred in 1906. In that year troops with machine guns were eventually called out by civic authorities to quell the violence that broke out after the Winnipeg Electric Railway Company imported "scabs" from eastern Canada to break a strike by motormen and conductors. The Vulcan Iron Works broke a metalworkers' strike with court injunctions and a lawsuit.[26]

A typical member of the commercial elite, E. F. Hutchings, reflects the attitudes toward labour shared by Winnipeg businessmen.[27] In 1911, severe comments had been made about the working conditions at his saddlery plant, and at the request of several employees, the city Ministerial Association had consented to talk to the owner. The issue at stake was not only the working conditions but also the fact that ten employees had been dismissed when they refused to sign a statement that they would have nothing to do with a union. The *Winnipeg Saturday Post* of November 4, 1911, told what happened to what it termed "ministerial meddlers":

> That super-serviceable body, the Ministerial Association, has been rushing in again upon a matter which was none of its business, and has again made itself ridiculous in the eyes of sensible persons.... Unfortunately for the fulfillment of its promises to the dismissed workers the Ministerial Association had figured without its host — no less a person than President E. F. Hutchings of the Great West Saddlery Company. Mr. Hutchings has no use for labour unions. He has built up and conducted a large business successfully without union labour, and is quite outspoken in his intention to keep on in the same old way. When the committee [met with him] to ask what he was going to do about the ten long straw workers, they were told it was none of their business, but that if they really wished to know, he did not propose to do anything, except manage his own business without help from labour agitators or the Ministerial Association. . . .

The *Saturday Post* went on to criticize the ministers for "condemning a reputable business firm" and to suggest that the value of the Ministerial Association's voice in public affairs was "in exact ratio to the infrequency with which it is heard."

In spite of poor labour-management relations, Winnipeg reached the height of its power and influence in the west in the years 1886-1913. It controlled wholesaling from the Great Lakes to the Rockies, the grain trade for the entire prairie region, its financial institutions operated throughout Canada, and manufacturing and retailing flourished. Although other cities such as Edmonton and Calgary were beginning to develop into important urban centres, Winnipeg was dominant by far.[28]

POPULATION GROWTH AND ETHNIC RELATIONSHIPS

Like their counterparts in other North American cities, Winnipeggers were fascinated with the growth of their community. The number of residents the city had at any particular time was considered to be of paramount importance, especially in comparing Winnipeg's advancement with that of other cities.[29] Almost as important in a community whose civic leaders and eminent citizens were exclusively Anglo-Saxon and Protestant — at least until the 1950s — was the ethnic and religious composition of the population. For although Winnipeggers were firm believers in the virtues of immigration, most did not easily reconcile themselves to the resultant polyglot population. The pride that came with the sharp rise in population was diminished by the knowledge that much of this growth was caused by so-called "foreign" elements. It has only been in recent years that Winnipeggers have seen the strong cos-

Main Street, 1904.

mopolitan makeup of their city as a major advantage; a point of view that was adopted only after considerable years of outright discrimination against "foreigners."[30]

During the first quarter century of its history as an incorporated city when Winnipeg was growing from a small cluster of wooden stores and homes housing eighteen hundred citizens to a major Canadian city of forty thousand people, three significant population trends were established. First, with the exception of a sharp increase in population in the early 1880s following the arrival of the CPR, growth was steady and unspectacular before 1900. Second, virtually all the growth achieved during this early period resulted from the influx of immigrants: natural increase was limited by a shortage of women (Appendix, Table II) and a high infant mortality rate,[31] and the expansion of the city's boundaries in 1875 and 1882 added relatively few citizens (see Map 4). Third, the early flow of immigrants into Winnipeg had its origin in two main sources: Great Britain and Ontario. This last was the most significant, and early established the essentially Anglo-Canadian nature of the city.

The rate of population growth in Winnipeg was from the outset far greater than the population growth rate of Manitoba and the other western provinces.[32] At an early date Winnipeg became and thereafter long remained the largest urban centre in all of western Canada (Appendix, Tables III and IV). Furthermore, by 1911 Winnipeg had become the third largest city in Canada, a position it held until the 1920s when it was bypassed by Vancouver.[33]

Before 1880, the population of the city of Winnipeg increased fairly slowly from about two thousand in 1874 to just over six thousand six years later. This was followed by a short burst of growth in the early eighties when the population climbed to over twenty thousand by 1886 (Appendix, Table V). By this time, however, the boom had already collapsed and for the balance of the decade growth was moderate. It was not until the late 1890s that all the conditions necessary for rapid population growth were present and a sustained boom could take place.

The slow rate of population growth in Winnipeg during this period did not go unnoticed, particularly by city council and the Board of Trade. Obsessed as these groups were with the expansion of their community, they set out to do something about the slow rate of growth. The methods adopted to attract immigrants varied

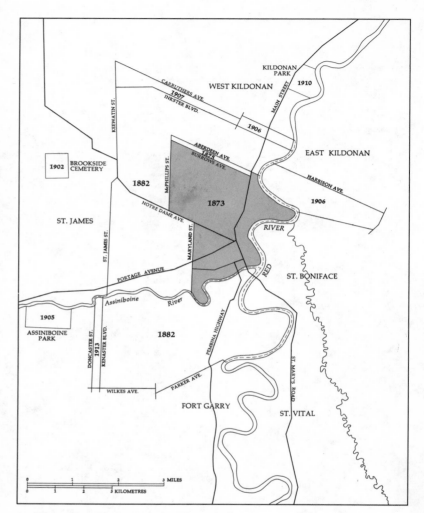

4 Boundary Extensions 1873-1913

The first CPR depot in Winnipeg was completed in 1883 but burned down three years later. A second station was soon built but it lasted only until 1905 when the present structure shown here was completed. The CPR depot was located close to Main Street and the federal immigration sheds and was the disembarking point for hundreds of thousands of immigrants over the years. This photograph shows the Countess of Dufferin being moved to Sir William Whyte Park.

over the years but included such practices as the publication of guides to Winnipeg and western Canada, the hiring of paid immigration agents, organized tours for newspaper reporters, advertisements in European, British and American newspapers, and the formation of such organizations as the Western Canadian Immigration Association and the Winnipeg Development and Industrial Bureau. The various programs had two things in common: all were costly and were largely financed by public rather than private funds.[34]

Not only did Winnipeg grow primarily because of immigration, it was immigration of a very particular kind. With the exception of small numbers of Jews, Scandinavians and Germans, the great bulk of immigrants arriving in Winnipeg came from Ontario and from Great Britain. Whether measured in terms of birthplace (Appendix, Tables VI and VII), ethnic origin (Appendix, Table VIII) or religious affiliation (Appendix, Table IX), the importance of the Protestant, British-Ontario immigrant in Winnipeg is striking.

The early arrival of a large number of Anglo-Saxons in Winnipeg is extremely important in understanding Winnipeg's subsequent history, as this group early established itself as the city's dominant charter group. The entry of Manitoba into Confederation in 1870 was followed by a mass influx of British and Ontario migrants into the province and as early as 1880 the original makeup of the community at Fort Garry — a balance of English, French, and Indian-Métis — was dramatically altered. The new majority of Anglo-Protestants quickly and effectively established their economic, social, political and cultural beliefs as the norm. Thereafter, all newcomers were expected to conform to an established British mould.[35]

This is not to say that the Anglo-Saxon majority was a completely homogeneous group. Encompassing, as it did, English, Scots, Irish and Ontario elements, the charter group was at one level culturally diverse.[36] Yet what was more important than this diversity was the fact that the dominant British-Ontario group felt themselves to be no less a unity than was Britain itself. The diversity that existed was almost completely obscured by the fact that the various elements were bound together by their common language, Protestant religion, and British heritage. The dominant group was further united in Winnipeg by its common experience: they had all migrated to Winnipeg and were working together to build a new community.

For those who came from other countries and non-Anglo-Saxon backgrounds adjustment was achieved only with the utmost difficulty. The sense of alienation experienced by the foreign newcomer is clearly revealed in the following penetrating comment by a Hungarian immigrant on the ethnic divisions of Winnipeg society:

> "The English," he whispered, " . . . the only people who count are the English. Their fathers got all the best jobs. They're the ones nobody ever calls foreigners. Nobody ever makes fun of their names or calls them 'bologny-eaters,' or laughs at the way they dress or talk. Nobody," he concluded bitterly, "cause when you're English it's the same as being Canadian."[37]

The intent of the dominant British population to enforce their cultural norms meant that ethnic pluralism was not even contemplated during this period. Rather, the British were determined to follow the melting pot approach of the United States, and it was the English majority who were "to provide the recipe and stoke the fire."[38]

Nothing sums up the nature of Winnipeg society in this period better than the reaction of its citizens to the Boer War. In 1899 thousands of Winnipeggers bid a rousing farewell at a mass rally on Main Street in front of City Hall to fifty Winnipeg members of the Canadian contingent. The editor of the city's social newspaper, *Town Topics*, voiced the sentiments of Anglo-Saxon Winnipeg when he declared: "I know nothing that would bind the Empire so strongly together as associations in an enterprise of this kind. It will show the world that . . . when we speak of the 'Soldiers of the Queen,' we mean all who carry arms whenever the Union Jack waves, from India to Australia, from Windsor Castle to [Winnipeg] Osborne Street Barracks."[39]

Led by a central core of Anglo-Saxons who by 1899 had had a full generation to establish themselves as community leaders, Winnipeg would remain in spirit, if not in fact, a "British" city for over fifty years.

While the years before 1900 witnessed relatively slow growth and harmonious ethnic relationships, the decade following the turn

Dominion Immigration Building. For most immigrants, their first few nights in Winnipeg were spent in the over-crowded and inadequate immigration hall.

of the century was marked by a rapid rate of growth and a sharp increase in tensions between the Anglo-Saxon Winnipeggers and the immigrant population. The growth of Winnipeg after 1900 was phenomenal. From a small city of 42,000 in 1901, it swelled to a sprawling metropolis of 150,000 by 1913 and rose from sixth place to third in the ranks of Canadian cities, surpassed only by Montreal and Toronto. Throughout the decade, Winnipeggers witnessed the most spectacular increase their community would ever undergo.

James Gray, in his book *The Boy From Winnipeg*, described this period of the city's history:

> The Winnipeg of my boyhood was a lusty, gutsy, bawdy fron-
> tier boom-town roaring through an unequalled economic
> debauch. . . . In a single decade more than 500,000 immigrants
> found their way from the four corners of Europe to Western
> Canada. All of them passed through Winnipeg, and a good
> one in ten of them went no further. . . . All summer long, Bri-
> tish and European immigrants trudged back and forth
> between the Canadian Pacific and Canadian Northern stations
> en route to their new homesteads. Carpenters, bricklayers,
> stonemasons, tinsmiths, plasterers, and painters worked from
> dawn to dusk putting up new railway shops, new warehouses
> for wholesalers, and new homes for the thousands of train-
> men, machinists, retail store clerks, bank clerks and bartend-
> ers who were flocking into town on every train from the east.

The official census returns which recorded Winnipeg's growth throughout the period tell only part of the story. Winnipeg also had a significant floating population. This group was made up almost entirely of single males who came west in search of work. Since Winnipeg served as the main recruiting centre for railway and bush contractors, farmers and manufacturers, nearly all of these men spent time in the city. Every summer, for example, easterners flocked west to help with the harvest; in 1912 there were 25,000 harvest excursionists in the city. Then, in the fall when the men were released from their summer occupations they again trekked to Winnipeg in search of employment. A few received positions in bush camps through the efforts of private employment agencies, but job opportunities during the cold winter months were limited. Some of the slack was taken up by casual work, whether stoking furnaces, splitting wood, or shovelling snow. Others left Winnipeg for a milder climate. Yet there remained a large number who stayed in Winnipeg, encouraged to remain by the facilities of a large city — its pool rooms, theatres, cheap cafes and rooming houses, and brothels.[40]

Although Winnipeg's rapid population growth delighted the residents, it also presented an almost countless series of problems. The ebb and flow of transient workers had an unsettling effect upon Winnipeg's social life, while the rapid increase in the number of permanent residents meant that the maintenance of social order and the protection of the public welfare required endless attention. The difficulties of enforcing laws, safeguarding public health, providing municipal services such as sewers and water, and securing consensus on social values were all magnified as the population grew.

Of all the problems faced during the decade, the question of assimilating large numbers of foreigners was uppermost in the minds of the city's British majority. The problems of absorbing large numbers of newcomers into the community was intensified when it was found that a large portion of immigrants arriving in Winnipeg after 1900 were Slavs and Jews, people who were feared as "strangers within our gates." This apprehension on the part of the city's Anglo-Saxons stemmed from the fact that these new arrivals, along with the inevitable differences of background, language, and religion, brought with them a resilient sense of ethnic pride that was new in Winnipeg. Moreover, large numbers of the newcomers tended to segregate themselves in "foreign ghettos" in the North End. In brief, the overwhelming numbers, the ethnic nationalism, the different — even strange — religions, and the tendency towards marked residential segregation all led to profound feelings of fear and apprehension on the part of Winnipeg's Anglo-Saxon charter group.

The dimensions of this hostility and apprehension can best be understood by recognizing that the dramatic increase in the number and variety of foreign-born residents in Winnipeg was a unique experience in Canadian urban development. While other cities were also receiving large influxes of immigrants, none received so many from such diverse sources in such a short period of time. The percentage of foreign-born in Winnipeg jumped from just under

Railway shop workers.

thirty-eight per cent in 1901 to over fifty-five per cent by 1911, an increase of over sixty thousand persons. Moreover, a comparison of Winnipeg with other Canadian cities reveals that only two other centres (Victoria and Calgary) had larger proportions of foreign-born in 1911. And in both cases the higher percentages were the result of large numbers of British-born residents rather than European-born or other non-Anglo-Saxon persons.[41] Uneasy with the increasing numbers of European-born Winnipeggers, the charter group attempted to avoid the immigrants by withdrawing into a solid, isolated group in the city's south and west ends. By the outbreak of war Winnipeg was a partitioned city, separated on the basis of language and ethnic origin.

Expressions of outright bigotry toward the Slav and Jew were voiced frequently in Winnipeg after 1900. The newcomers' use of alcohol offended many, especially the ladies of the Women's Christian Temperance Union, who invariably linked "foreigners, liquor dealers, and politicians in a chain of corruption and degradation."[42] Comments such as: "The Slav has not thus far proved himself the equal of the northwestern European as an immigrant," and "They are the unfortunate product of a civilization that is a thousand years behind the Canadian," were both expressed and believed by the charter group.[43] Some Winnipeggers became so concerned over the presence of large numbers of Slavs and Jews that in a rare abandonment of their belief in the merits of growth they advocated a policy of exclusion or, at the very least, a strictly controlled quota system. The following excerpt from the *Winnipeg Telegram* is typical:

> There are few people who will affirm that Slavonic immigrants are desirable settlers, or that they are welcomed by the white people of Western Canada. . . . Those whose ignorance is impenetrable, whose customs are repulsive, whose civilization is primitive, and whose character and morals are justly condemned, are surely not the class of immigrants which the country's paid immigration agents should seek to attract. Better by far to keep our land for the children, and children's children, of Canadians, than to fill up the country with the scum of Europe.[44]

The key agent in the immigrant assimilation process was the public school system. Most Anglo-Saxon Winnipeggers looked to the school "as the mightiest assimilation force for elevating the immigrant to the level of Canadian life."[45] The city's leaders felt strongly that on the school "more than any other agency will depend the quality and nature of the citizenship of the future; that in the way in which the school avails itself of its opportunity depends the extent to which Canadian traditions will be appropriated, Canadian national sentiment imbibed, and Canadian standards of living adopted by the next generation of the new races that are making their homes in our midst."[46]

From the standpoint of Winnipeg's charter group, however, there were serious problems associated with using the public school system as an assimilating agent. First, there was the problem of providing adequate facilities and teaching staff to serve the rapidly growing student population.[47] But the second difficulty, that of language, was even more severe. It was difficult to train a sufficient number of teachers who could speak both English and the language of the immigrants they faced in the classroom. The situation that developed was described by the principal of one North End school:

> Imagine if you can, a young girl, herself only a few years out of school, facing a class of fifty children, none of whom could understand a word spoken by her pupils. The children could not converse with each other, excepting in small groups of those who had learned the same language in their homes. Obviously the first task was to get teachers and pupils to understand each other.[48]

The city's Anglo-Saxons realized, moreover, that they had to reach more than school-age children if the process of assimilation through education was to be successful. Accordingly, Mayor Ashdown was instrumental in having the Winnipeg School Board establish a system of evening classes in 1907. During that year ten English-language evening classes were opened for foreigners and six more were soon added, twelve of which were north of the CPR tracks. To attract students to the classes advertisements were run in the city's numerous foreign-language newspapers and handbills in five languages were printed and widely distributed.[49]

The efforts of the Winnipeg School Board to use the educational system as an assimilating agent were frustrated by problems other than facilities and language. One of these was the tendency of the

GRAFLEX CAMERA PHOTOGRAPH

This photograph appeared in the 1912 Annual Report of the superintendent of neglected children for the Province of Manitoba (Winnipeg).

School and students, 1893.

Settlers' goods at CPR depot, 1909. One of the major reasons for Winnipeg's prosperity was that it serviced the needs of the hundreds of thousands of immigrants who went west. Settlers needed farm implements, lumber, hardware goods, wagons, harnesses, consumer goods, etc., and the merchants of Winnipeg reaped fortunes supplying these goods.

The rapid growth of Winnipeg, coupled with the authorities' callous attitude, meant that many Winnipeggers could not find — or could not afford — cheap rented accommodation. This man built his own shelter, taking care to insulate it by banking earth against the exterior wall.

city's ethnic groups to take upon themselves the task of educating their children in the language and culture of their particular group. This was true for almost every nationality, be it Scandinavian, German, Slavic or Jewish. It was estimated that in 1911 at least three thousand foreigners were attending private or separate schools in Winnipeg. Thousands more attended evening or weekend classes conducted by the religious and cultural organizations of the various ethnic groups.[50]

The education-assimilation question was eventually brought to a head by two other problems: the lack of compulsory school attendance legislation and conflict over the language of instruction.[51] The Public Schools Act of Manitoba permitted bilingual schools but did not provide for compulsory attendance. The clauses of the Public Schools Act dealing with language of instruction had been enacted in 1897.[52] In the first few years of operation the legislation worked as it was intended, to allow French children to be taught in their mother tongue. But since even this compromise was less than satisfactory to most Winnipeggers, it became intolerable when instruction in languages other than English was sought not only by the French but by the Ukrainians, Poles and others. The editor of the *Manitoba Free Press*, John W. Dafoe, noted with unconcealed horror that this had led by 1907 to some thirteen different languages being used in provincial schools as the language of instruction.[53]

The hostile reaction of Winnipeg's charter group to the use of languages other than English in public schools was intensified when they saw their taxes being used to train teachers to meet the demands for non-English speaking teachers. During this period the provincial government established at least two special training schools for bilingual teachers: a Polish Teachers' Training School and a Ruthenian Training School. Indeed, much to the consternation of the charter group, the Ukrainian teachers even established their own teachers' organization, held conventions in the city and published a weekly newspaper,[54] a journal which the *Winnipeg Tribune* described in June 1914 as being "subversive and destructive of Canadian citizenship and Canadian nationality."

The reaction of the charter group to the lack of a school attendance law was equally hostile. Many Winnipeg children were receiving little or no education. To make matters even worse, this was particularly true in the case of new immigrants who, owing to economic need or just plain ignorance and fear, kept their children away from classes. Faced with this situation, there arose in Winnipeg a demand for compulsory education as an absolute necessity. The problem was explained as follows:

> [Immigrant] children are growing up without an education, save in wickedness. Every day they are becoming a serious menace to the country. The future, if this continues, is very alarming. There must be compulsory education. There must! The party, the parliament, the government which permits a venerable obstacle to stand in the way of this absolute necessity to the very safety of the Dominion, which permits love for office or power to delay the enactment or proper enforcement of proper legislation whereby every child shall be compelled to attend school has forefeited all right to the respect of the people, and whatever its merits, must be replaced by those who have vision and courage to discern and do what is imperative.[55]

These opinions received widespread support among the English community in Winnipeg. In 1902, for example, a delegation headed by Mayor John Arbuthnot met with members of the provincial government and strongly urged the necessity of compulsory education.[56] And in 1909 a "citizen's meeting," attended by such well-known Winnipeggers as ex-mayors Ashdown and Ryan and Alderman Riley, reported that "thousands of children never attend a school and were growing up absolutely illiterate and that such a condition will work as a menace to the community. The opinion prevailed that the solution of the question . . . lay in the immediate passage by the provincial government of a compulsory education bill."[57]

Given the apparently unanimous agreement among the English majority on the need for compulsory education and unilingual schools, it is necessary to explain why their views were not met by the provincial government.[58] The Conservative government, headed by Premier Roblin, drew heavily on the ethnic vote to maintain its hold on office.[59] Indeed, Roblin had made a compact with the Roman Catholic Archbishop of St. Boniface that stipulated he would not disturb the status quo in return for the relatively small

Although by eastern standards Winnipeg was a young city, it had developed large slum areas by World War I. This view of the interior of an immigrant "home" shows the poverty and crowding. In many cases, several families shared the same dwelling.

but powerful (in terms of provincial seats) French vote. The agreement was a good one for Roblin and served him well until 1915. The government's only efforts to appease the rising tide of protest in Winnipeg against this attempt to curry favour with the minority groups were the unsuccessful attack on truancy in the city by tightening the enforcement of the provincial Children's Act,[60] and the passage, in 1906, of flag legislation that required all provincial schools to fly the Union Jack during school hours.[61]

In the face of this attitude on the part of Premier Roblin and the Conservatives many in the city turned to the provincial Liberal party and its leader, T. C. Norris, who took a firm stand on the education question. And, shortly after a Liberal victory in 1915, the new provincial government established a unilingual school system and passed a compulsory attendance law. Although the matter of bilingual schools has since remained an issue of some importance in Manitoba, the settlement achieved in 1916 is still in effect. In general, the legislation had the desired impact so far as the charter group was concerned and in subsequent years all immigrants of school age learned English as a matter of course. On the other hand, the heated rhetoric of the campaign itself intensified interracial hostility in Winnipeg for decades.

The attempt of the charter group to assimilate the non-Anglo-Saxon was only one side of the coin. The other was the formidable adjustment problem faced by the immigrants themselves. The most pressing concern, of course, was to obtain employment. For those whose background had equipped them with a specific trade or skill there was little difficulty in adjusting to the economic conditions of their new surroundings. Many, however, were poverty-stricken peasants with neither training nor capital. The second major area of adjustment was more complicated. This was the matter of social and structural assimilation, a process that could be considered complete when the immigrant had learned the language and social usages of the city well enough to participate in its economic, political and social life without encountering prejudice. The emphasis here was on externals such as the ability to speak English, and the adoption of the dress, manners, and the social rituals of the dominant group. Finally, and most difficult of all, was cultural assimilation, a process of inter-penetration and fusion in which the immigrant acquired the memories, sentiments and attitudes of the city's dominant group, and by sharing their experience and history became incorporated with them in a broad and all-embracing cultural life.

In pre-World War I Winnipeg only the process of economic adjustment was achieved to any great extent; social assimilation was just beginning when the tensions of the war and the Winnipeg General Strike temporarily halted the process. Cultural assimilation, the most difficult and gradual process, usually requiring two or three generations, did not get underway until well into the thirties, forties, and fifties.[62]

In the process of economic adjustment all immigrants in Winnipeg were aided by the fact that the city enjoyed economic prosperity throughout the pre-war period. Except for a few severe but shortlived recessions — such as in 1907-1908 — employment opportunities were plentiful.[63] But finding employment did not necessarily mean that the newcomer achieved economic security. A study conducted by J. S. Woodsworth in 1913 indicated that a normal standard of living in Winnipeg required an income of at least $1,200 per year. Yet, Woodsworth continued, "It is difficult to find an actual workingman's family budget which maintains a normal standard. Large numbers of workmen are receiving under $600 per year, many under $500, half of what is necessary."[64] These economic realities meant that many immigrants were forced to resort to drastic measures in their struggle for survival. Often families broke up as mothers and even children went to work to supplement the incomes of their husbands and fathers. The immigrant, already tested by the new conditions of life in Winnipeg, was further demoralized by the effects of low wages.

The fact that thousands of families had an inadequate standard of living in an apparently prosperous city was brought to the attention of city council on several occasions, particularly after 1900. Private charities, individual investigators, the Trades and Labour Council, and even the municipal health department reported on the inequities of income and called for improved health and building bylaws, municipal housing, fair wage schedules, public works programming, and a host of other progressive measures. For the most part these pleas were ignored. Although Winnipeg had a relief committee as early as 1874, its work never extended beyond aiding those in particularly desperate straits and in the period 1900-1913,

All Peoples' Mission was sponsored by the Methodist Church and was one of Winnipeg's most effective assimilation agents.

for example, the city spent, on the average, only $6,200 a year on relief.[65]

There are several factors which help explain Winnipeg's failure to deal with its social problems in a progressive manner. First of all the city's governing elite was obsessed with the need for growth and tended to discourage financial support for any activity which did not promote direct economic returns. The drain of capital, both public and private, into economic enterprises and promotional schemes, such as the Winnipeg Development and Industrial Bureau, left little for community services.[66] Another factor was the age-sex ratio of the city's population (Appendix, Tables II and X). The absence of a large older age group during these early years may well have relieved the pressure upon health and welfare institutions but it also removed the steadying influence of tradition and deprived the community of the leadership of those not strenuously engaged in making a living.[67] Similarly, with relatively few children among the early settlers, extensive educational, medical and recreational facilities were not required in the early years. But when the situation changed rapidly with the heavy influx of immigrant families, problems of maternity and infant welfare and education quickly assumed considerable importance.[68]

Still another element that accentuated the city's social problems was the fact that those persons who had the strongest voice in the direction of institutional policies and community services were the very ones who were least exposed to the disturbing conditions faced by the newcomers. Sheltered in their lavish homes in Armstrong's Point, Fort Rouge, and Wellington Crescent, and engaged in a social and business life centred around the Manitoba Club, the Board of Trade, and the St. Charles Country Club, the governing elite's callous stance was often the result of ignorance. While some of these people supported social improvement efforts such as foreign mission work, for the most part they gave little serious thought to the problems in their midst. Temperance, direct legislation, the single tax and woman's suffrage were middle-class diversions which overrode the pressing problems of poverty, overcrowding and disease faced by the city's poor.

Fortunately, however, the process of economic adjustment and assimilation did not rely exclusively on the inadequate agencies of the civic corporation. Both were aided by a host of voluntary associations. Winnipeg's groups were legion. They included the Sons of England, the St. Andrew's Society, the Irish Association, the German Society, the Icelandic (Progressive) Society, the (Polish) St. Peter and Paul Society, the Zionist Society, the Ruthenian National Society, and numerous others. Exclusive without being invidious, such clubs served as guideposts for the bewildered immigrant. They identified other residents with similar backgrounds and interests and encouraged participation in common activities. Coupled with the churches, unions, and ethnic newspapers, membership in these organizations alleviated economic insecurity by providing funds, assistance and insurance in cases of destitution, illness and death. Finally, ethnic-based political and commercial associations promoted involvement in matters involving municipal authorities and even the federal government. Voluntary organizations first introduced the immigrant to the community and afterwards linked him to it.[69]

The voluntary nature of these organizations also meant, however, that they had neither the inclination nor the means to help every immigrant, even if the newcomer belonged to the appropriate ethnic group. The general lack of affluent membership among the Jewish and Slavic organizations, for example, meant that when need was discovered often little could be done.[70] In Winnipeg, as in other cities, the void was partially filled by private charities organized to meet specific needs rather than to serve particular groups.[71]

Winnipeg was fortunate in having several such charitable agencies, led by what can only be called practical idealists. Although the best known was All People's Mission, other such as the Margaret Scott Nursing Mission and the Salvation Army were also active.[72] All People's was founded in 1898 by the Methodists to carry out traditional religious salvation work but by 1910, under the leadership of J.S. Woodsworth, it was doing far more than that. A partial listing of its program includes the running of two kindergartens; visits to immigrants' homes; boys' and girls' classes and clubs; a fresh-air camp; the provision of swimming and gymnasium facilities; night classes in English and civics; Sunday schools; free legal advice; pressure for a Juvenile Court (established in 1908); hospital visitation; welcoming immigrants at the federal immigration buildings; mothers' meetings; dispensation of relief; concerts and debates; and numerous other activities.[73]

One of the chief values of the work of All People's, and other agencies like it, was the publicity its work gave to conditions in Winnipeg's "foreign ghetto." Winnipeg's daily newspapers gave generous space to the activities of the Mission and until the war — when charges of catering to "enemy aliens" were laid — praised Woodsworth unreservedly. Also, the work of All People's and other such missions is noteworthy since they were usually staffed, led and financed by Anglo-Saxons. The genuine commitment of such agencies to Winnipeg's poor (of whatever ethnic origin) clearly indicates that not all of the city's charter group were concerned only with economic growth. At the same time, however, it must be noted that these agencies were no less intent on assimilating the immigrant than were either the Winnipeg School Board or the Orange Order. What distinguished the social service agencies from the others was the generally humanitarian nature of their proselytism.

THE URBAN LANDSCAPE

Winnipeg's urban landscape was built in the years before 1913 according to a strict pattern determined by history, geography and economics. One of the first issues that confronted city council after incorporation in 1874 was the layout of Winnipeg's streets which had been largely determined by river-lot farming and fur trade routes.[74] Main Street was already well established as the most important street in the city. This former trail along the Red River, which had been a main route of travel between the early Selkirk Settlement and the Hudson's Bay Company's post of Upper Fort Garry, was never straightened, however; and its crookedness was to cause city council many headaches over the years. But the adoption of a 132-foot right-of-way for Main Street and Portage Avenue partially compensated for their irregular courses. The widths of Portage Avenue and Main Street were not dictated by visions of eight-lane traffic but were based on the mode of travel of the early Red River carts. The carts tended to move in a rough echelon pattern which took up a great deal of space. The reasons for this were that a long single file of carts would have been vulnerable to ambush, and by travelling in a random fashion the deep, muddy ruts of the carts ahead could be avoided.[75]

The familiar and historic pattern of long, narrow strips of land fronting on the river provided the basis for new street plans. Thus all the streets north of Notre Dame, which ran west from the Red River and crossed Main Street, closely followed the boundary lines of the early lots. Similarly, in the area between Notre Dame and the Assiniboine River, the streets ran north from the latter, meeting Notre Dame at a sharp angle (see Map 5).

In these early years Notre Dame was intended to become, after Main Street, the most important street in Winnipeg. Notre Dame Avenue formed an axis; streets leading north from the Assiniboine River swung east at Notre Dame and then ran out at right angles across those running west from the Red River. Significantly, in these early plans, Portage Avenue (then called Queen) and the area south of it were unplanned and undeveloped.

Given this real and planned importance of Main Street and Notre Dame Avenue, it is not surprising that the residential sections of the city tended to group around them. In the area between Main Street and the Red River were located most of the residences built before 1874. Point Douglas, surrounded by the river on three sides, was, prior to the coming of the railroad, one of the most desirable locations in the young community. Many of the founders of Winnipeg had homes there, including James H. Ashdown, W. G. Fonseca, Robert and Stewart Mulvey, Dr. Schultz, and others.[76] Close to Main Street was also the desired location of a large number of boarding houses which were a very prominent feature of the growing city. The lack of sufficient space in hotels and the shortage of housing for the large floating population had led many homeowners to provide accommodation to meet the great demand.[77] The streets leading to the waterfront and wharves were also dominated by boarding houses. Finally, it was in the area west of Main Street, and particularly along the streets running parallel to and adjoining Notre Dame Avenue, that most of the post-incorporation residences were situated.

Prior to 1877, then, the built-up portion of the newly incorporated city comprised only a small fraction of its political extent, probably about one-fifth of the administrative area of Winnipeg. This concentration was largely the result of the speculative manipulations of the Hudson's Bay Company. The Company had opposed incorporation because it would have had to pay large amounts of taxes on the 450 acres of land that it owned within the proposed city's boundaries. Following incorporation the Company at first sold only a very limited number of lots in its reserve in the area bounded by Notre Dame Avenue, Main Street, and the Assiniboine River. Consequently, up to 1877 Winnipeg tended to spread north of Notre Dame, leaving this southern section almost untouched. After 1877 the Company sold a large number of lots in the reserve and by 1883 had apparently reaped profits of over $2,000,000. This area quickly developed and became the most desirable residential district in the city. Soon Company officials, government officials, and successful businessmen either located or relocated (moving from Point Douglas) here.

The physical amenities of life that existed in Winnipeg at this time were notable by their absence. Material comforts such as hard-surfaced roadways and sidewalks and a public transportation system simply did not exist. Main Street and Portage Avenue became an impenetrable mass of mire during spring and fall. Indeed, during the 1870s and early 1880s the city was famous for its mud. In wet weather the few patches of wooden sidewalk, to quote a visitor, "floated like barges." Newcomers were told that if they ever saw a hat floating in the mud they were to throw it a line — there would be a man under it.[78]

In this early period there was little residential segregation by either ethnicity or class. The preponderance of the British and Ontarians precluded any significant cultural conflicts that might have been manifested in residential segregation. At incorporation Winnipeg had been divided into four wards — North, South, East, and West[79] — but these divisions generally served only as convenient electoral and administrative boundaries and none of them acquired the distinctive characteristics that would mark the different wards of the city in a later period. It must also be emphasized that at this time there was no pronounced working-class residential district anywhere in Winnipeg. This development did not take place until the appearance of more industry and the routing of the mainline of the Canadian Pacific Railway through Point Douglas.

The commercial and industrial development of the city tended to follow the spatial patterns established by residential building. The part of Main Street between "Portage Road" and Point Douglas contained most of the commercial establishments, and even as early as 1875, the corner of Portage and Main was the centre of most

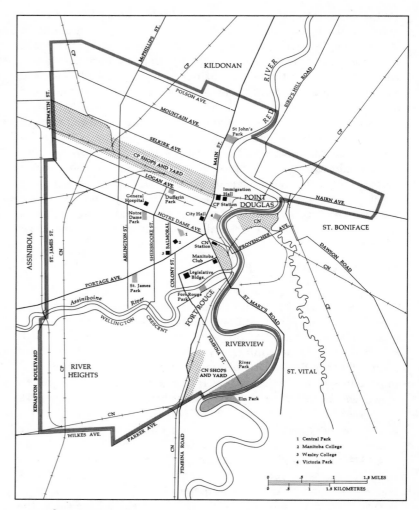

5 Winnipeg in 1907

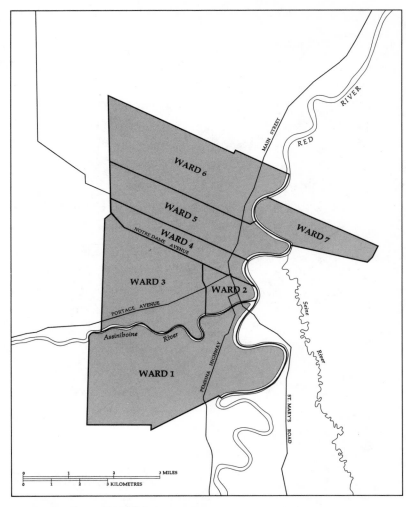

6 Ward Boundaries 1882-1919

business activity. The southern part of Main Street was dominated by Upper Fort Garry, the walls of which cut across the southern end of the street. This was the chief reason why only a few commercial buildings existed there. By 1881, however, Fort Garry had lost much of its reputation as the major component in the commercial life of The Forks and during the boom of 1882 all the Fort except for one gate was torn down to make way for more profitable land use.

The industries of the city during this period consisted mainly of saw and grist mills which were located on the waterfront of the Red River. Two breweries occupied sites at a considerable distance from the built-up area, and a distillery and a soda water factory were located in the centre of Winnipeg. To complete the industrial picture mention need be made only of several carriage and wagon factories and two foundries.[80]

At the beginning of 1881 Winnipeg was a thriving yet relatively small settlement with tenuous connections with its hinterland and the eastern provinces. But all this changed with the routing of the CPR through the city. The real estate boom and the great influx of newcomers after 1881 had marked effects on the urban landscape of Winnipeg. One of the most obvious changes was the expansion of the city's boundaries and the adoption of a new ward system. Winnipeg was divided into six wards in 1882 and a seventh was added in 1906 (see Map 6).

In the years following the real estate boom of 1881-1882, there developed in Winnipeg a series of distinctive environments. The clustering of economic activities, the segregation of classes and ethnic groups, the unequal distribution of municipal services, and different types of residential construction: all created a considerable variety of specialized and unique districts within the city. Indeed, the presence of neighbourhoods of distinctive character distinguished the large City of Winnipeg from its more jumbled predecessor, the small, almost rural community of 1874-1884.

It is impossible in a brief canvass to survey all the variations of neighbourhood which existed in Winnipeg in the years 1884-1913, but by dividing the city into three large districts, and by discussing suburban growth separately, the most important variations can be described and analysed. In general, Wards 2 and 4 became the Central Core; Wards 5, 6, and 7 became the North End; and Wards 1 and 3 formed the South and West Ends respectively. By 1910 a few areas in Winnipeg had been fully built up and some industries and residents were spilling over into new suburbs beyond the city's boundaries. These districts and suburbs, radiating as they did from Portage and Main, reflected the general directions of growth Winnipeg took in this period (see Map 7).

The Central Core

The intersection of Portage and Main had become by 1885, and thereafter remained, the core of the city's commercial focus. Commercial land use spread along Main Street and on streets east and west of this major thoroughfare. Buildings in residential use before 1885 eventually gave way to this growing commercial district. In the central portion of the city real estate prices were relatively high, and in the years after 1885 only business enterprises could afford to purchase lots here. In general, lots on Main Street were priced about twenty times higher than those on the fringe of the central business district. As an example, a lot twenty-eight feet wide on Main Street was assessed at $19,600 in 1885 while one on the eastern fringe of Ward 3 was assessed at only $1,000.[81]

Besides a large number of retail stores and service-oriented establishments (such as real estate agencies), Winnipeg's central core was dominated by the institutions connected with the grain and wholesale trade. With the construction of a Grain Exchange Building near City Hall in 1882, Winnipeg became firmly established as the headquarters of the western grain trade. This new function in the economic structure of the city resulted in the establishment of grain companies, facilities for handling the grain, and new and larger financial institutions. By the early nineties there were the beginnings of a concentrated financial section in the vicinity of City Hall. By 1901 no fewer than twenty-six companies and brokers dealing in grain had their offices in the Grain Exchange Building, and three banks opened branch offices in the neighbourhood. And as a complement to the grain trade a marked concentration of dealers in agricultural supplies appeared in the vicinity of the Grain Exchange Building. In 1901 there were eleven such dealers, including Massey-Harris Co. Ltd., the McCormick Harvesting Machinery Company, and Cockshutt Plow.[82] In 1906 a new Grain Exchange Building was built close to the corner of Portage and Main and this move resulted in a similar step being taken by banks, stockbrokers, and grain merchants. By 1913 more than twenty-five

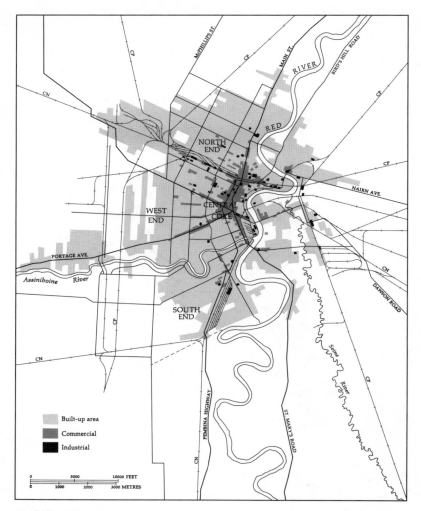

7 Winnipeg in 1913

Grain Exchange Building, c. 1915. The Winnipeg Grain Exchange was organized in 1887 as the Winnipeg Grain and Produce Exchange. The first trading place for the exchange was in the basement of city hall, followed by new quarters on Princess Street in 1892. The Grain Exchange Building shown here was located on Lombard Avenue and was opened in 1903. It was later expanded with the addition of several floors.

Ogilvie Flour Mill. The Montreal-based Ogilvie Milling Company was established in Winnipeg during 1876. The mill shown here was completed in 1882.
The six-storey building is of brick construction with the then popular mansard roof. In its early years the mill had a daily capacity of nine hundred barrels of flour.

The McIntyre Block was built between 1898 and 1900 to replace an earlier structure which was destroyed by fire. The limestone facade of the building made this block one of the most architecturally appealing structures in Winnipeg.

buildings used exclusively for banking and stockbroking were concentrated on Main Street, just north of Portage Avenue. This district was the headquarters for the financial and grain marketing operations of the Canadian west and over the years it gained international recognition.

With the emergence of retail stores in the new agricultural communities along the railway lines, Winnipeg merchants began to profit from an extensive wholesale trade. Within a short time after 1885 this trade assumed a dominant position in Winnipeg's economic structure; in 1890, for example, there were over eighty wholesale firms in the city doing an aggregate turnover of $15 million annually.[83] And the establishments of the wholesale dealers were almost entirely located in the central core, in the area just west of City Hall.

In the period following 1885, warehouses and other commercial buildings rapidly began to supplant the frame buildings of the central core. Stovel's Printing Company erected their new building on the site of a number of old houses, while the Gault Company built their massive 1898 building on the site of the 1876 Methodist-Episcopal Church. By 1905, the commercial district of the central core had been so filled with new structures that smaller 1880s buildings, considered large in their day, were removed for still larger versions. Thus the Merchants' Bank was demolished in 1900 for an eight-storey building. The Robertson Block, built in 1880, was partially demolished to make way for a new Imperial Bank in 1906. And the eleven-storey Union Bank, considered to be Winnipeg's first skyscraper, rose during 1904 from the ruins of an 1887 structure.[84]

In choosing a location for their premises the wholesale companies tended to avoid main thoroughfares such as Main Street and Portage Avenue. The loading and unloading of goods required space which was unavailable in suitable amounts and at a reasonable cost on these streets. Yet a central location was still required, preferably close to the local concentration of retail stores and not too far from the railroad. Consequently the streets branching off Main Street were allotted to the wholesale trade.

The concentration of the wholesale trade in the core was encouraged by two other developments. In 1904 the CPR built a spur from its main line into the heart of the district to serve the many wholesale firms located there. And between 1910 and 1912 the Midland

Railway was also constructed to serve this district. Its right-of-way ran almost the whole length of Ward 4 and warehouses were built on both sides of the tracks. Thus even the western portions of Ward 4 became marked by extensive development of the wholesale trade.

In terms of industrial development the central core did not dominate the city as it did in retail and wholesale trade. Most of Winnipeg's heavy and medium industry was located in other districts. Light industries, such as the garment and printing industries, cigar manufacturing and saddleries, were, however, spread throughout the central area of the city.

It was in the central core as well that the great majority of Winnipeg's other non-residential structures were located. Ward 2 had within its boundaries the Legislative Buildings, Fort Osborne Barracks, the University of Manitoba, the Court House, Provincial Gaol, Post Office and numerous other administrative structures. Here, too, were many of the city's leading hotels and clubs including Hotel Fort Garry and the prestigious Manitoba Club. Similarly, Ward 4 contained City Hall, the Winnipeg General Hospital, and the Winnipeg, Orpheum, Pantages, and Walker theatres.

It was the hotels of the area, however, that had the greatest impact on the character of the central core. The area between the CPR and CNR stations was Winnipeg's hotel row, and along this portion of Main Street were upwards of sixty hotels. In this pre-Prohibition era hotels were first and foremost places to drink, and because of the high concentration of bars, "pedestrians were never beyond the aroma of booze that wafted through the windows and doors of the hotels." The hotels also often had poolrooms attached while in between the hotels were "wholesale boozeries" and "Free Admission Parlours." In the latter customers could choose between flicking-card movies, slot machines, target practice, and a prostitute in the back room.[85] It was this area of pickpockets, pool sharks, prostitutes, confidence men, and booze that inspired one writer to suggest that the city deserved to be called "Winnipeg the Wicked."[86]

The increasingly commercial nature of the central core resulted in its gradual deterioration as a residential area. This decline occurred simultaneously with the development of other accessible and desirable residential locations. Accessible was the key word, for it was not until Winnipeg's rivers had been bridged and the street railway came into general use that the South and West Ends,

The Leland Hotel.

both far removed from the central business district, became viable residential areas. The long period of economic prosperity enjoyed by Winnipeg promoted rapid class turnover in old central city housing and large-scale migration to the new upper-class and middle-class wards and suburbs.

To refer to old central city housing in a city as young as was Winnipeg is not, of course, perfectly accurate. Naturally some of the homes built in the seventies and eighties had deteriorated by 1913. But a large number of the original homes, built as they often were for quite well-to-do persons, remained fine, useful structures which continued to command substantial rents and prices. Thus as original inhabitants moved out, their places were not quickly filled by the lower class for whom the rents and prices remained too steep. Rather, the residential areas of the central core declined very gradually. The result was that Winnipeg escaped a core of poverty simply because of its newness as a settled community. The growing working class and the large numbers of disadvantaged immigrants tended to gravitate to the North End, where land was cheap and a large number of working-class homes were constructed in the years after 1895. In general, then, Winnipeg's spatial growth was marked by a core of middle- and working-class elements, surrounded on the south by the upper class, on the west by the middle class, and on the north by the working class.

The ethnic mix of the central core changed little between 1886 and 1913.[87] Like all districts in Winnipeg in 1886 it was dominated by those of British-Ontario stock, with this group comprising over eighty per cent of the area's population. In the years between 1886 and 1913 the British remained the core's dominant group. While all the other ethnic groups except for the Scandinavians increased their percentage of the district's population during this period, the core's general ethnic mix was substantially retained. Thus, without attempting to account for all the variations that occurred in this thirty-year period, it can be noted that in terms of ethnic composition the central core was the "middle" district of Winnipeg. For while it contained fairly large numbers of all the city's ethnic groups, none except the Germans had a majority of their group located in this district. The great majority of the Slavs, Jews and Scandinavians were situated in the North End, and it was the South and West Ends that had the greatest percentage of British by 1901.

In the trend to ethnic segregation in Winnipeg, the central core was the city's most stable district.

The North End

Wards 5, 6 and 7 comprised the North End, a label that then and since has carried with it a good deal more than geographic meaning. The North End was a synonym for the "foreign quarter", "New Jerusalem", and "CPR Town." Perhaps the best description of the image Winnipeggers held of the North End is found in a novel written about that area. The central character, an East European immigrant, lives amid the "mean and dirty clutter" of the North End; "a howling chaos, . . . an endless grey expanse of mouldering ruin, a heap seething with unwashed children, sick men in grey underwear, vast sweating women in vaster petticoats."[88]

The image of the North End as an undesirable residential location for prosperous Anglo-Saxons was not, of course, formed overnight. Indeed, in the years before the coming of the railroad and the great influx of immigrants, Point Douglas in Ward 3 was the most prestigious residential location in Winnipeg. But this designation did not survive the routing of the CPR main line through Ward 5. By 1895 the North End had in fact become dominated by the working class and by large groups of foreign immigrants.

The development of railway facilities in the North End went through two stages. Between 1882 and 1884 the CPR built its yards, shops and roundhouse in Ward 5. These original facilities did not last beyond 1903. In that year the CPR, in response to the growth of Winnipeg as the commercial and grain centre of the Canadian west, began a vast expansion program.

The role of the CPR in changing the character of the North End was apparent in four general areas. The construction of a large station, locomotive shops, stores and office building, foundry, freight car shops, power house, scrap yard, and immense marshalling yards (120 miles of tracks and space for 10,000 cars) itself represented a considerable industrial development. The huge CPR facilities were the dominant physical feature of the North End. No one could enter that portion of the city without being vividly aware of a maze of buildings and tracks, noise, dirt and smell. In contrast to the central core and the South End, which also had considerable railway facilities located within their boundaries, the CPR yards

Jewish stores like this one in Winnipeg's North End were one of the reasons this area attracted so many Slavic immigrants. The owners of these stores, being natives of eastern European countries, could speak or at least understand most Slavic languages. They also used to sell goods on credit, an arrangement familiar to many newcomers from the small towns of eastern Europe.

were in the heart of the North End and not on the periphery.

The continuing development of Winnipeg as a major railroad centre meant that the railways employed thousands of Winnipeggers. By 1911 over 3,500 persons were employed by the CPR, more than in any other institution in the West. The workers located themselves on either side of the tracks in Wards 5 and 6. The growth of the North End as a working-class area was also a result of the role the railway played in attracting heavy and medium industry. Easy access to the railroad, as the predominant means of transport, was of vital importance for most of these industries. This factor became so important that old established companies left their sites on the Red River and moved west to locations near the railway tracks. In 1901, for example, north Point Douglas was the location for the Ogilvie Flour Mills, Vulcan Iron and Engineering Works, and several saw mills. And by 1913 the location or relocation of medium and heavy industry on both sides of the tracks from Point Douglas to the western boundary of the city was most apparent. Medium industries, such as the manufacturing of carriages and wagons, farm implements, electrical appliances, and malt liquors occurred in the vicinity of Higgins and Jarvis Avenues. Heavy industries, such as bridge and iron works, machine shops, and concrete companies also located on both sides of the tracks, particularly in the western areas of the North End. Although harmful and unsuited to the residential districts around them, these industries, and particularly those in the Point Douglas area, remained in their locations long after it was obvious that more suitable sites were available on the outskirts of the city. The large capital investment and high expense involved in moving prevented their relocation.

Finally, the running of the CPR main line across Ward 5, followed by growth of that company's facilities and the attraction of other industries, effectively cut off the North End from the rest of the city. The result of this large area of industrial development was described in 1912:

> For many years the North End . . . was practically a district apart from the city. . . . The true cause of this isolation was the level railroad crossing intersecting Main Street. The traffic grew immensely; there were many passenger trains constantly going in and out of the station just east of Main Street, and in addition hundreds of freight trains choked the tracks to such

an extent that traffic on Main Street was often blocked for hours. The street cars did not cross the tracks and passengers for the North End had to transfer at the crossing, often waiting many minutes in all kinds of weather. Naturally, with such conditions, . . . those who located north of the tracks were not of a desirable class.[89]

This major impediment to a free movement of residents in and out of the North End was overcome slowly. By 1913 only two overhead bridges and two subways provided access to the North End. And it was not until after 1908 that the city's street railway had more than one crossing of the rail yards.

The general character of the North End as the home for the working class and immigrant was encouraged by Winnipeg's developers and real estate agents. Since Winnipeg had no large stock of old housing to accommodate the thousands who entered Winnipeg in the years after 1896, a great demand arose for new and cheap dwellings. To meet this demand, large tracts of land in the North End were purchased, developed and sold to the newcomers. In order to make large profits, the developers pinched the land: the average lot in the North End was only twenty-five or thirty-three feet wide. Because the land was so crowded with structures, eventual modernization could only be achieved by the enormously cumbersome, disruptive and expensive process of urban renewal.[90]

The North End was also sharply different from the rest of the city in terms of municipal services. Fewer than half the dwellings in the North End were connected with the city's waterworks system. One effect of this disparity in water services is revealed when the infant mortality rates for Winnipeg are examined by districts. In 1913 the North End had a mortality rate of 248.6 deaths per 1,000 births, while in the central core it was 173.1, and in the South and West Ends 116.8. Unfortunately for North End residents, only the City Health Department recognized the connection between these mortality rates and the waterworks situation. Most civic officials and politicians attributed the poor showing of the North End to the ignorance, laziness and immorality of the North End's population, and attempts to improve municipal services in this area were few and inadequate.[91]

The validity of the image of the North End as Winnipeg's "foreign quarter" cannot be questioned. In the early years immigrants

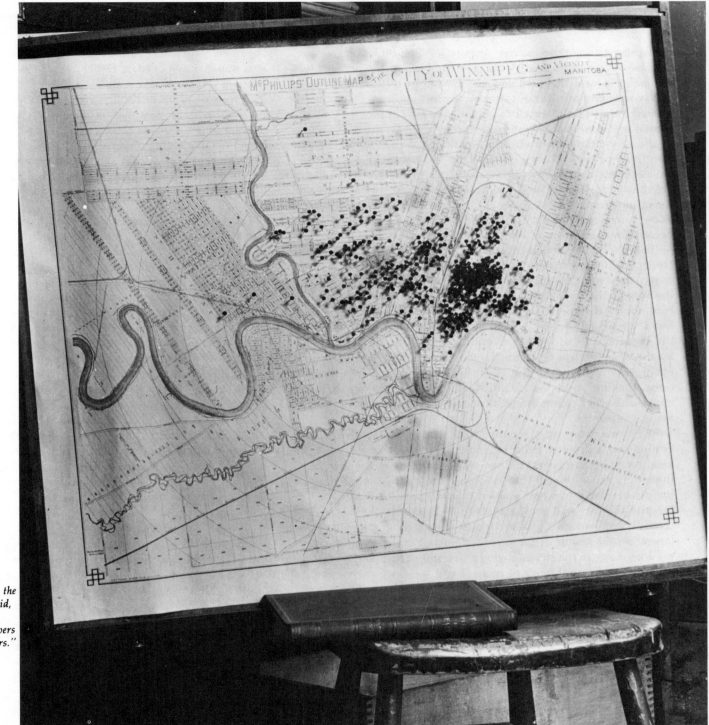

Smallpox was a common disease in pre-war Winnipeg. As this map illustrates, the disease, along with others such as typhoid, was concentrated in the North End, an area poorly serviced with water and sewers and inhabited by Winnipeg's "foreigners."

tended to concentrate in the vicinity of Point Douglas where, because of this area's relative age, some old and cheap housing was available. Their early example was followed by others and by 1913 the North End was unquestionably cosmopolitan. Here were located 87 per cent of the city's Jews, 83 per cent of the Slavs, 67 per cent of the Scandinavians, and 22 per cent of the Germans.

The economic factors already mentioned — the lack of a sufficient quantity of old cheap housing in the central core, the rapid development of a supply of cheap homes in the North End, and proximity to places of work — played the largest role in attracting the immigrant to this area. But in time, as churches and lay institutions were located in the North End to serve the population, these became by themselves one of the factors attracting the newcomer. Still another factor which contributed to the foreign makeup of the North End's population was the desire of the immigrant to enjoy a lively social life. Since ignorance of the English language separated the immigrants from social intercourse with the Anglo-Ontarian community, they preferred to settle down in areas where they could interact with fellow immigrants. Moreover, slowly and gradually the concentration of foreigners in the North End was strengthened by the development of distinctive business and professional establishments operated by the city's Jews and Slavs. These institutions, together with the establishment of churches, synagogues, clubs, and other communal institutions, gave the North End a distinctive character.

The "foreign invasion" of the North End by disfavoured ethnic groups had a decided effect on the Anglo-Saxon residents of the area. As one contemporary noted, "The newcomers not only filled the empty spaces but in time displaced the original inhabitants of the district, most of whom moved to other parts of the city. . . ."[92] Despite the fact that the percentage of British in the North End steadily declined, this group remained throughout the period the largest ethnic group in the district. This, of course, reflects their predominance in the city as a whole. In terms of residential segregation, however, the important point is that only twenty per cent of the British population of Winnipeg were located in specific parts of the district; places that were as much ghettos as were areas where the non-Anglo-Saxons congregated. One of these concentrations was in the western portion of Ward 5, close by the CPR shops on

Logan Avenue where railway employees lived. A more prestigious area was that east of Main Street in the vicinity of St. John's Park in Ward 6.

In spite of Winnipeg's high incidence of ethnic residential segregation, it is significant that large numbers of the city's non-British citizens settled outside the foreign ghettos. Both the Germans and Scandinavians were proud to point to their dispersal throughout the city, which suggests that this group not only had more cultural affinities with the British-Ontarians, but also that they had the financial resources and work skills to advance their economic status.

The inclusion of large numbers of Anglo-Saxons in the North End and the dispersal of some foreigners to other parts of the city did not change the fact that this district's character was determined by its large foreign element. The poverty and illiteracy of the foreign immigrants and their ignorance of the language and customs of the dominant British group had a detrimental influence upon the appearance of the district. Overcrowded houses and tenements, lack of sanitary installations, dirty back-yards, muddy, foul-smelling streets, and poor lighting conditions made up the atmosphere in which the population of North Winnipeg had to live in the years prior to 1913. Yet the entire responsibility for this state of affairs could hardly lie with the foreigner, since the civic authorities and commercial elite neglected the area. There were never a sufficient number of schools for the immigrant child; there were few day-nurseries, kindergartens, dispensaries, or parks; drunkenness was widespread and gambling dens and brothels were wide open. Indeed, it was not for many years after 1913 that the city officials and general public opinion became interested in an overall improvement of conditions in the North End.

South and West Winnipeg

The South End — "home of the economic upper-crust" — and the West End — the district of the prosperous middle class — were the last areas of Winnipeg to develop. The greatest periods of growth in the West End were 1890-1895 and 1900-1912. In the South End it was only in the latter period that large numbers moved into Fort Rouge. Both districts contained low population densities.

There are many factors that explain the relatively late develop-

A middle-class home.

ment of South and West Winnipeg. Prior to 1895 there was sufficient room in the central core for a good deal of expansion and it was only in the years after that date that population pressure began to force residents of the core, and newcomers, to look for new areas in which to live. Coupled with this was the development of new means of intra-urban transportation. An article in the *Manitoba Free Press* in March 1899 noted "No more remarkable development has been witnessed in our day than the growth in the use of the bicycle. It has furnished a new means of locomotion, has solved for a great many people the old problem of rapid transit in the cities."

More important than the growth of the use of the bicycle, however, was the aggressive expansion of Winnipeg's street railway system in the years after the turn of the century. During this time lines were not only considerably lengthened, but service was increased and improved. Thus in 1900 fewer than three and one-half million passengers were carried; in 1904 the paid fares reached nine and one-half million, in 1908 twenty million and in 1913 almost sixty million. These substantial increases were also reflected in the gross earnings of the Winnipeg Electric Railway Company, which jumped from $28,000 in 1900 to over $4,000,000 in 1913.[93] This continuous expansion of public transportation facilities had a cumulative effect on Winnipeg's spatial growth.[94] The pace of suburbanization, at first slow, went forward with increasing acceleration, until by 1910 it attained the proportions of a mass movement. In the period 1900-1912, for instance, South and West Winnipeg gained more new residents than did any of the other districts of Winnipeg.

The construction of bridges across the Assiniboine River also facilitated the growth of South Winnipeg. The first Osborne Street Bridge was built in 1882, the Maryland Bridge in 1894, and the Main Street Bridge in 1897; the latter replacing a private toll bridge built in 1881. Only two of these, however, were crossed by street railway lines before 1900.

Two other factors deserve consideration in the development of the South and West Ends. Unlike the other districts, these areas had relatively little commercial or industrial development. Although the Canadian Northern Railway yards and the retail and service establishments along Portage, Ellice, and Sargent Avenues employed some residents, these districts were inhabited primarily by com-

muters who travelled long distances to places of work. Only with the development of intra-urban transportation and the willingness to use it could these areas grow. The second restraining factor on the development of these districts was that developers, in contrast to the North End, clearly thought of these areas as desirable residential locations. With wider streets, larger lots, and building restrictions only the more affluent of Winnipeg's residents could move to these areas.

The conscious desire to develop exclusive districts in West and South Winnipeg is apparent in the following advertisement placed in local newspapers. Referring to Armstrong's Point in the West End, one advertisement read:

> This most desirable resident portion of the City is now controlled by a syndicate who have authorized us to offer a limited number of Lots for Sale, with building restrictions, ensuring the construction of handsome residences. The improvements now being made by the city and those contemplated by the syndicate with the serpentine drive. . .will make the Point not only the finest locality for artistic and stately homes, but it will become. . ."The Faubourg St. Germain" of Winnipeg, the most fashionable drive in the city.[95]

Besides generous lot sizes, building restrictions, magnificent trees, and proximity to the river, both these areas had other attractive features that would have appealed to Winnipeg's upper crust. The peninsular configuration of Armstrong's Point, for example, kept rapid traffic from the streets and tended to give the area privacy and a sense of identity. The combined effect of all these restrictions and natural advantages were described by one Winnipegger:

> There were no houses in [Armstrong's Point]. There were only castles, huge castles three full stories in height, some with leaded glass windows, and all, certainly, with dozens of rooms. They were built in an assortment of architectural styles and peopled by names from Winnipeg's commercial and industrial *Who's Who*. I was awe-stricken by the sheer size of the houses.[96]

The substantial number of brick dwellings in the South and West

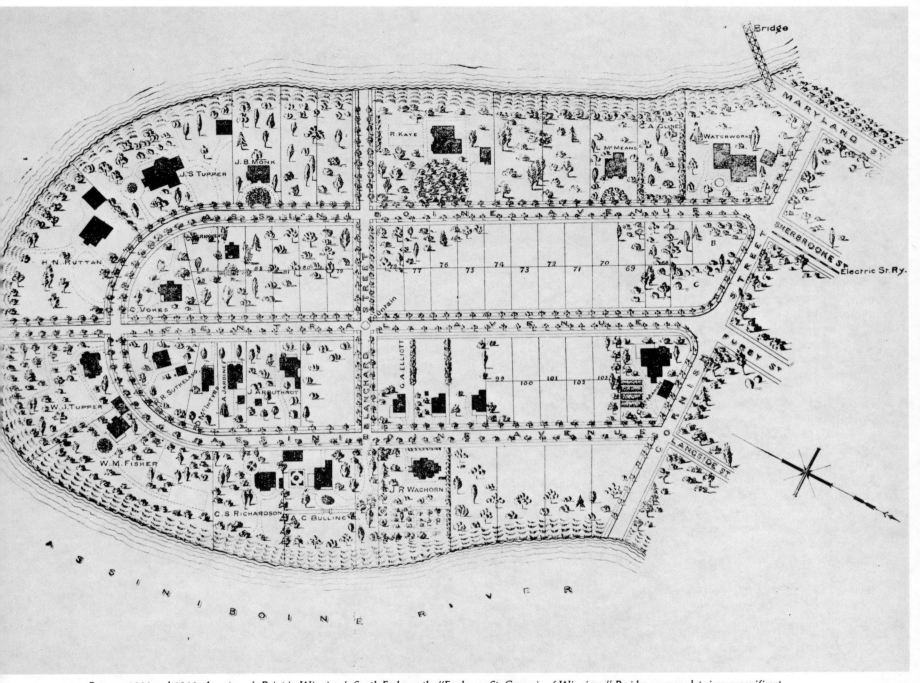

Between 1900 and 1910, Armstrong's Point in Winnipeg's South End was the "Faubourg St. Germain of Winnipeg." Besides generous lot sizes, magnificent trees, and proximity to the Assiniboine River, the Point had other attractive features that appealed to Winnipeg's economic upper-crust. The Point's peninsular configuration prevented heavy traffic, and the privacy this afforded gave the area an aura of luxury.

Interior and exterior views of J. H. Ashdown's home on Wellington Crescent.

Ends reflects the affluence of the areas' residents, but building statistics reveal that both areas had a large number of more modest structures as well.[97] Indeed, the exclusive and upper-class nature of South and West Winnipeg must not be exaggerated. In the area between Notre Dame and Portage Avenue, for example, a great deal of development occurred that differed but little from that carried out in the North End. The area between Portage Avenue and the Assiniboine River, of course, yielded higher land prices because of closeness to the river, and a distinctly middle-class development occurred here. Thus a reporter in 1909 observed that homes north of Portage ranged from "scores of shacks which have cost $150 to $200" to "new cottages and houses averaging $3,000 a piece," while in the area south of Portage homes "usually cost from $3,000 to $5,-000." And, to complete this cost comparison, it was further reported that in the "middle-class areas of central and southern Fort Rouge" homes ranged in cost "from $2,000 to $15,000."[98]

Another dimension of the distinctive character of South and West Winnipeg was its ethnic makeup. All of the South End and most of the West End were inhabited overwhelmingly by those of British origin. It was only in the northern portion of the West End, particularly along Ellice and Sargent Avenues, that significant concentration of Germans and Scandinavians occurred. It was, moreover, usually the more successful of these groups who lived in these areas, those who by education or economic success had "graduated from Point Douglas to the West End."[99]

With the development of South and West Winnipeg as the domain of Winnipeg's largely British upper and middle-class the city's spatial and social patterns were firmly established. By 1913 there was a distinct north-south dichotomy in Winnipeg which, despite the passage of more than fifty years, has changed but little. Indeed, the ethnic and class segregation of Winnipeg survived almost intact into the 1970s.

Suburban Development

Except for St. Boniface, it was not until after 1901 that the first traces of suburban growth appeared in Winnipeg. (Appendix, Table XI). It was only with the increased popularity of the bicycle and the extension of street railway lines that settlement of these outlying areas was possible. Also, as long as there were a sufficient amount and variety of building sites within the city of Winnipeg, there was little reason to settle in areas that were far from places of employment and shopping and entertainment facilities. But in the years after 1901 the transportation problem was solved and expansion into suburban areas began to occur.

St. Boniface was organized as a municipality in 1880 and then successively became incorporated as a town and a city in 1883 and 1908. The first signs of an urban pattern appeared in St. Boniface in 1883 when some of Winnipeg's residents and businessmen took advantage of the drastic differences in land values and tax rates between that town and Winnipeg, and built their homes or industrial plants there. But prior to 1901 only a small area of St. Boniface, close to the Red River, was built up. Great strides were made after the turn of the century, however, in both residential and industrial building. It was during these years that the St. Boniface landscape became marked with flour mills and abattoirs, and the city established itself as a noted meat-packing centre.

The development and growth of St. Boniface were not, however, entirely dependent on differences in land values and the growth of industry. For it was also the cultural centre of French Canadians in western Canada. Here were to be found the important buildings of the Roman Catholic Church — its cathedral, hospital, college, schools, and so forth. Thus in 1916 St. Boniface's population of 11,-021 was made up of 4,530 persons of French origin. Moreover, the French were the largest single group in St. Boniface at that time, outnumbering even those of British origin.

St. James was the suburb second in importance and size. Situated on the western outskirts of Winnipeg's West End, St. James served primarily as a residential suburb for the city. It was reached directly from the business centre of Winnipeg by way of Portage Avenue. This single major access route tended to cause the development of St. James to cling closer to the southern part, near the Assiniboine River, than it might otherwise have done had there been another major thoroughfare to provide a connection from St. James to Winnipeg.

St. James offered an excellent area for residential purposes. No drainage problems, a reduced flood danger, low municipal taxes, and large lots favourably competed with residential areas in Winnipeg. The development of an independent street railway system in

WARWICK APARTMENTS.

By the early 1900s apartment buildings began to make their appearance in Winnipeg. In these early years, however, most were designed for and occupied by "a well-to-do class of tenants."

St. James, along with street lighting, cement sidewalks, and asphalted roads were also attractive features. All gave St. James distinct advantages over the eastern and northern suburbs of the city.

St. Vital was incorporated as a municipality in 1903. It was made up of parts of the old municipality of St. Boniface and was situated east of the Red River, immediately south of the urban area of the town of St. Boniface. By 1913 a residential community had come into existence in the northern sections of St. Vital. St. Mary's Road and some streets branching off to the east were developed by this time but the greater part of St. Vital remained in agricultural use.

The only other concentrated development in Winnipeg's suburbs took place in Kildonan and Transcona. The former was where many of the Selkirk settlers had established themselves and the area had grown sufficiently by 1919 to cause it to be divided into two municipalities, West Kildonan and East Kildonan, on respective sides of the Red River. Winnipeg's Main Street extended into West Kildonan and it was here that the first northern suburban growth took place in the years after 1901. A similar but smaller suburban development took place in East Kildonan, mainly along Bird's Hill Road (now called Henderson Highway). The town of Transcona was incorporated in 1912 and it developed as a residential community for those working in the Grand Trunk Pacific yards and shops which had been established there.

In general the growth of Winnipeg's suburbs was just getting underway when war broke out in 1914. Yet even at this early date a distinct pattern emerged that was to be followed for several decades. The areas of greatest growth were those to the west (St. James), south (St. Vital and Fort Rouge), and east (St. Boniface). The northern expansion of Winnipeg's urban area, while significant, was never of the same proportions as any of these other areas.

By World War I, Winnipeg's urban landscape had undergone a fantastic change and the city's patterns of physical growth were firmly established. In less than half a century Winnipeg had grown from a small fur-trading post with fewer than two thousand inhabitants to a sprawling metropolis almost one hundred times that size. The physical expansion that accompanied this growth in population was equally great. When incorporated in 1874, over 3.1 square miles were included within the boundaries of the City of Winnipeg; much of which was undeveloped land. Yet by 1913 the city's boundaries had not only grown to include 23.6 square miles, but most of this area was in either residential or commercial use. Indeed, by 1913 Winnipeg's population and industry were spilling over into surrounding municipalities. The rapid growth of Winnipeg brought numerous other major changes. It was transformed from a city of pedestrians to one of bicycles, street cars, and even a few automobiles. The old residential area of the 1870s and 1880s had become by 1913 the industrial, commercial, financial and communications centre of the Canadian West.

Winnipeg in 1913 was very much a city divided: divided into areas of work and residences, rich and poor, Anglo-Saxon and foreigner. By this time, too, many of the familiar modern problems of urban life were beginning to emerge: the sudden withdrawal of whole segments of an old neighbourhood's population; the rapid decay of entire sections of the city; and the spread of the metropolis beyond its political boundaries. The establishment of such patterns of growth had serious consequences for Winnipeg. In the short run, of course, residential segregation had a pacifying effect. Class and ethnic segregation held conflicting groups apart. The upper class of the South End, the middle class and prosperous working class of the West End and central core were separated from the lower class and foreigners of the North End. Each district had a neighbourhood homogeneity that gave it a sense of place and community. On the other hand, many Winnipeggers had never lived in mixed neighbourhoods and thus failed to develop the tolerance and respect for different goals and values which sustain a diverse community through times of economic and social stress.

Another legacy of this period that is still apparent in Winnipeg is found in architectural styles. Prior to the boom of the early 1880s, building styles followed one of two patterns. Most of the public buildings and substantial houses of this early era were built of limestone and with few exceptions followed patterns imported from Europe. More common, however, was a unique construction technique and style known as "Red River Frame." This involved building with square logs which were grooved to hold the thinned ends of other logs laid horizontally. This indigenous building style was altered somewhat in the 1880s when a few of the buildings in the frontier community adopted brick-veneer fronts. In the years after the coming of the railway in the early 1880s, however, Winnipeg's

Settler's home, c. 1890.

era of independence in building styles came to an end and the architecture of the city came to resemble that of any other city of the time. In general, the availability of new building materials and the growing prosperity and importance of the prairie metropolis resulted in more pretentious styles. For while many of the city's buildings continued to be simple and utilitarian structures, an increasing number copied styles then in vogue elsewhere — late Victorian, Edwardian, and those of the "Chicago School." As Winnipeg developed, its architectural styles became largely derivative and lost the local charm of the earlier period.

THE URBAN COMMUNITY: SOCIAL AND POLITICAL LIFE

The social and political evolution of Winnipeg, tied as it is to so many other facets of the city's development, is difficult to examine in isolation. The social conditions experienced by the city's population in the years before 1914 were in large part a reflection of the age of the community, the state of technology and general economic conditions. Similarly, municipal politics in Winnipeg reflected in large measure the economic and social relationships among various groups within the city, and between the city and provincial and federal governments. Moreover, the conflict, confusion and tension that were inescapable facets of life in Winnipeg were often juxtaposed with examples of co-operation, order and harmony.

As early as the mid-1880s, Winnipeg was a socially divided city, and municipal politics followed a similar pattern. Throughout the period the civic corporation was controlled by the city's foremost businessmen while the vast majority of citizens, the artisans and workers, were effectively excluded from public decision-making.

These social and political patterns did not develop overnight, however; during the decade of the 1870s Winnipeg was still an egalitarian, pioneer community and the elections of this early period were casual affairs. The city's first municipal election in the fall of 1875, for example, was rambunctious with both mayoralty candidates and their supporters sparing nothing in their attempts to smear the opposition. Charges of corruption and bribery abounded. One of the candidates, Francis Evans Cornish, the eloquent and impetuous former mayor of London, Ontario, was charged with

having gained that position by questionable methods. It was said that in London he had taken undue advantage of a local law granting the franchise to anyone with twenty-four hours' residence in the town when he bribed some two thousand soldiers stationed nearby to move their tents onto city property the day before the election. Unfortunately for his opponent, William Fisher Luxton, editor of the *Manitoba Free Press*, such charges had little impact on the outcome, because Cornish employed similar methods in the Winnipeg elections.[101]

After a sizzling six-week campaign, Winnipeggers turned out on January 5th, 1874, to choose their first mayor. Twelve aldermen were also to be elected, but the spotlight centred on the mayoralty contest. Election day was clear and frosty, with wood smoke curling up from chimneys and stovepipes. Business in the small community was almost entirely suspended, except for hotels and saloons, which did a thriving trade. At 10 A.M. the polls opened and the rush was on. Cutters and sleighs caused traffic jams as eager citizens hurried to record their votes, their choices entered openly, for all to see, beside their names in the poll book. Supporters of the various candidates were decorated with flags and banners, and processions paraded from poll to poll. Although there were only 388 legal votes to be cast, 562 were counted. Despite the obvious irregularities, Winnipeg had its first mayor in the person of Francis Evans Cornish.

Winnipeg's first mayor was typical of many of Winnipeg's leading citizens, although he was certainly more flamboyant than most of his contemporaries. He was born in London, Upper Canada, in 1831, and subsequently trained as a lawyer. He served for a time as both alderman and mayor of London but following his unsuccessful bid for the London seat in the Ontario Legislature, he came to Winnipeg in 1872. That same year he was one of the first lawyers called to the Manitoba Bar. He quickly rose to prominence in the public life of the young province; he was, for example, deeply involved in the trial of Ambroise Lepine for the "execution" of Thomas Scott.[102]

In 1873, Cornish was one of the most active petitioners for the incorporation of Winnipeg and thereafter successfully ran for mayor. As mayor, Cornish proved himself to be a true character. One story about him states that sitting one morning as Police Mag-

City Hall, 1906. Winnipeg's "gingerbread house" city hall built in 1886 captured the full exuberance and optimism of the pre-war era. It was demolished in the early 1960s amid substantial protest.

istrate, he laid a charge against himself for driving a horse and carriage while in a drunken state. Having charged himself, he left the chair, said "Guilty, Your Honour," resumed his place, fined himself five dollars, then immediately rescinded the fine since it was his first offence.[103]

Despite Cornish's irreverence, Winnipeg city council did get things done under his leadership and that of his successor, William N. Kennedy (1875-1876). One of the most noteworthy activities of these early years was the construction of Winnipeg's first city hall. In the two years following Winnipeg's incorporation, city council meetings were held in a variety of buildings in the young city, including a furniture store. By August 1875, however, Winnipeg's first city hall had been begun amid great ceremony. On August 17, 1875, a "grand civic holiday" celebrating the placing of the cornerstone of the new structure occurred. The ceremony began with a large procession down Main Street and concluded with the ritual of laying the cornerstone.

> In what must have been the largest iron casket ever entombed in a cornerstone were samples of money, all the way from early Hudson's Bay Company pounds and shillings to Canadian currency, British money, even Russian kopeks and Prussian coins brought in by Mennonite immigrants. There were photos galore, including the mayor and council, street scenes, dog trains, oxcarts, even Louis Riel and his rebel government; newspapers, copies of charters, bylaws and progress reports; the prize list of the first annual show in 1874 of the Industrial and Agricultural Society of Manitoba; a copy of the city's charter of incorporation and its "rules and regulations" for 1875.[104]

Winnipeg's first city hall, constructed at a cost of almost $40,000, was formally opened in March 1876 with a concert in aid of the Winnipeg General Hospital. During these early years, when the city hall was one of only a handful of substantial buildings in the young city, it served many purposes. In September 1876, for example, a group used the council chambers to organize Winnipeg's first philharmonic society.[105]

Almost from the outset, however, this first city hall proved to be structurally unsound. It had been built over Brown's Creek, which crossed Main Street near William Avenue. The land fill on which the structure was erected could not support the building and as early as 1876 ominous cracks began to appear as the city hall slowly settled into the creek bed on which it had been built. During the winter of 1882-1883 an addition was made to the city hall but it too was soon in difficulty. The addition had been constructed during the excessive cold weather of that winter and when spring arrived "the building showed unmistakeable signs of being unsafe. Huge cracks appeared in the walls, an arch fell down, the woodwork became warped, and so many hasty signs of construction were apparent that the building was propped up for several weeks and ultimately pulled down" in April 1883.[106]

The first advertisements calling for plans and specifications for the erection of Winnipeg's second city hall appeared in the city's daily papers of Saturday, June 16, 1883. A year later, on a sweltering hot 19th of July, 1884, Mayor Alexander Logan and other members of city council gathered on scaffolding for the official ceremony of laying the cornerstone. The second city hall was surrounded by controversy from the beginning. Disputes over the material used in the construction of the building and over fees paid to the architectural firm of Barber and Barber raged throughout 1884 and 1885. Indeed, the circumstances surrounding the construction of Winnipeg's second city hall even drove one disgruntled citizen, George B. Brooks, to write a pamphlet entitled *Plain Facts About the New City Hall: Its Inside History From the First Down to the Present — Interesting Disclosures.* Other pamphleteers also commented on the facts surrounding the construction of the city hall.[107]

Yet out of this turmoil there finally emerged in 1886 a substantial and solid structure that was to last until the 1960s, when it was demolished. Winnipeg's second city hall was a Victorian fantasy that captured in its layers of stone and brick, its turrets and picturesque clock, more than any other building of the time the exuberance and optimism of the period.[108] And like its predecessor, the great Victorian city hall quickly became a focal point for Winnipeg. It not only served the needs of municipal government, it also provided a home in the years immediately following its construction for the Board of Trade, the library and reading room of the Historical and Scientific Society of Manitoba, and the club rooms of the St. George's and St. Andrew's Societies.[109]

Market Square, 1908. The market building behind city hall was built in 1897, replacing an older structure torn down shortly before. Market Square was the centre of trade and commerce for many years, with hotels, stores, agricultural businesses, and livery stables near at hand. After World War I two storeys were added to the building and it was converted into civic offices. It was demolished, along with city hall, in 1964.

Volunteers from Citizens' Committee on Winnipeg fire truck, 1919.

Winnipeg Police Department on parade, 1913.

The demolition of one city hall and the construction of another indicated that Winnipeg was by the early 1880s a thriving young city. Indeed, Winnipeg was rapidly becoming a highly organized society as a host of clubs and institutions were established in the young community. The Winnipeg General Hospital received its first patient in a little whitewashed building at McDermott and Albert in 1872. It was reported that "patients were brought to this crude hospital in muddy-wheeled buck-boards. There was no organized staff — the nurses being the unskilled but kind-hearted womenfolk of the Red River Settlement." During the next ten years, the hospital was moved five times but in 1883 a building was erected on what was to become a permanent site.[110] The exclusive Manitoba Club was organized in 1874, a club in which membership "was practically a certificate of leadership in the commercial community of Winnipeg."[111] The first of its kind in western Canada, a symbol of the fledgling western expansion, the members successfully brought elegance to the newly incorporated city. Similarly, a number of professional associations were taking shape: the Manitoba Law Society was incorporated in 1877, the Manitoba College of Physicians and Surgeons in the same year.

Another significant and longlived institution made its appearance in 1879. Aside from its cultural import, the Historical and Scientific Society of Manitoba provided a sort of social bridging between the business and academic worlds, bringing together merchants, lawyers, doctors, clergymen and teachers to hear and present papers of an historical or scientific nature.[112] Meanwhile, churches, schools, and ethnic benevolent societies were also established with the aid and enterprise of the business community. In the field of public education, for example, there was rapid expansion. In 1876, Winnipeg had only four teachers, two schools, and just over four hundred registered students. Ten years later there were forty-nine teachers in eleven schools with a student population of almost three thousand.[113] Equally noteworthy, since curling was to become the most popular winter sport in Winnipeg, was the beginning of the Caledonian Curling Club in 1876.

The most significant development of the period, however, was the emergence of the Winnipeg Board of Trade. Abortive attempts had been made to establish a business organization earlier in the 1870s, but the Winnipeg Board of Trade was successfully organized only in 1879. Prominent at its early meetings were Aldermen Ashdown, Alloway, Eden, and W. H. Lyon, all well-to-do businessmen. The first elections of the Board made A.G.B. Bannatyne president for 1879-1880, Lyon vice-president, and put Eden, Alloway, Ashdown, and D. H. McMillan on the council. With these leading citizens on its first council, the Winnipeg Board of Trade rapidly became the most important organization in the city, the very exemplification of the city's commercial elite. Throughout the years the roster of the presidents and council members of the Board of Trade came to read like a social register of Winnipeg commerce and finance. Together with their colleagues on city council, the members of the Board of Trade had a major influence in shaping Winnipeg's growth. These individuals wielded enough power in the city to make major decisions regarding the commitment of public funds and the allocation of municipal resources in response to the problems and possibilities that emerged in their community.[114]

Very early in Winnipeg's existence as an incorporated community, the city's businessmen reached a fundamental agreement on the role the municipal corporation should play in the affairs of the city. They sought an administration that would attend to the finances and day-to-day processes of municipal government in a businesslike manner and, when called upon, would use public funds to promote the growth they desired, and thus protect and further their own interests.

Although the Board of Trade played an important role in civic politics from its inception in 1879, it first took a direct and major part in the crucial civic election of 1884. The three years preceding this election had been extremely important ones for the development of Winnipeg, but they had also been years when scandals, mismanagement, and "culpable negligence and incompetence marked the administration of the city's affairs," a condition, the editor of the *Winnipeg Times* was sure, "that no businessman would tolerate in the management of his business or estate."[115] The problems with the city halls were only part of a larger picture that included the collapse of the Winnipeg real estate boom in 1882 and the almost $2,000,000 debt the city had incurred by mid-1883. It was as a result of these problems that the President of the Board of Trade, C. J. Brydges, supported by members of a newly formed Property Owners' Association, set out in May 1883 to "place civic

Nurses with babies, Grace Hospital.

affairs on such a basis as will ensure the economical and advantageous expenditure of money."

Several plans for reforming civic government were put forward in ensuing months, culminating in a citizens' convention held in October 1884. The convention was called "for the nomination of fit and proper persons" to constitute the city council for 1885, and the meeting soon decided that civic affairs could be straightened out only by electing a slate of candidates "with proven business ability."

The Citizens' Ticket was headed by Charles E. Hamilton and included such prominent realtors and businessmen as G.F. Carruthers, George H. Campbell and T. Ryan, all members of the Board of Trade. The incumbent, Mayor Alexander Logan, was rejected by the convention because "although he is admitted to be a good intending upright man . . . he lacks discernment and decision [and] has an unwarranted trust in others." The Citizens' Ticket candidate, Charles Hamilton, was a lawyer in the firm of millionaire Winnipegger, J.A.M. Aitkins. Hamilton was considered tough enough to solve Winnipeg's problems and received the enthusiastic backing of the Board of Trade.[116]

It was the expressed intention of the Citizens' Committee that the slate of candidates they put forward should be elected by acclamation, a step that would restore confidence in the city. But while this would be the case the following year in most wards, the civic election of 1884 turned into one of the most intensely fought campaigns in Winnipeg's history. Both sides came out for reform of one sort or another and the election turned on personalities. The result was an acrimonious contest that left considerable bitterness.

It was clear from the outset that the Citizens' Ticket was immensely popular but the former aldermen "quite naturally made up their mind not to stand calmly by and hear themselves denounced as boodlers."[117] The incumbents received support from the civic officials who were apprehensive that the reform advocated by the Citizens' Ticket would mean "either that their salaries will be reduced to something in keeping with the stringency of the times and that they will be expected to earn that by doing the work now performed by numberless assistants, or that their services will be disposed with entirely and they be thrown upon the world to earn their livelihood in the same manner as the ordinary citizen."[118]

The elections of December 8th left no doubt that the electorate agreed with the position of the Board of Trade. With the exception of two aldermen, the entire slate offered by the Citizens' Ticket was elected, including mayoralty candidate, Charles Hamilton. The two "old guard" candidates, moreover, were elected by majorities of only seven and fifty votes respectively.

Following the 1884 elections, the Board of Trade and its members and supporters were never again forced to take such a direct role in civic politics, as their views concerning the need for business-like efficiency in government now dominated. An analysis of the various elective offices in Winnipeg in the years before 1914, for example, reveals several significant facts. The most important is that the commercial group dominated every elective office throughout the period. This suggests that Winnipeg's businessmen took more than an occasional interest in politics. For although their early involvement in municipal affairs may have assured such things as effective transportation facilities, there was, they felt, a continuing necessity to control the municipal government. Attracted by the role the local government could play in promoting prosperity, in building the city, and in increasing the value of their property through improvements, the commercial elite remained actively involved in civic politics.

The continuing and consistently high degree of involvement of Winnipeg's commercial class in municipal government is also noteworthy from another viewpoint. In many other North American cities businessmen gained control of the local government only by pushing aside an old and established social elite. Then, often in a short time, they were themselves pushed out of politics by other groups such as "professional politicians" or men who depended on the ethnic vote for their political success.[119] Winnipeg's commercial class did not have to depose an aristocracy because of the circumstances surrounding the city's foundation; Winnipeg was established by businessmen, for business purposes, and businessmen were its first and natural leaders. In fact, Winnipeg's commercial and social elites were indistinguishable; membership in one group was almost always accompanied by membership in the other group. The second possibility — the businessmen themselves being

Governor-General Earl Grey and the Countess, Manitoba's Lt.-Gov. Sir Daniel McMillan and Lady McMillan, and two unidentified young women on the steps of Government House during the vice-regal visit in 1911.

Foote

pushed out — was forestalled until the post-1913 period, and even then the commercial elite retained substantial control over the affairs of the city.

Two other patterns are also apparent from an occupational classification of elected municipal office holders. First, the city's professionals — doctors, lawyers, engineers — succeeded in gaining an average of only ten per cent of the various elective positions, a level of representation that remained the same throughout the period. At no time were they driven out by the businessmen. Indeed, there was never any serious conflict between the supposedly distinct professional, social, and commercial groups of Winnipeg. Secondly, the occupational classification reveals that Winnipeg's artisans and workingmen were grossly under-represented. Between 1874 and 1913 they elected no representatives to the mayor's chair and out of a total of over five hundred aldermen and controllers elected in this forty-five year period, less than five per cent came from these groups.[120]

While a classification of Winnipeg's civic leaders by occupation says much about who governed Winnipeg during this period, it does not tell the whole story. Several other factors played an important part in determining a man's success in municipal politics. It was not enough, for example, to merely be a member of the business community, one also had to achieve a high degree of financial success. For while it is true that businessmen dominated politics, it was also true that wealthy businessmen — the richer the better — were most successful.

This connection between financial success, high social status, and political success is often a distinguishing characteristic of any new urban centre. In older established cities such factors as intellectual excellence and reputation, or social prestige derived from something other than money, were often the basis of political power, but in Winnipeg numerous men of humble origin and often little formal education were able to rise quickly to positions of prominence. The reward of political office went to the organizer, the projector, the risk-taker — in short, the man who had proved himself in the demanding business world.

Next to financial success, participation in various business organizations was probably the most important political asset. The successful municipal politician did not limit his membership to only one organization. Most belonged to many such bodies and took active roles, often serving on the executive or on committees. These business organizations included the Winnipeg Board of Trade, the Real Estate Exchange, the Winnipeg Development and Industrial Bureau, the Builder's Exchange and so on. Equally significant, however, is the fact that many of the mayors, and a large number of the controllers and aldermen, were also members of regional and even national business organizations. These included the Canadian Manufacturers' Association, the Canadian Industrial Exhibition Association, the National Association of Real Estate Exchanges, the Western Canadian Real Estate Association, the Northwest Commercial Travellers' Association, the Western Canadian Immigration Association, and several others. Membership in these organizations implies that Winnipeg's commercial elite was something more than a parochial oligarchy.

Membership in many non-business organizations was also a characteristic of Winnipeg's civic leaders. These ranged from the prestigious Manitoba Club to such clubs as the Carleton, Union, Adanac, St. Charles, Commercial, and others. Moreover, the successful politician and his family took part in an endless round of various social and cultural activities. The Winnipeg Operatic and Dramatic Society, the Women's Musical Club, and the Women's Art Association were all active organizations. From the activities of the latter group during the period 1900-1912, for example, a considerable growth in art took place. The enthusiasm of the time resulted in the formation of numerous smaller groups — the Studio Club, the Arts and Craft Society, the Winnipeg Art League, to name a few — which held exhibitions on their own, generally in the spring. The result was that in 1912 the Industrial Bureau, assisted by finances from individuals and City Council, erected an addition as part of the Industrial Bureau Building, and an art gallery was formally opened in December 1912.[121]

Amateur athletic associations sponsored diverse sporting activities and Winnipeg's middle and upper class took part in sleighing, snowshoeing, skating, cycling, cricket, horseracing, curling, canoeing, and rowing. The first bonspiel was held in March 1889 and thereafter Winnipeg quickly became the major centre in North America for winter curling. Bonspiel Week, in February of each year, brought many rinks from all over Canada to Winnipeg. In

Assiniboine Park Bridge, 1912.

A women's curling team in Winnipeg.

Skating on the Assiniboine River.

FOOTE. PHOTO.

Foxhunting, Charleswood, c. 1912.

Winnipeg Beach was a popular resort for city residents served by the CPR. One advertisement for the beach stated that "to hundreds of thousands of western and Winnipeg folks there is probably no more musical combination than that of Winnipeg Beach where every conceivable form of good, wholesome outdoor sport may be indulged in. The beautiful safe beach for bathing, the glorious shade trees, the virgin lawns and, for those in quest of more exciting amusement, the roller coaster, ending the perfect day with a dance in the new spacious pavilion with its democratic freedom and perfect terpsichorean music."

Mrs. A.C. Ross and daughters, 1917.

Winnipeg Canoe Club.

Camping at Grand Bend.

Parade preparation to Red River for Greek Orthodox Church baptism, c. 1910.

1903, for example, one hundred and twenty rinks, including nearly five thousand curling enthusiasts, gathered in Winnipeg to compete for the championship offered by the Manitoba branch of the Royal Caledonian Curling Association. Curling was only one of the many organized sports, however. Other clubs included the Winnipeg Rowing Club, the Winnipeg Swimming Club, the Winnipeg Cricket Association, the Winnipeg Canoe Club, the Lake of the Woods Yacht Club, the St. George's Snowshoe Club, the St. Charles Country Club, and several others.[122]

Financial success and active participation in business, social, athletic, charitable and traditional political organizations — these characteristics go far to suggest the attributes necessary for political success in Winnipeg. But there were still other elements of almost equal importance to these: ethic origin and religion. Winnipeg's civic leaders were, almost to a man, of Anglo-Saxon origin and Protestant religion. Despite their growing numbers, especially in the years after 1896, the city's Slavs, Jews, Germans, and Scandinavians gained but a fraction of the seats they may have expected. Significantly, it was not until 1956 that Winnipeg elected its first non-Anglo-Saxon mayor, and even then it was a shock to many Winnipeggers. All of this leads to the conclusion that Winnipeg was governed between 1874 and 1913 by a very select group of men who comprised a social, cultural, and, above all, commercial elite. Two men who held various elective offices in Winnipeg during this period provide excellent examples of the type of leadership the city received during this period.

James Henry Ashdown was mayor in 1907 and 1908, retaining the office by acclamation for his second term. Often described as a thoroughly self-made man and Winnipeg's "Merchant Prince," Ashdown was born in London, England, in 1844. He came to Canada with his parents in 1852 and at eighteen began a three-year apprenticeship with a tinsmith in Hespeler, Ontario. Once this was completed in 1865 he spent some time in Chicago, finally coming to Winnipeg in 1868. He purchased a small hardware store which over the years grew into a thriving wholesale and retail business. By 1910 Ashdown was a millionaire, being successful not only in business but in real estate speculation as well.

Ashdown was involved in the Red River Rebellion of 1870, as one of Schultz's "citizen guards." He was duly arrested and jailed

by Riel. Following the entry of Manitoba into the Dominion of Canada he was given a commission as Justice of the Peace. In 1874 he became chairman of the Citizens' Committee which secured incorporation of Winnipeg from the province. He then served as alderman from 1874 to 1879. Ashdown was equally prominent in other activities. He was an original member of the Board of Trade and served as its president in 1887. By 1910 he was one of the most important businessmen in western Canada. He was a director of the Bank of Montreal, the Northern Crown Bank, the Northern Trust Company, and the president of the Canadian Fire Insurance Company. In the social sphere he was a member of the Masonic fraternity, the Commercial Club, and the very exclusive Manitoba Club. He was a Liberal in politics and a Methodist in religion. In the latter connection he was one of the founders of Wesley College and later sat on its Board of Governors. He also took part in the meetings and discussions of the Historical and Scientific Society of Manitoba. By 1912, Ashdown lived on the prestigious Wellington Crescent in Ward 1. His mansion boasted a green tile roof, limestone walls, sixty-four rooms, and a garage with an automobile turntable and grease-pit.

Ashdown's return to active politics in 1907, after a long absence, came about when he was persuaded to run for mayor by "a citizen's committee composed of the best businessmen of Winnipeg." His nomination papers included the signatures of most of the city's financial elite and he won an overwhelming victory. Significantly, his opponent was supported by organized labour.

Another representative of the elite, William Sanford Evans, was also mayor for more than one term, holding office from 1909 to 1911. Born in Spencerville, Ontario, in 1869 he attended public school in Hamilton, and went on to obtain a Bachelor of Arts degree at Victoria College in Cobourg, Ontario. Evans then did post-graduate work at Columbia University, receiving his Master of Arts degree in 1896. Journalism was Evans' first area of interest and he joined the editorial staff of the Toronto *Mail and Empire* in 1897. In 1898 he made his first attempt to gain political office, running as a Conservative candidate for South Wentworth in the Ontario provincial elections. After being defeated Evans retired briefly from newspaper work and became treasurer of the National Cycle and Automobile Company of Toronto. In 1900 he married Mary Irene

Gurney, the daughter of a former mayor of Toronto, and in 1901 they moved to Winnipeg. There Evans became editor of the *Winnipeg Telegram* and president of the Telegram Printing Company.

To this point Evans' education and career did not fit into the mould of Winnipeg's other mayors. But in 1905 Evans resigned as editor of the *Telegram* (he remained owner) and established the financial concern of W. Sanford Evans and Company. He was instrumental in establishing a stock exchange in Winnipeg, and served as president of the Winnipeg Stock Exchange and president of the Royal Canadian Agencies, Canadian Industrial Securities Company, Estevan Coal and Brick Company, and Gurney Northwest Foundry Company. He was also vice-president of the Canadian Bond and Mortgage Corporation, a director of the Sovereign Life Assurance Company, and a member of the executive council of the Board of Trade. It was this impressive business record that guaranteed Evans' success in municipal politics. In 1907, when Winnipeg was experiencing financial difficulties, he ran for the Board of Control and was successful. He served as controller until Ashdown declined to run for a third term, and was then elected mayor.

As controller and mayor, Evans took a keen interest in municipal government. He served as vice-president (1909) and then president (1910) of the Union of Canadian Municipalities. In other organizations he served a term as president of the Winnipeg Canadian Club and one as the first president of the Associated Canadian Clubs of Canada. Indeed, Sanford Evans was a co-founder of the Canadian Club movement. He was also president of the Winnipeg Development and Industrial Bureau (1907-1908), chairman of the Town Planning Commission and a member of the Winnipeg Industrial Exhibition.

Mayor Evans was listed in the *Who's Who of Western Canada* as being a member of the Methodist Church "or any other [church] that makes for the highest good." His other activities included serving as a councillor of the University of Manitoba and as a member of the Masonic Order, and the Manitoba, Carleton, Adanac, Commercial and St. Charles clubs. Evans resided in Ward 2 and after his career in municipal politics sat as a Conservative member of the Manitoba legislature for fourteen years.[123]

The political domination of Winnipeg by an Anglo-Saxon commercial elite was the result of more than their numbers. First of all, non-Anglo-Saxons, especially after 1896 made up a significant proportion of Winnipeg's populace and thus should have been able to elect more representatives. This is particularly true of the aldermanic positions, since these were ward-elected representatives and several of the city's wards contained non-Anglo-Saxon majorities from as early as 1901. Secondly, the group most likely to oppose the policies of the commercial elite, the city's workers and artisans, were organized early in Winnipeg. The city had a local of the Knights of Labor from 1884 and in 1886 a central Trades and Labour Council was formed. By 1895 an Independent Labour Party had been organized, the first in Canada. Even these labour groups however, were run mainly by Anglo-Canadians.

It is true, of course, that Winnipeg's labour organizations quarrelled as much among themselves as with the "capitalist enemy," and a part of their failure to elect representatives stems from this basic fact. Compared with the stability, homogeneity, and singleness of purpose displayed by the commercial elite, organized labour remained splintered throughout this period. There was continuous and often bitter in-fighting among various labour and socialist organizations and this caused a division of forces that labour could ill afford.[124]

There are, however, other important reasons for labour's lack of political success at the municipal level. For a variety of reasons the city's labour organizations directed their major political efforts at the provincial and federal levels of government. They did so not because they felt municipal politics unimportant; it was rather a result of their assessment that they stood a better chance of electoral success at the higher levels. There, at least, they did not have to overcome a series of election laws and practices that, at the municipal level, effectively disenfranchised labour and over-represented the commercial class. Moreover, if labour could have wielded sufficient political power at the provincial level they could have removed the impediments contained in the City Charter which was granted by the province.

The means whereby Winnipeg's artisans and workingmen were effectively excluded from participation in civic politics are easily pinpointed. Beginning at incorporation and continuing throughout the period, voters and candidates for municipal election had to meet a series of qualifications that differed from those required in provincial or federal politics. The most important of these was a property qualification and although it never exceeded $2,000 for candidates — and was less for electors — it did, in fact, disenfranchise thousands of Winnipeggers. In 1906, for example, when the population was over 100,000, there were only 7,784 registered voters.

An interesting and, at first sight, progressive measure was one introduced in 1895 that gave females the right to vote in municipal elections. What this meant in reality was that those who held sufficient property would now have added influence. In other words, to the labourer who barely, if at all, met the property qualification for himself this move meant little in terms of giving his wife a vote. But for the affluent merchant or manufacturer, with property valued at several thousands of dollars, it meant that both he and his wife could vote. Significantly, women were not allowed to hold office until after 1916 and although the first, Jessie Kirk, was elected to office in 1921, she was not followed by a second until the election of Margaret McWilliams in 1933.

The importance of property in municipal politics did not end there. With the institution in 1890 of the plural vote, the commercial elite effectively removed any possibility of sheer numbers carrying a municipal election. After 1890 a person could vote in every ward "in which he had been rated for the necessary property qualification." Until 1906 this meant that certain wealthy electors could possibly qualify in six wards, while after that date (when a new ward was added), seven wards. The importance of such a law is revealed by the fact that in 1910 it was estimated that the civic voters' list had six thousand repeaters.

The changes to the Municipal Act that instituted the plural vote did, however, specify that this privilege extended only to votes for aldermen, controllers, and money bylaws, and that each voter could vote only once per ward. In mayoralty elections the elector was restricted to only one vote "at the polling subdivision in which he is a resident." But these limitations were only rarely acknowledged. Throughout this period the civic voters' list did not incorporate the qualifying provisions made in the act. In 1910, for example, when there were seventy-two polling subdivisions, "Names of scores and hundreds of citizens . . . appear on the printed (and official) voters'

list as many as ten, fifteen, twenty, thirty times and upwards, even into the sixties. As instances, the name of ex-Mayor Andrews appears in no less than sixty-six subdivisions, and that of Dr. D. E. Sprague in over sixty subdivisions." Given this situation, it is not surprising to learn that the defeated mayoralty candidate in the 1910 election called for an investigation. But the charge that the real public opinion of Winnipeg could be defeated practically at any election did not disturb the governing commercial elite because prior to 1913 no changes were requested or made in the plural vote provisions of the Municipal Act and some Winnipeggers continued to have inordinate electoral power. Indeed, it was not until 1965 that plural voting was abolished in Winnipeg civic elections.

The aim of these qualifications was to represent property, not people. This was made abundantly clear in 1914 when city council approached the provincial legislature with a request for an amendment to the Municipal Act that would have provided for any joint stock company owning property within the city the right to instruct its manager, a director, or an employee to vote on money bylaws and other questions of civic government. In defending the request Mayor T. R. Deacon and the city solicitor argued that:

> All collections of property were . . . the result of an expenditure of human energy. The heads of many business organizations in Winnipeg had worked up from poor boys, had established themselves in the confidence of their associates and built up a business. In his own case, [Mayor Deacon] had worked his way through university and when he came to Winnipeg did not have enough capital to establish the business that he wished. He had interested friends in his proposition and had formed a joint stock company. That company [Manitoba Bridge and Iron Works] owned valuable property in Winnipeg, yet had no vote. On the other hand, the man owning a lot adjoining a lot made valuable through the efforts of the company did have a vote. A vote through a company was not a vote on bricks and mortar, but a vote on the energies of men. He could see no objection to instructed voting.[125]

Labour, of course, was vehemently opposed to the measure and attacked it as "a bad principle, vicious, and the worst piece of class legislation that the legislature had ever been asked to pass." Fortu-

Organized labour in Winnipeg had its own newspaper, The Voice, *as early as 1900. It was for many years edited by Arthur W. Puttee, Winnipeg's first labour MP (1900-1904).*

nately for labour, the amendment never came out of committee.

One significant change did occur in 1906, however, with the addition of an elected, four-man Board of Control in addition to the fourteen aldermen. These men were to serve as full-time civic representatives, their main task being to "restrain any rashness on the part of city council in guiding the growth of the booming city."[126] By the creation of this full-time, salaried executive committee, elected by the entire city rather than by wards, the commercial elite effectively centralized the system of municipal government. During the existence of the Board (it was disbanded in 1919), the continuous day-to-day processes of civic government were fully in the hands of a very small group of individuals. Together with the restricted franchise and plural voting, the Board of Control further assured Winnipeg's businessmen that their policies would prevail.

While Winnipeg's politics were thus being directed largely along the lines the commercial elite desired, the needs of other groups in the city were being ignored. Since the majority of the city's people were not involved in the political process the commercial elite who occupied positions in the municipal government did not have to bother about strong public backing. They could pursue their growth ethic at public expense and with a minimum of argument. Their concentration on growth at any cost ignored such crucial issues as social welfare and comprehensive city planning and in so doing left to their successors problems of enormous magnitude.

Examples of this neglect of social issues are numerous. Perhaps the most glaring was in the area of public health. Indeed, the development of an active civic health department was undertaken only in 1905, in the wake of a severe typhoid epidemic.[127]

Typhoid is a disease that flourished in frontier settlements where there were inadequate supplies of pure water and poor sanitation facilities. By the early 1900s, despite the fact that Winnipeg had been an organized community for over twenty-five years, such conditions still existed. In the area of waterworks, for example, certain districts in the city were much neglected. While the generally prosperous south end of the city had over seventy-eight per cent of the houses connected to the waterworks system, the North End, where most of the foreign immigrants lived, had only forty-two percent of the homes and tenement buildings hooked up.

Waterworks connections were, however, only one part of the

problem. During this period, the city derived its water supply from frequently inadequate artesian wells. Accordingly it was common practice for the city to rely on water from the polluted Red and Assiniboine Rivers during periods of peak demand. Yet despite the admitted connection between typhoid and the use of polluted water, it was not until 1913 that steps were taken to solve the city's water supply problems. In that year construction began on a $13.5 million aqueduct to Shoal Lake, ninety-seven miles east from Winnipeg. When completed in 1919, the Shoal Lake aqueduct did provide the city with a pure and plentiful supply of water.

Still another aspect of the city's sanitary problems was the generally filthy conditions of certain neighbourhoods. A report in 1904 noted that the sanitary conditions of the area surrounding the CPR tracks "was bad in the extreme." On one street, for example, the three doctors who wrote the report found a continuous line of outdoor toilets only a few feet apart. These were allowed to drain freely into a ditch on either side of the roadway and "there being little or no soakage into the ground," the ditches were practically a long, open latrine. The report compared conditions to those of a European village in the Middle Ages.

Turning to the city as a whole, the doctors recorded some startling statistics. Excluding the suburbs, Winnipeg had over 6,500 "box closets," even on such thoroughfares as Main Street and Portage Avenue. And in the North End, "the filth, squalor, and overcrowding among the foreign elements is beyond our power of description." Finally, the report suggested that city council immediately undertake remedial measures. Those suggested were enforced sewer connections; the abolition of box closets and their replacement by iron pail closets where sewer connections were not possible; the abolition of all public wells; an increase in the scavenger service; and the frequent flushing of sewers under water pressure.[128]

Unfortunately, this sound advice was not taken and the results of these and other similar conditions, combined with a lack of any effective public education program dealing with proper sanitation, were recorded in the number of typhoid cases in the city. Between 1900 and 1905, for example, Winnipeg had the following number of cases and deaths: 1900 — 582 and 34; 1901 — 349 and 36; 1902 — 356 and 29; 1903 — 489 and 46; 1904 — 1,276 and 133; 1905 —

Banquet in a sewer, in celebration of completion of the construction project, 1912.

1,606 and 138. Not only were the number of typhoid cases and deaths for 1904 and 1905 greater than those experienced by any other major North American or European city, they were coupled with extremely high infant mortality and general death rates. In both areas, Winnipeg consistently had one of the worst rates on the continent. To further compound the problem, it was found that the high infant mortality rate was concentrated in the immigrant neighbourhoods. In 1912, for example, fifty-four per cent of the infant deaths took place in the North End although this area only had thirty-four per cent of the city's population. The response of the elite to this situation was to blame poor sanitary conditions on the ignorance, laziness and immorality of the North End's foreign-born population.

In retrospect the typhoid epidemic of 1904-1905, while tragic in itself, did have positive effects. After 1905 the city health department slowly began to receive the support necessary to enable it to deal with some of the city's massive health problems in a more aggressive and positive manner. And this fact, together with the completion of the Shoal Lake aqueduct in 1919 and a decline in the city's rapid rate of growth, led to markedly improved health conditions in the 1920s. In the interim, however, Winnipeg remained one of the continent's most unhealthy cities, especially for the poor.

The inability of Winnipeg's civic council, dominated as it was by a booster-oriented commercial elite, to deal effectively with important social issues was also demonstrated in the controversy surrounding the existence of a red-light district in Winnipeg. As early as March 1874, only months after the city's incorporation, city council received a petition from a resident calling for the removal of "houses of ill-fame." Other reports followed this one and during the period 1874-1883 prostitution was periodically raised in the local press. In 1883, however, two significant events took place that were to affect the issue of prostitution in the city for the next thirty years. One was the city's first "Anti Social Evil Crusade" mounted by the Ministerial Association; the other was the adoption of a policy of "segregated vice" by Winnipeg city council.

The 1883 crusade began when a group of concerned citizens and clergymen sent a petition to city council calling for the removal of the houses of ill-fame that were located on Queen Street West (later to become Portage Avenue) in the vicinity of Colony Street. City council responded by moving the prostitutes to a different area of the city where regular police patrols were soon established. This policy was in fact a tacit agreement between the madams and the city authorities that prostitution would be confined to houses on the outskirts of the city; that there would be no soliciting in the settled portions of the community; and that prostitutes would ride only in closed carriages. The prostitutes were also told that it was to their benefit to carry on a quiet business for there was no telling what might happen if the clergy got wind of this arrangement for "clergymen are not the most intelligent men, nor do they reason the best."[129]

Winnipeg thus entered the 1900s with an official policy of "segregated vice" and with prostitution flourishing. The unequalled prosperity and growth of Winnipeg during this decade brought a corresponding increase in the number of houses of prostitution, and even attracted prostitutes from other cities to operate there. By 1909 there were one hundred bawdy houses which were no longer confined to the segregated area on Rachel and McFarlane Streets on Point Douglas.

This expansion of the trade coincided with a general public movement toward moral reform that grew up after 1910. The reform movement, which was sweeping all of North America, was in Winnipeg at least partially a result of the reaction among the settled members of the community to the radically changing social conditions of a rapidly expanding urban population. Whatever the cause of this spirit of reform, it resulted in a campaign, dominated by clergymen, to combat prostitution. Groups dedicated to the abolition of commercialized vice in the United States, such as the National Vigilance Committee, the American Purity Federation and the Alliance for the Suppression and Prevention of the White Slave Traffic, soon spread into Canada with the establishment of the International Purity Federation and the Moral and Social Reform League. Rev. Dr. J. G. Shearer, a respected official of both the Purity Federation and the Moral Reform Council, and a central figure in the controversy in Winnipeg, described the Purity Federation: "It not only preached the gospel of better social and moral conditions, but investigated as well many phases of the purity problem of social vice, the white slave trade, and how best to secure the teaching of the purpose and the problems of sex legislation and law enforcement."[130] Spurred on by a deep-rooted, rural puritanism which still influenced many people in a new city like Winnipeg, the mass support for the reform movement came from the Protestant denominations. Methodists, Presbyterians, Congregationalists and Baptists accounted for over fifty thousand of the city's population in 1911, almost forty per cent of the total. To this group the policy of segregation of prostitution was equivalent to condoning vice.

It was the Moral and Social Reform League, formed in 1907, that proved to be the strongest advocate of the anti-segregation policy. A contemporary weekly tabloid sponsored by the organization characterized the group as a "federation of the religious and social reform bodies for consultation and cooperation with respect to legislative reform growing out of their common Christianity."[131] Groups affiliated with the League, at one time or another, were the Trades and Labor Council, the Icelandic Lutheran Synod, the Women's Christian Temperance Union, the Unitarian Conference, the Scandinavian Anti-Saloon League, the Polish National Catholic Church, the Ruthenian Catholic Church, the Russian Orthodox Greek Church plus, of course, the Methodist, Baptist, Congregationalist and Presbyterian churches whose clergymen dominated the organization.

The activities of the Moral and Social Reform League in respect to prostitution and other social concerns began soon after its formation in 1907 and continued well past 1910.[132] Their greatest effort came in 1910, however, when the League began a major campaign to rid Winnipeg of the segregated area on Point Douglas. The chief weapon the League employed was the publication of a thirty-two page pamphlet entitled *The Problem of Social Vice in Winnipeg*. Written by one of Canada's most eminent Protestant clergymen, Rev. Dr. F. DuVal, the pamphlet was a passionate indictment of the policy of segregation.[133] Segregation was dismissed as being just as detrimental to the moral health of the community as legal toleration. DuVal contended that what had happened in Winnipeg was that the police had been given the exclusive right to legislate, execute, and enforce the laws regarding prostitution because city council had shirked its duty. This was a flagrant violation of the sacred traditions of western Christian civilization. The pamphlet also exhorted the citizens of Winnipeg to fight the growing evil since, according to DuVal, the struggle in Winnipeg was far more than a local issue. It was a holy war to save western Canada, indeed the whole country, so that it might yet prove to be the "noblest edition of national life in the world."

Despite the League's extensive efforts, the Police Commission persisted in its policy of segregated prostitution. The fact was that city council, and especially Mayor Sanford Evans, refused to be put on the defensive and simply ignored the Moral and Social Reform League and their supporters. Even more important, however, was the fact that powerful and influential groups like the Board of Trade, by staying out of the controversy, lent tacit approval to the status quo.

This situation was sharply changed early in November 1910 with the publication of the following sensational headlines in the Toronto *Globe*: SOCIAL EVIL RUNS RIOT IN WINNIPEG, VICE DISTRICT GROWING, EVERY DEN AN ILLICIT LIQUOR DIVE. The ensuing story was based on an interview with Rev. Dr. J. G. Shearer, general secretary of the national Moral and Social Reform League and a respected Presbyterian minister known for his role in persuading Parliament to pass the Lord's Day Act in 1907. Accusations of civic graft and a portrayal in eastern newspapers of Winnipeg as a vice-ridden city triggered a violent reaction among respectable Winnipeggers and particularly in city council, the main target of the allegations. That Winnipeg should be vilified as the "rottenest city in Canada" by the eastern establishment was too much for the adolescent pride of the western community to bear. Perhaps even more important, public attacks such as this would certainly not help in the city's efforts to attract immigrants and industry from the east.

In the weeks following the Toronto reports, prostitution became the major issue of the upcoming mayoralty election. The *Free Press* noted that Shearer's charges were being "hotly commented upon in Winnipeg." The same paper went on to add that city council felt that the charges were only a part of the campaign of Mr. E. D. Martin, the anti-segregation mayoralty candidate supported by the reformers. "The impression is general around the city hall that Dr. Shearer's aspersions are simply a portion of a campaign organized with the intention of boosting the chances of the anti-segregation candidate for the mayoralty chair."[134] Given this interpretation, Evans and his supporters adopted a policy of no comment on

Shearer's charges. But within a week this calm was shattered when the *Telegram*, owned by Evans, began running angry editorials denouncing Shearer as a "monomaniac" and a "liar and a slanderer."[135]

The prostitution issue reached a peak early in December when Mayor Evans announced his decision to run for a third term. The 1910 election campaign was one of the most strenuous and hotly contested in the history of municipal politics. Evans emerged as a master of political strategy. His campaign was highly polished, well-organized and ruthlessly efficient. With the active and strongly partisan support of the *Telegram*, and the more passive support of the *Free Press*, the mayor succeeded in pushing the issue of segregation to the background and replacing it with the issue of Winnipeg's "good name."

> As citizens of our community, we should be, if possible, even more jealous of the good name of our city than of our homes. . . . It is patent that those who have the welfare of the city at heart would not advertise it abroad as the rottenest city on the continent. I stand for the best and cleanest and purest city in the world — for Winnipeg to have the reputation of such.[136]

Evans' tactics had the desired effect of putting Martin and his supporters on the defensive. The anti-segregationists diligently presented their arguments, but this issue had been overshadowed by their need to repudiate the various charges levelled by Evans and company. In one speech, for example, Martin devoted most of his time to defending himself from Evans' charge that he was a candidate of foreign agitators. Of course, Martin and the reformers were not naive about Evans' strategy. It was evident that they realized the reputation of the city issue was a red herring. As Martin stated, ". . . he [Evans] tried to hide himself behind the good name of the city [but] it is not the good name of the city that is on trial at this election; [it is] the action of men who, in defiance of the law, set up conditions which inevitably reflected upon the city's good name." Martin's efforts to bring the "real issue" into sharp focus, however, were largely unsuccessful.[137]

Evans was amply rewarded for his skillful campaign when the results were declared. He was elected by a vote of 7,634 to 5,744, winning fifty-seven of the city's seventy-two polls. Furthermore, in ensuing years, the social vice issue was mentioned only infrequently and the brothels on Rachel and McFarlane streets continued to operate openly for a full thirty years until the trade fell victim to amateur competition.[138]

The prostitution issue was yet another example of the commercial elite's laissez-faire attitude to social problems. By 1910 divisions in the city had become entrenched, foreshadowing the social strife Winnipeg was to endure in the years following World War I.

Parade on Portage Avenue, c. 1915.

Decoration Day Parade, 1916.

Peace Day Celebrations, June 1919.

Chapter Two

Crisis and Decline
1914-1945

The General Strike was Winnipeg's . . . climactic event. . . . The victory was a Pyrrhic one for Winnipeg's commercial aristocracy: the city over which it presided, after 1919, was a city in decline. Like other inland centres, it suffered from the drop in ocean freight rates that followed the opening of the Panama Canal, in conjunction with the rigidity of inland railway freight rates which coastal interests were careful to maintain. At the same time the wheat economy, key to Winnipeg's earlier growth, lost its ebullience and ceased to expand significantly. The loss of young men in the War was another blow: Winnipeg's business in the 1920s was in the hands of tired old men. But the handicap created by the crushing of the General Strike — a weak and defensive labour movement and a steady slippage of wage rates within the Canadian spectrum — may have been most important. . . . [The effect of these conditions was] to sap the strength and drawing power of the local consumer market, and to dissuade employers from making the effort to improve efficiency and to innovate. It was an effect all too visible among the capitalists of Winnipeg, notoriously unenterprising after 1919. In this sense, what the Citizens' Committee put down turned out to be their own future.

H. C. Pentland,
Canadian Dimension, 1969.

WAR AND STRIKE

While the rise of Winnipeg was meteoric, its relative decline was a slow process. Winnipeg's problems began with the recession of 1913, when a condition of overinvestment in the capital goods industry had come about in anticipation of a rapid rate of development in western Canada. By the fall of 1913 had there been a depression it would have been severe and prolonged. The war, however, prevented this collapse and for a few years restored western prosperity.[1] Markets for agricultural produce expanded and prices rose; wheat acreage increased and there was a substantial rise in the value of exports from western Canada. By the end of the war prices were still moving upward and Winnipeg's future, especially in manufacturing, looked bright. However, the occurrence of the Winnipeg General Strike[2] interrupted this prosperity and marked the beginning of a thirty-year period of stagnation. The factors responsible, aside from the tremendous impact of the strike itself, included generally unfavourable world economic conditions (evident in several recessions as well as in the Depression); the rise of other western cities such as Vancouver, Calgary and Edmonton; the loss of key freight-rate advantages; and the growth of new marketing methods. Together they combined to make the period from 1914 to 1945 the most difficult in Winnipeg's history.

By 1913 Winnipeg was the largest city in western Canada and was that area's industrial, financial and marketing centre. Moreover, the city's leaders envisioned a golden future for Winnipeg based on increased industry and trade, a future that could best be achieved if the conditions conducive to the free operation of commerce were maintained. This meant, in effect, freedom from organized labour. But the presence in Winnipeg of the main repair shops, yards and roundhouses of three transcontinental railways and their related industries had also created a large and fairly cohesive labour force which was early organized into unions and determined to expand. Strikes in 1906 and other years helped to increase the polarization of labour and management, and although the war put labour strife temporarily in the background the resentment and discontent of Winnipeg's workers continued to grow.[3]

War increased the demand for labour and the cost of living without any corresponding improvement in real wages. Both of these factors worked to regenerate labour unrest when the recession ended in late 1915. Prices of almost all commodities began to rise sharply while the size of the underpaid workforce increased. Trade union membership grew and prompted the unions to begin flexing their muscles with demands for recognition, higher wages and better working conditions. The result was greater militancy among Winnipeg's unions and by 1918 strikes in the city became frequent. At one point in May thirteen unions were simultaneously off their jobs and the more than 6,800 strikers included workers from such crucial municipal services as fire, water, light and power, and public transportation.[4]

The growing militancy of labour in Winnipeg, and in other parts of Canada, was further spurred on by the federal government's scheme for the conscription of manpower for military service. Labour opposed this measure both because they objected to being forced to fight fellow workers of different nationalities and because they thought it was a first step toward industrial conscription. Through industrial conscription, the government could force workers to work in certain factories and thus effectively destroy their right to strike.

Following the war, the direction in which the tide was running became clearer. In March 1919, when representatives of western labour unions convened in Calgary, Winnipeg sent forty-seven representatives, the largest delegation at the convention. The most important result of the Calgary Convention was to approve the creation of the One Big Union. The O.B.U. was the institutional expression of the demand for industrial organization and was based on the organization of all workers, skilled and unskilled, into one working class movement. Their new political and economic strength, it was argued, could then be deployed to accomplish the objectives of the working class. Equally important, in the aftermath of the convention, was the Marxist rhetoric which accompanied the various resolutions. The convention demanded the release of all political prisoners and sent fraternal greetings to the new Soviet government of Russia.[5]

It was in this heady atmosphere that the Winnipeg General Strike began a few weeks later on May 15, 1919. The strike lasted six weeks and concluded in riot, bloodshed, and the arrest of the strike leaders. During the massive walkout, Winnipeg became a community caught in the grip of fear, a fear spawned and fed by lack of effective communication between opposing elements.

The strike actually began in the city's metal industry. Members of the metalworking unions had fought three difficult and futile campaigns for employer recognition of their union since 1906 and in the spring of 1919 opened a new campaign and ran into the same stiff opposition. Workers in the building trades in the city had already gained recognition but had suffered during the war as increases in the cost of living rapidly outstripped their wages. They were determined in 1919 to make up for lost time with substantial new gains. When their bargaining met little success, they struck on May 1st and were followed the next day by the metalworkers. As far as these workers were concerned, the fundamental issues of union recognition and a reasonable living wage were at stake. When they appealed to the local Trades and Labour Council for help, an overwhelming majority of Winnipeg union members voted to begin a general strike to support them on May 15.

The response to the general strike call was immediate and by 11:00 A.M. on May 15 Winnipeg was paralyzed. Approximately seventy unions backed the call as did thousands of unorganized workers. Within three days about 35,000 workers walked off the job — bakers, barbers, bricklayers, cab drivers, caretakers, carpenters, clerks, culinary workers, elevator operators, firemen, plumbers, postal workers, printers, street railway workers, teamsters, and many more. The city's policemen, who also voted to strike, stayed at their jobs only at the request of the Strike Committee.

The Winnipeg General Strike of 1919 represented the result of decades of class polarization heightened by depression and war. Labour's discontent sprang from genuine and legitimate grievances — long hours, low wages, bad housing, and rising prices. Times were hard for the working man: the cost of living had increased by seventy-five per cent while the increase in earnings was only eighteen per cent over 1913 levels. The average construction worker earned approximately $900 per year while studies showed that the minimum requirement for an average family in Winnipeg was $1,-500.[6]

These grievances were real but the issue that triggered the strike was one of principle — the refusal of many employers to engage in collective bargaining. Trade unionists felt humiliated and degraded by the stubborn attitude of management and their frustration sought release in a massive walkout by the whole labour force. The influences of American radicalism and Marxism were present to some extent, but the strike was not "Communist-inspired" as some charged. In spite of these facts, the atmosphere in Winnipeg was so tense that many in the city saw the strike as an attempt to overthrow the constitutional authority and replace it with an alien economic and political system.

With the onset of the strike, the divisions in Winnipeg society were clearly revealed. On one side were the workers, led by a general strike committee of about three hundred delegates from member unions and a central strike committee of fifteen which acted as an executive. Although they had struck for union recognition and a living wage, the strike was really the result of many deep-rooted and complex factors. Union leaders had been powerless in Winnipeg for decades. Class division had long split the community and the general strike was only the latest and most serious manifestation of a lack of unity of economic or political purpose among the city's residents. The workers believed that if they won this strike and forced the employers to back down, they would have won the most important fight of all and would wipe out past defeats.

While labour undoubtedly exaggerated the possibilities of change in 1919, employers were just as unrealistic in their striving to retain outmoded power relationships. Typical of employers was a view of labour as a commodity to be bought as cheaply as possible. Most employers were reluctant to yield up a paternalistic "master and man" relationship and negotiate terms with workers collectively.[7]

The views held by Winnipeg's employers found a home in the Citizens' Committee of One Thousand, an organization which purported to be representative of the neutral citizenry but which was actually fiercely anti-strike. The committee was *ad hoc* in the sense that it was not elective, nor was it responsible to any constituted authority, but there is no doubt that the Citizens' Committee was composed of prominent and powerful business and professional men commonly dedicated to the defeat of the strikers. In pursuing that goal they enjoyed extremely close relations with all three levels of government. Together they realized the far-reaching significance of this strike and concluded they could not afford to lose such a crucial battle.

The Citizens' Committee and their supporters fought the strike with every weapon at their disposal and asserted that it was an O.B.U. plot, supported by aliens, to initiate a Canadian revolution. When, for example, the workers' General Strike Committee permitted certain essential services to operate and issued cards stating that the men working at these specially designated jobs were doing so with the permission of the Strike Committee, their opponents charged that the strikers had taken over civic government and were thus fomenting revolution. Throughout the strike, the Citizens' Committee directed strike-breaking activities, recruited volunteers for the fire halls and postal services, counselled the employers, and worked closely with all levels of government. It was largely at their instigation and with their help that some two thousand Special Police were organized and the regular police fired. This assured control of the streets by forces unfriendly to the strikers.

The federal government undertook even more stringent anti-strike measures. The federal authorities built up the Royal North West Mounted Police contingent in the city and arranged the organization of a large, heavily armed force of volunteer militia. When it became clear that the strikers could not be forced to accept a dictated settlement, ten men considered to be strike leaders, including R. B. Russell, William Ivens, John Queen, George Arm-

June 21, 1919, "Bloody Saturday" as it was termed, was the culmination of the Winnipeg General Strike. The city's photographers must have known that they were recording history, and so many photos have been preserved of that day that it is possible to follow events on almost a minute-by-minute basis.

(1) Early that Saturday afternoon, a crowd gathered on Main Street in front of city hall to watch a "silent parade" that was called not by the strikers but by the pro-strike returned soldiers.

(2) Winnipeg's mayor rushed to Osborne Barracks and requested that the Mounties come to "the aid of the civil power." The response was 54 police on horseback, shown in this photo riding north on Main Street.

(3) The RNWMP at Portage Avenue. Some of the "Mounties" near the rear were in army uniforms, and had been transferred from military to civilian authority. The Mounties rode three times up and down Main Street, to clear the crowd from in front of city hall and to prevent the parade.

(4) The first time, they broke into a trot as they passed the Union Bank Building, shown top right. About this time, the mayor read the Riot Act. The Mounties rode another six blocks up Main Street.

(5) The crowd closed in again as the Mounties completed their first ride up Main Street.

(6) Some streetcars were being operated by Citizens' Committee volunteers and armed militia. This was considered a provocation by pro-strike forces, since the street railwaymen were on strike. As one streetcar passed in front of city hall, "a bunch of men got together, most of them teenaged boys, and heaved," recalled an eyewitness. Then the Mounties returned from their first ride up Main Street, and were hit by "a rain of stones and bricks."

(7) The second ride north of the RNWMP, this time without the men in khaki and with clubs in hand. A number of Mounties were hit by stones taken from a nearby construction site; two fell from their horses and were dragged to safety.

(8) The third charge. The clubs were in the left hand, and .45 revolvers were drawn. The Mounties turned left on to William Street, charging directly into the crowd, and as they did so they fired a volley. At least one onlooker was hit, an old man standing by the Union Bank.

(9) While the Mounties were behind city hall, one man lay on the sidewalk in front of city hall, apparently shot. Another was kneeling at the curb. Many people thought the RNWMP were firing blanks, until they saw men falling down shot.

4

5

6

10

11

12

13

14

(10) The return of the third charge. Recalled one eyewitness: "They were running out of stones . . . and another fellow — he was a real fanatic — ran up to pick up half a brick — it was only fifteen feet in front of a Mountie. He had just straightened up when — he got it." The man was probably Mike Sokolowiski, who was killed instantly by a shot in the heart in front of the Manitoba Hotel. In this photo one man is lying on the curb, and as people run to his aid the Mounties are turned around looking at him.

(11) As special constables armed with clubs marched out to clear the streets, some members of the crowd set the streetcar on fire.

(12) By 3:45, the streets were clear. These special police, lined up across Main Street at Market Street, were carrying clubs and wore white armbands.

(13 & 14) Trucks with machine guns mounted on them were brought out. Here Mounties with rifles and militia line up after the charges on Main Street just south of city hall. Police and military patrolled the empty streets as the city waited for the response of the strike committee. The strike organizers were incensed by the violence of the authorities, but they felt that they could not win in the face of the intransigence of the government and the city's employers.

strong, A. A. Heaps, and R. E. Bray, were arrested by being roused from their beds at gunpoint in the early hours of June 17 and hustled off to Stony Mountain penitentiary. It was the clear objective of the government either to settle the strike in favour of the employers or to crush it by force.

The strikers were in a difficult position. The attempt of the Strike Committee to maintain order, revealed by their policy of urging the strikers to stay at home and avoid demonstrations, was constantly challenged by the Citizens' Committee and their supporters. Furthermore, the strategy of paralyzing an entire city and then allowing some essential services to function only with Strike Committee consent stimulated a belief on the part of the authorities that the strikers were after a revolutionary usurpation of power.[8]

Following the arrest of the strike leaders on orders from Ottawa, a group of war veterans sympathetic to the strikers organized a mass rally on Saturday June 21, in defiance of bans on public demonstrations issued by Mayor Charles F. Gray. By 2:00 P.M. Saturday the large crowd that had gathered in front of city hall on Main Street had become an unruly mob. Streetcars were blocked and one was eventually set on fire. At this point Mayor Gray called in the Royal North West Mounted Police to disperse the crowd. They moved north down Main Street in line, endeavouring to clear the street, but were met with stout defiance. Mayor Gray then read the Riot Act and in a second charge, which earned for that day the title "Bloody Saturday," the police used firearms and one man was killed and several others wounded. The "Specials" then lined up across the width of Main Street and with clubs in hand proceeded to clear the area. Finally, the militia moved into the downtown area from Fort Osborne, armed with machine guns. By evening Winnipeg was an armed camp; hundreds were wounded; one man was dead, another dying. Faced with the reality of brutal, naked force, the Strike Committee admitted defeat and called the strike off at 11:00 A.M. on June 26th.

The strikers had failed to achieve their major objectives and after six weeks of effort the futility of the strike had become painfully clear. All the strikers were able to gain was an agreement on the part of the provincial government to appoint a royal commission to conduct an impartial investigation into the causes of the dispute. Yet, although the Winnipeg General Strike came to an abrupt, inglorious end, the passions it provoked would live on for decades.

The Winnipeg General Strike of 1919 had a profound effect on the economic, political and social history of the city. It marked the city's passage from a relatively simple, pioneer, rurally oriented community to a more complex, technological and highly urbanized metropolis. The significance of this major event in Winnipeg's history is that it crystallized in one occurrence the tensions that had been developing in the community since its inception. It also spelled the end for several decades of much of the goodwill that certain groups in the city had been attempting to foster. Many of the economic, social and political dimensions of life in post-1919 Winnipeg can only be understood if the strike and its aftermath are viewed as key factors in the determination of the character of the city.

ECONOMIC GROWTH AND METROPOLITAN DEVELOPMENT

After the General Strike there followed a period of recession with falling wheat prices being the main cause. This recession was short-lived and by 1925 prosperity returned. Higher wheat prices, falling transportation costs, and a general improvement in world business conditions paved the way for substantial increases in Canada's export trade. General recovery was also strengthened by American investments abroad, part of which came to Canada. There were also larger supplies of domestic capital available. The result was a renewed expansion in the capital goods industries and in railway building in western Canada. The west and its metropolis again began to expand. The distributing trades in particular experienced great prosperity. By 1930, 768 wholesale establishments gave employment to over 8,300 persons and had net sales of $635 million. Retail merchandising and service establishments numbered 3,577, gave employment to over 17,000 people, and had sales of $145 million. In short, under the impact of local and western production and growing consumer needs, commerce in Winnipeg thrived.[9]

Manufacturing also made considerable progress during the late twenties. The gross value of manufactured products increased from $75 million in 1921 to $109 million by 1929 (Appendix, Table XI).

Eley Brothers Plant.

The foremost industry in the city was still the processing of farm products — particularly flour milling, and slaughtering and meat packing. The other large establishments, such as printing and publishing, cotton and jute bag manufacturing and electric light and power production, were complementary.[10] Increased building activity after 1926 and mining development in the north contributed to manufacturing activity. The exploitation of mineral, timber and hydro-electric resources in northern Manitoba and northwestern Ontario furnished Winnipeg with a valuable new hinterland. Producers of copper and brass, iron and steel products, and lumber all benefited. The widespread use of the automobile aided the tourist industry, and afforded superior access to Winnipeg from the surrounding countryside, with favourable effects upon local retail trade.[11]

In the development of both manufacturing and tourism, Winnipeg's Board of Trade played a leading role. In 1924 it was instrumental in the formation of the Industrial Development Board of Manitoba. The Board's activities were financed by the province, the city of Winnipeg, the Board of Trade, and other business organizations and its goal was to encourage the purchase of homemade products to assist existing industries, and to encourage new development. During 1924 and 1925 the Board of Trade was also involved in the creation of the Winnipeg Tourist and Convention Bureau, which "energetically developed tourist traffic" through such activities as a "Pine-to-Palm" motor trip headed by Mayor R. H. Webb.[12]

Perhaps no individual contributed more to the recovery of Winnipeg after World War I than James A. Richardson. Scion of a wealthy family, he came west in 1919 to take charge of the Winnipeg branch of the family firm. He revolutionized it, became spokesman of the grain trade and, to some extent, of the farmers. His breadth of vision was inspiring. He saw the prairie west as a complex place, not just a breadbasket. And he saw the businessman's role as a creative one that involved not only making money but also promoting a balanced development of the wealth of the country.

In 1925, he started Richardson Securities, now one of the largest investment firms in Canada. By 1926 the daring experiments of the first bush pilots had so proved the value of the airplane in the north that Richardson brought the wealth of the grain trade to support the new venture, and formed Western Canada Airways Limited. Then Richardson switched his attention from airlines to airwaves and established Radio Station CJRC.[13]

These and the numerous other ventures by Richardson provided the Winnipeg business community with an example of the creative leadership the city so desperately needed, but few followed the example. Indeed, even before the onset of depression in 1929, it was apparent that Winnipeg had severe problems as an alarming number of adverse trends became clearly discernible. Industry was not yet sufficiently diversified to absorb seasonal workers during the winter months. The result was an unemployment problem which became particularly acute in the winter of 1921-22 and required expenditures by all levels of government to overcome. Most significant, however, were changes in transportation and in merchandising methods which were beyond the control of the Winnipeg business community.

With the stabilization and decline of ocean freight rates after the war, and the opening of the cheaper sea route via the Panama Canal in 1914, European shippers and eastern Canadian manufacturers tended to use the ocean route instead of railways. Vancouver became a new gateway to the west and was soon able to capture a large part of Winnipeg's grain and wholesale trade. Indeed, during the decade of the 1920s Vancouver bypassed Winnipeg as the third largest city in Canada.

To this factor was added the effects of increased development in the provinces of Alberta and Saskatchewan. The rise of other prairie cities challenged Winnipeg's traditional freight rate privileges, which were declared discriminatory and extended to other western cities.[14] The growth of these rival centres seriously undermined Winnipeg's primary function as a distributing centre. A substantial number of wholesalers emerged in the smaller western cities, particularly in the hardware and grocery lines. In such staple items, sold at low profit margins, the new freight rate structures enabled distributors in these centres to compete on better than even terms, within their respective trading areas, against the wholesalers of Winnipeg. The growth of such cities as Saskatoon, Regina, Edmonton and Calgary, along with their respective trading areas, strengthened their capacity to offer services comparable to those supplied by Winnipeg firms. Between 1924 and 1930, for example,

Grain Exchange.

Street asphalt crew at Portage and Toronto.

A business in Winnipeg's central core.

8829-1

'F00.

The CPR yards were an important psychological as well as physical barrier in Winnipeg. As one Winnipegger put it, "the so-called foreigners occupied one gigantic melting pot north of the CPR tracks."

The clothing industry or "needle trade" has been a major component of the city's economy since 1900. The industry grew steadily over the years, even during the Great Depression. During the 1930s small scale garment, glove, shoe and dress factories proliferated as unemployed workers and businessmen occupied empty warehouse space in the city's wholesale district. Since then the apparel industry has grown to the third largest in Canada, preceded by only Montreal and Toronto. It is also the second largest employer in Winnipeg, following the food and beverage industry, and the largest employer of women.

the wholesale trade of Winnipeg declined from $96.7 million to $72.9 million. In Calgary it rose from $24.6 to $30.5 million and in Edmonton from $18.1 to $24.7 million.[15]

Additional factors aggravated the adverse effects on Winnipeg of the growing encroachments by other Western cities. The increased use of automobiles during the 1920s enabled farmers to shop in larger centres and the loss of patronage by small town merchants imposed severe pressures on Winnipeg wholesale houses which had given these merchants credit and relied upon their business. The emergence of mail order companies also caused problems since wholesalers and retailers of hardware, clothing, and domestic items were bypassed by the consumer who enjoyed the convenience of the mail-order catalogue. To compete as best as possible with mail order firms, large city stores purchased directly from manufacturers. This trend made it very difficult for wholesalers to sell profitably to retailers. Finally, the emerging tendency, developed in the United States, for manufacturers to advertise their brands directly to the consuming public created consumer brand consciousness and further reduced the dependence of manufacturers on wholesalers to distribute their merchandise for them.[16]

Locally owned retail establishments experienced other difficulties during the 1920s. During this decade, independent retailers in Winnipeg received stiff competition from large department and chain stores owned or controlled by interests in eastern Canada or the United States. Competition from these large stores substantially reduced the profit margin of independent retailers and ultimately drove some out of business. It also had a detrimental result in other areas. Employment levels were reduced since chain and department stores employed fewer staff per capita sales than did smaller, independent stores. Profits from retailing were drained from the city, purchasing power was reduced, and the city's tax base was adversely affected.[17]

These problems, combined with the legacy of bitterness and polarization left by the General Strike and a lack of economic leadership, were largely responsible for the erosion of Winnipeg's position.

The stock market crash of October 1929 marked the end of the preceding era of troubled expansion. The gross value of manufactured products in Winnipeg which had been over $109 million in 1929, dropped to $59 million in 1933. The wholesale trade of Manitoba, seventy-five per cent of which was in Winnipeg, declined from $99 million in 1930 to $65 million in 1933. Eaton's mail-order business slumped from $22 million in 1930 to $17 million by 1932. The value of the tourist trade fell off by $1.5 million between 1928 and 1933.[18] Dramatic evidence of economic trouble could also be found in the sharp decline in building activity. In 1929, $11.1 million worth of building permits had been issued in Winnipeg. This figure shrank to $6.6 million in 1930 and then to a low of $700,000 in 1934 (Appendix, Table XII).

The collapse of 1929 evolved into the Great Depression. The decline in the incomes of western farmers as prairie drought persisted seriously affected Winnipeg businesses. The virtual cessation of developmental activity throughout the west practically ended the demand for the products of the city's large and diversified construction materials industry, while depressed agricultural income in the hinterland brought huge reductions in demand for the goods which the city manufactured and distributed.

As the farm economy crumbled, industry and commerce suffered; the running of trains in and out of Winnipeg slackened; numerous factories closed. In the winter of 1929-30 the unemployment Winnipeg had experienced in the early twenties returned with a vengeance. Where 405 persons had registered for relief in 1928-29, 2,094 registered the following year. And in the bleak years that followed, the figure continued to climb until thousands of workers were idle and hundreds of families on relief. Relief works were provided by the city, province and federal governments but none were able to lift the city, or for that matter the country, out of the Depression.

Winnipeg, like other western cities, entered a period of severe financial stress. Tax revenues fell drastically just as the demand for city expenditures increased. The decline in revenues was due chiefly to a decline in the assessed value of real estate in Winnipeg (from $288 million in 1915 to $194 million in 1937) and to tax arrears (thirty per cent of taxpayers were in arrears for a year or more in 1936). The result was that in 1936 the city's revenues fell short of meeting expenditures by $3,313,955. Relief costs soared. In the years 1931-1936, they totalled $20,452,000 in Winnipeg alone, and the city had to pay over forty per cent of this staggering figure.

WE'RE **FULLER** PEP

I'M FINE & DANDY!

How Are You?

I'M FINE & DANDY!

How Are You?

FOOTE

— SUCCESS CLUB —

4TH FIELD MANAGER'S SCHOOL. WESTERN CAN. DISTRICT. APR. 15·16·17·1926.

9042-1

9042-1

Delegates to the Fuller Brush Company's Field Manager School, 1926.

Vegetable gardens planted in the grounds of the legislative buildings, c. 1938.

WINNIPEG M-65

Construction of the Winnipeg Civic Auditorium was one of the public works programs of the Depression. The auditorium now serves as the home of the Provincial Library and Archives.

By 1937, the city told a federal commission that it was "absolutely impossible for it to continue to function" without assistance.[19]

Yet the Depression brought unexpected benefits to a few residents of Winnipeg. With depressed conditions prairie retailers pursued a hand-to-mouth policy with the result that more emphasis was laid on the quickness of manufacturing and delivery. This factor gave Winnipeg's industries and commercial establishments a measure of advantage over larger, more firmly established eastern firms that were a considerable distance from the market.

The prairie impoverishment which thus indirectly aided local manufacturers in the marketing of their products aided them in production as well. Drought, depressed agricultural prices and mechanization drove many thousands of persons off the land to seek opportunities in the cities. The presence in Winnipeg, all through the 1930s, of a large unemployed population supported by public relief ensured an adequate supply of labour to all manner of local firms. Furthermore, difficult conditions discouraged the location of eastern Canadian or American branch plant factories. Instead, unemployed workmen, tradesmen, and mechanics frequently entered into business in a small way.[20]

Other factors also contributed to Winnipeg's economic survival during the difficult years of the Drepression. The large hydro-electric power plants developed both by the city and the province in earlier years provided ample power at low rates.[21] The huge contraction of the wholesale trade released large amounts of space in warehouse and wholesale buildings, suitable for light industry. Promotional activity, suspended in 1933 for lack of support, was resumed in 1935 when the Industrial Development Bureau began again to receive adequate financial assistance from local business firms and city council.[22]

Together, these factors enabled Winnipeg to survive the Great Depression. The number of manufacturing establishments in the city, for example, increased steadily throughout the period (from 519 in 1930 to 648 in 1939) with the most notable expansion occurring in the needle trades.[23] By the time war broke out in 1939, the city had regained a good deal of its lost momentum. Buses bulged with workers bound for the garment factories now established in old warehouse buildings. There were increasing numbers of new automobiles on the streets and retailers were once again optimistic.

Portage Avenue stores scrubbed the gloom from their display windows and basement bargain hunters at Eaton's ventured into upper floors. With lineups at movie houses and clubs Winnipeg again resumed its reputation as a lively town.

The real, dramatic change, particularly for the unemployed, came only after the outbreak of war, however. The war provided, for the first time in a decade, adequate jobs. Not only did men now find work, but so did hundreds of women. They were needed in the industries which were quickly put into high gear producing military equipment and supplies. Uniforms, boots, and other military equipment poured from rapidly expanded facilities. The various ironworks in the city turned to the manufacture of shells, while the infant aircraft parts operations in the city expanded greatly. In short, the war provided for Winnipeg the solution to unemployment that it could not find in peacetime.

POPULATION GROWTH AND ETHNIC RELATIONSHIPS

While the period from 1900 to 1913 was one in which intolerance and hostility toward the European immigrant in Winnipeg increased, it was in fact an era of relative calm compared with what transpired in the years after the outbreak of World War I in August 1914. In the months and years following Canada's declaration of war a number of issues — some new, others pre-dating the war itself — and events brought into very sharp focus the deep divisions that already existed in Winnipeg between Anglo-Saxon and foreign residents. For while the war was certainly a major contributor to the heightening of tension in Winnipeg, other forces also had a significant impact on social relationships between various ethnic groups in the city. Although issues such as temperance, sabbatarianism, compulsory and unilingual education, and unemployment, and events such as the Russian Revolution, the Red Scare and the Winnipeg General Strike had different and usually unrelated causes, they also all managed in their own way to increase or exacerbate ethnic divisions in Winnipeg.[24] Indeed, together with the war, they combined to make the years from 1914 to 1920 the worst in Winnipeg's social history: ethnic discrimination was rampant; foreigners lost their jobs, were disenfranchised and deported; property was destroyed; lives were threatened. Most important of all,

Workers at the Winnipeg Electric Railway Company's Fort Rouge Yards in 1929.

the events of these years left scars on the tissue of Winnipeg society that took decades to heal.[25]

In the years prior to 1914, the charter group in Winnipeg had viewed the foreigner and his assimilation to a way of life as serious but ultimately solvable problems. The war, however, caused a dramatic change in this attitude. The outbreak of hostilities in Europe brought an immediate heightening of pro-British feelings among members of the city's charter group. At the same time the emotional hysteria that was generated by the war made certain ethnic groups in Winnipeg automatic targets of attack. The most obvious result was that Germans — who had hitherto been regarded as worthy immigrants — were immediately placed on the list of "undesirable aliens." During the course of the war the natual reaction of British Winnipeg to the German enemy was fed by crude but persistent propaganda until, by 1919, the charter group was proclaiming that the term Anglo-Saxon was a misnomer and that the proper term should be "Anglo-Celtic." Thus the *Winnipeg Telegram* declared: "All Scottish, Irish and Welsh people, and most English folk, would do well to remember that they are not the descendants of an insignificant German tribe."[26]

Winnipeggers of German descent were not the only objects of derision during the period 1914-1918. War psychology brought everyone who was not obviously British under suspicion. The problems faced by Europeans in Winnipeg were detailed in a letter printed in the *Winnipeg Tribune* in 1915. Written by a group of Ukrainians, it stated:

> Owing to the unjust classification of all Slavs as Austrians and anti-allies, and owing to irresponsible utterances in the press and otherwise, a certain degree of intolerance and hatred towards everything that is foreign has been transplanted in the public mind, resulting in indiscreet looting of property, disturbing divine service in the churches, raiding of private homes, and personal assaults of the gravest kind, to all those who have the appearance of foreign birth, thus rendering our lives endangered.[27]

The "alien" problem in Winnipeg was further intensified as a result of the Russian Revolution of 1917. When the Russian Bolshevists surrendered to the Germans in November, a "Hun-Bol-shevist" conspiracy designed to destroy "the civilization of Anglo-Saxonism the world over" was immediately perceived, with predictable results for Winnipeg's Slavs.[28]

The intense feelings of hostility and hatred generated by the war did not soon subside after 1918. Instead, if anything, they became worse. There were at least four reasons for this. First, the months following the end of the war were marked by a mounting fear of a "combined alien-revolutionary threat" that plunged most of North America into the infamous Red Scare of 1919. In Winnipeg, manifestations of the general paranoia — fed by pro-alien and pro-revolutionary statements by Winnipeg labour leaders at the founding convention of the One Big Union in March 1919 — were more apparent than in most other cities on the continent.[29] Second, the months following the war saw a severe unemployment problem in Winnipeg, particularly among returned soldiers. "Frustrated by the fact that many of them were unemployed while Germans and Ukrainians and other 'alien enemies' held down good jobs, it was they who most persistently demanded that the alien-pacifist-Red element be deported immediately."[30] This bitterness led to serious rioting in January 1919. Third, the Winnipeg General Strike of 1919 was perceived by many in the city as a revolution led and supported by the same elements that had proven disloyal during the war. The fact that there was little evidence to support this view — there were no foreigners prominent in the labour movement in Winnipeg — mattered little, and the association between strikers and foreigners persisted. Finally, throughout the period the supporters of prohibition, sabbatarianism and compulsory and unilingual education generally perceived the foreigner as an opponent of their goals and these feelings provided a constant undercurrent of anti-alien feeling well into the 1920s.[31]

But whatever the cause, manifestations of anti-European feelings were apparent on many fronts during 1919 and 1920. Indicative of the mood of Winnipeg's charter group during these years was the fact that in January 1919 a group of war veterans and opportunistic hoodlums prowled around the city, smashed the windows of stores in the North End, broke into homes and demanded that everyone who had even the appearance of an alien kiss the Union Jack. The club building of the Austro-Hungarian Society was literally left in ruins and Edelweiss Brewery in Elmwood was made a shambles.[32]

Although Winnipeg received the bulk of its immigration during the early 1900s there were other influxes during the 1920s and post World War I period.

The city's Ukrainian residents were also a target.

> The attackers did not limit themselves to physical beatings of individuals [of German descent] but attacked the halls and centres of Ukrainian organizations. Drunk veterans broke into buildings, demolished the furniture, destroyed libraries and musical instruments, throwing them out into the street through broken windows. Attacking the Prosvita Reading Society premises, the hooligans smashed all the windows, destroyed the library and theatre costumes.[33]

No charges were laid against the marauders by the authorities.

During the twenty-five years stretching from 1920 to 1945, the struggle for harmonious relationships between ethnic groups was aided by several trends that affected both the city's growth rate and the ethnic characteristics of its population. Most important was the fact that during the period the city grew at a very slow rate compared with the pre-World War I era. The sharply reduced growth rate was evident in the fact that Winnipeg was bypassed by Vancouver as Canada's third largest city in the 1920s (Appendix, Table IV), and in the fact that Winnipeg's average five-year growth rate for the period 1921-1946 was only 8.3 per cent compared to an average rate of 45.4 per cent between 1901 and 1921 (Appendix, Table V). Indeed, during the period 1931-1936, the city's population actually declined by three thousand persons. Only in its position in the urban hierarchies of Manitoba and the prairie provinces did Winnipeg hold its own (Appendix, Tables IV and III).

The reason for this sharp decline in the population growth rate was an abrupt end to the vast influx of immigrants which had in previous years swelled the city's population. There were, of course, periods when the city received substantial numbers of newcomers, particularly during the late 1920s, but these influxes were slight compared with the great movements of an earlier period. Furthermore, many of the people who came to Winnipeg during this period were from the rural parts of Canada rather than immigrants from abroad. This was an important trend since in most cases the newcomers to the city had already gone through some of the stages of assimilation and could fit into the community with less difficulty than those who came directly from foreign countries.

The declining percentage of foreign-born residents in Winnipeg was also the result of the fact that natural increase played a role of increasing importance in the city's growth rate. Continuing declines in the city's infant mortality rate, an increase in the number of females in the city (Appendix, Table II), and the drop in the number of immigrants all increased the importance of natural increase as a factor in population growth. The result was that more Winnipeggers were actually born in the city. Between 1921 and 1941, the city's foreign-born population declined from forty-seven per cent to thirty-five per cent (Appendix, Tables VI and VII).

Together, these factors had much to do with a decrease in ethnic hostility in Winnipeg in the years after 1920. The proportion of British in Winnipeg as compared with other ethnic groups continued to drop throughout the period but at a much slower rate than during the pre-1913 era when it had declined by over ten per cent in one decade (Appendix, Tables VIII and IX). The city's Anglo-Saxons, more secure in their own positions, were less prone to feel threatened as the years passed and gradually tempered most of the strident feelings of superiority.

Indeed, as the years passed and the city's other ethnic groups became more settled and secure they too shed some of the protective coverings that had shielded them in earlier years. As the immigrant stream dwindled and ethnic groups no longer received large numbers of fresh recruits from the mother country, the cultural identity of the groups slowly waned and increasing numbers were absorbed into the broader community. The Winnipeg-born offspring of the original immigrants identified more with Canada than their mother country. They were more adaptive than their parents and easily learned the language and the social customs of the city and in time even began to participate in its economic, political and social life without encountering overt prejudice. Driven by an intense feeling of inferiority, the immigrants' children rushed to adopt the ways of the city's Anglo-Canadian majority. Unlike their parents or grandparents, the second and third generation desired, above all, to be accepted by the Anglo-Saxons.[34]

One measure of this yearning for acceptance was the fact that many Europeans decided to change their names. In the novel *Under the Ribs of Death* by John Marlyn, set in Winnipeg during the 1920s, the central character changes his name from Sandor Hunyadi to Alex Hunter. The explanation given for his action says much about

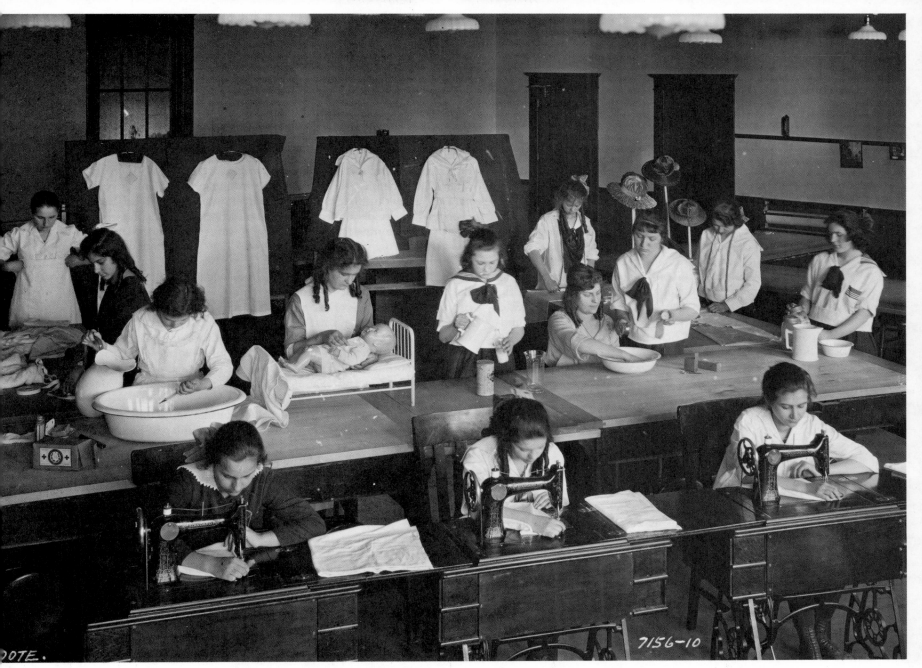

The William Whyte School was designed "for training in standards of living for girls." According to a 1924 school management report, provision was made "for specific training in those departments that bear on the work of women in the home. This includes instruction in food values, selection, purchase and preparation of food, serving of meals, the care and cleansing of the house, sewing, cutting, fitting and making of garments, choice and purchase of materials, testing materials, the relation of dress to income, millinery, house furnishing and decoration, and laundry work. The instruction is practical and cannot fail to have an influence on the ideals of the girls and their work in their own homes. The training is offered to all girls, independent of their standing in academic studies."

the nature of Winnipeg during this period. "No one stared, snickered, or gaped when this name was spoken; it came easily to the tongue. Eyebrows remained in place at its mention. A new name . . . seemed to absolve him of . . . his previous existence."[35]

Still other factors affected Winnipeg's relatively peaceful absorption of its immigrant population during this period. One was the rapid rate of suburban growth. Although the movement to the surrounding municipalities began in the early 1900s, it continued rapidly throughout the years after World War I. Outward urban migration arose from a desire on the part of different ethnic groups and classes to establish new residential subcommunities with church, school, and recreational areas distinct from older, more mixed neighbourhoods.[36] The process was made possible by the advent of cheap urban transportation in the form of both streetcars and automobiles. The result of this migration of residents was an increasing differentiation of residential life in Winnipeg and the surrounding suburbs. Much of the growth achieved by greater Winnipeg in the years after 1921 was concentrated in the surrounding municipalities of Assiniboia, Charleswood, the Kildonans, Fort Garry, St. Boniface, St. James, St. Vital, Transcona, and Tuxedo, rather than in the city of Winnipeg itself (see Appendix, Table XI).

Thus, by 1921, the area north of the CPR tracks contained sixty per cent of the city's Germans, eighty-six per cent of the Ukrainians, eighty-four per cent of the Jewish and seventy-six per cent of the Polish. In the years after 1921 this pattern was extended to the suburbs as Ukrainians tended to congregate in the Kildonans and Transcona, as well as in the North End, while a large proportion of the Jewish group located in West Kildonan. A firmer sense of community evolved out of this continued segregation as each group was able to protect and affirm its cultural values within the homogeneity of its own neighbourhood, instead of being thrust into the melting pot of the North End.

Ethnic tensions in Winnipeg eased also owing to the fact that the immigrants who arrived in Winnipeg in the post-1921 period were of a distinctly different type than those who had come earlier. A wider variety of ethnic origin categories, social classes, and occupations were included in this final phase of immigration. This phase also included many immigrants who came as refugees displaced by political disruptions in their homeland. These disruptions had a great impact upon persons from all social and economic levels; many of them came from urban centres and were generally well-educated people with professional training, artistic talents, and linguistic skills, along with experience in business or government, or a skilled trade. Possessing better education and training these recent immigrants were better able to adjust to their new surroundings.[37]

Taken together, the decline in Winnipeg's growth rate and the changes in the ethnic composition of its population in the years after 1920 generally had the effect of reducing hostilities between various groups in the city. But the process was slow and no great changes were evident overnight. By the end of the 1920s, the overt bigotry of Winnipeg's Anglo-Saxons toward foreigners that had characterized the years between 1914 and 1920 had softened somewhat but discrimination took other forms. A quota system, for example, was established at the Manitoba Medical College during the 1920s. Its goal was to keep Slavs and Jews out of the medical profession, regardless of their scholastic achievements. This system operated effectively and without much contradiction until the end of World War II. By the end of World War II, however, significant changes had occurred in the city. For while World War I had released emotions that victimized the city's non-Anglo-Saxons, the Depression and World War II ameliorated their condition somewhat. The otherwise disastrous period of economic depression during the 1930s brought an abrupt halt to further immigration and gave those who had already arrived the opportunity to blunt the sharpness of differences which were so strikingly evident to the city's Anglo-Saxons. In addition, the years of the Depression relieved the attention of the Anglo-Saxons to matters connected with the foreigners in the city as most groups simply struggled to survive the decade.[38] Then, during the second world war, "the demand for manpower knew no ethnic limits."[39] The war also brought human rights issues to the fore for the combatting of genocide and totalitarianism aroused a new spirit in Canada which led eventually to a demand that it set its own house in order.[40] Generally, then, as Winnipeg entered the postwar period, there were growing indications that the discrimination toward foreigners which had for so long been a part of Winnipeg's social environment was moderating.

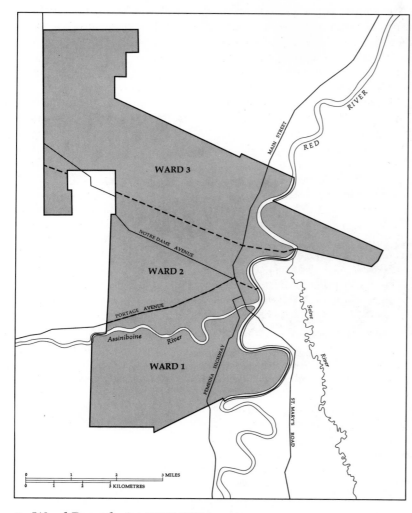

8 Ward Boundaries 1920-1971

THE URBAN LANDSCAPE

During the thirty-one year period stretching from the outbreak of World War I to the end of World War II in 1945, most of the patterns of physical growth established in the preceding decades were maintained. The urban landscape of Winnipeg by 1945 was only slightly different from that established by 1913. In terms of the city's size, the location and desirability of residential areas, the segregation of classes and ethnic groups, the pattern of suburban development, and even generally the location of industry and commerce, Winnipeg remained attached to established patterns.

Among the few changes of the period 1914-1945 was an alteration in Winnipeg's ward boundaries in 1920 when the city's seven wards were collapsed into three. Ward 1 and parts of Wards 2 and 3 became the new Ward 1; the remaining parts of Wards 2 and 3 and Ward 4 became the new Ward 2; while Wards 5, 6, and 7 became the new Ward 3. These ward boundaries were to remain in effect until the formation of Unicity in 1972. But even though they had a major impact on civic politics — and were, in fact, a very neat gerrymander by the city's establishment — the new ward boundaries had virtually no other effect on the urban landscape save that of creating new lines on the map of the city (see Map 8).

One of the more significant events that did occur in the inter-war period was the removal of the Univeristy of Manitoba from its buildings on Broadway Avenue in central Winnipeg to a new site in the southern part of Greater Winnipeg. The move actually took place in the early 1930s but was in fact the long awaited result of a controversy that had begun in 1907. In that year F. W. Heubach, manager of the Tuxedo Park Company, had offered the overcrowded university a site of 150 acres opposite the south entrance of Assiniboine Park southwest of the city. But even though this site was accepted in 1910, the university did not move there. Instead, following the move of the separate Agricultural College to a site in St. Vital in 1912 and a series of reports and commissions, and a good deal of public controversy, the present southern site was decided upon in 1929.[41] Although it was little appreciated at the time by Winnipeggers, this move was a significant step in the integration of the city and the surrounding municipalities and was further supported by the relocation of St. John's and St. Paul's Colleges from their central city locations to the university site in the 1950s.

The result of a Commonwealth competition, the Manitoba legislative building was not opened until 1920. An incredible assembly of exact details from numerous classical buildings, it is nevertheless a well devised composition. On top of the building is the "Golden Boy," a well known Manitoba symbol.

The legislative building under construction in 1915.

11391.

One of the last major buildings constructed in Winnipeg prior to the Depression was the huge Hudson's Bay Company retail store on Portage Avenue. It was built in 1926.

8503.-1

FOOTE.

The Hotel Fort Garry, built on the site of Upper
Fort Garry, is an example of the grand manner of
architecture. The building created by the
architectural firm of Ross and MacDonald was
"in the Francois I style recalling the old French
chateaux in Normandy and Touraine." Each
major public room also had its own appropriate
stylistic garb, hence the Adam style Palm Room
(now the Drummer Boy Lounge), the Louis XIV
rotunda, and the Jacobean dining room.

Across Main Street from the Hotel Fort Garry is Union Station and the CNR Yards, occupying one of the most attractive sites in Winnipeg on the banks of the Red River. These yards indicate that in its earlier days railway companies were able to obtain almost anything they wished from city council. The station itself commands a view down tree-lined Broadway Avenue and was conceived in the grand tradition as the gateway to a great city. The imposing arched entrance which reflects the domed rotunda within is clearly related to the design of Grand Central Station in New York, designed by the same architects.

Only the United Colleges of Wesley and Manitoba, to become the University of Winnipeg in 1967, remained in a downtown location.

Other particularly noticeable changes occurred in the areas of government and commerce, most notably with the completion of the massive neo-classical Legislative Buildings on Broadway Avenue in 1921 and the construction of a huge Hudson's Bay Company retail store on Portage Avenue in 1926. Less spectacularly, the T. Eaton Company, which in 1905 had marked a new era with the construction of its enormous retail store on Portage Avenue, began to build warehouses and a printing plant and to develop a research department that would make it a leader among the merchandising firms of North America. In other areas of building activity, the short-lived boom of the late twenties resulted in the construction of other public buildings, warehouses, stores, apartment blocks and houses as the few remaining vacant spaces in the city filled up and growth continued in the suburbs — most notably in St. Vital, St. Boniface, and East Kildonan. The substantial housing construction that went on in the suburbs was made possible by an ever expanding street railway system, which linked these districts to the city centre.

In general, however, Winnipeg experienced a housing shortage during this period and the economic structure of the city grew but slowly. New construction consisted primarily of dwellings and institutional buildings rather than wholesale structures or factories. Prominent among the new commercial buildings erected were those connected to recent innovations and technological developments. A new downtown movie theatre was completed in 1921; an automobile show room, the Medical Arts Building, and the Film Exchange Building were built in 1922. Two race tracks, Whittier and Polo Parks, were also opened in the 1920s. The provincial government built a new million-dollar institute for the deaf and dumb in Tuxedo in 1922. The large Olympia (now Marlborough) Hotel was also reopened in 1923.[42]

The increased mobility of Winnipeg's population during this era created demands for more park facilities. Although two large parks had already been secured by the Winnipeg Parks Board — Assiniboine Park in 1904 and Kildonan Park in 1910 —there was still no major park to the south. With the intention of providing a third major park for Winnipeg, the City Parks Board entered into negoti-

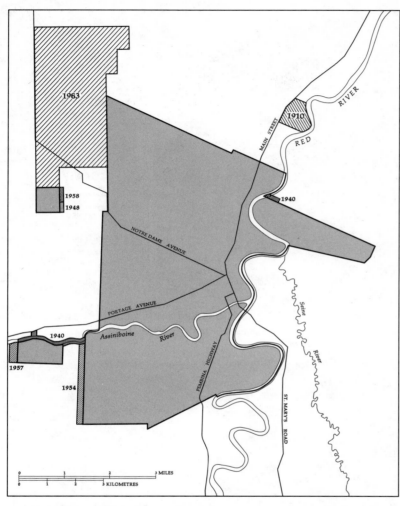

9   Boundary Extensions 1914-1963

ations with the Municipality of St. Vital in 1928 and acquired 110 acres of fertile, undulating riverbank property. A plan for the new park was completed following the English landscape style with its curvilinear system of traffic and pedestrian movement. Work was then begun in 1931 but it was only in the years after 1960, when the park was taken over by the Metropolitan Corporation of Greater Winnipeg, that the park was completed. Although numerous other smaller parks were also acquired by the city, most of its attention was focused on St. Vital Park and its two counterparts, Assiniboine and Kildonan (see Map 9).

With the arrival of the Depression of the 1930s building in Winnipeg almost came to a standstill. Perhaps the most significant developments of the decade were the construction of an auditorium and such necessary but unattractive items as subways and sewers under the federal public works program, and the expansion of the municipal airport in St. James. The latter was the result of Winnipeg's being designated as the main base of the newly organized Trans Canada Airline in 1937.

The Depression also brought an end to the pretentious building styles of the earlier periods, with their extravagant adornment and, in a few cases, imagination and vigour. As a result of both economics and a change in attitudes, there was a return to more simple and straightforward design. But this change in style had little impact until the postwar period because there was simply little construction. The value of building permits dropped from a high of $11,000,000 in 1929 to a low of $700,000 in 1933 and was not to pass the $11 million mark again until 1946 (Appendix, Table XII).[43] Throughout the Depression real estate values remained low, houses were allowed to deteriorate and the slums along both sides of the CPR tracks from Point Douglas westward became ever more dilapidated. Many businesses went bankrupt and deserted warehouses in the central core were saved from continued vacancy only by a sharp rise in the number of firms involved in the labour-intensive needle trades.

Most alarming, however, was that the economic difficulties of the Depression actually resulted in many buildings being demolished by owners in order to escape the burdens of taxation. Among the numerous demolitions of the decade were many of the city's notable mansions, including the former homes of such well-known

These views of the home of A.N. Nanton indicate that many members of the city's commercial elite lived in a grand style. Nanton came to Winnipeg in 1883 and opened the firm of Osler, Hammond and Nanton in 1884. He served as President of the Board of Trade in 1898.

Opened in 1907, the Walker Theatre had a splendour that surpassed anything in the entire West. The plush seats, luxurious fittings, crystal chandeliers, gilt trim — all were a foretaste of glories to come. For many years the most famous artists of the English-speaking world appeared here — there were plays, grand and light opera, concerts, and pantomime. But the Walker did not survive the rise of movies and was sold for taxes in 1936. It reopened in 1945 as the Odeon moving picture theatre.

members of Winnipeg's elite as Sir Augustus Nanton, Sir William White, Sir Daniel McMillan, and the Honourable Robert Rogers. A number of other houses of the same type were abandoned by owners and were acquired by the city for tax arrears. In addition, many business properties were torn down, including the old Hudson's Bay Departmental Store on Main Street which had occupied half a city block. Title through tax sale proceedings was also taken on many valuable business properties in the very heart of the city, including Robinson's Department Store, almost at the corner of Main Street and Portage Avenue, the Forum Block, the Walker Theatre, the Playhouse Theatre, and several warehouses.[44]

The general downturn in building activity, accompanied by hundreds of demolitions, aggravated Winnipeg's already severe housing problem. In 1930, the city had 587 houses (1.6 per cent of the total number) and 1,047 suites (10.4 per cent) vacant. By 1940 the situation had deteriorated to an alarming degree since in that year there were only 157 houses (.4 per cent) and 180 suites (1.6 per cent) available. By the end of World War II there were but 11 houses (.03 per cent) and 2 suites (.02 per cent) vacant. Put another way, it was estimated that Winnipeg had a shortage of no fewer than ten thousand housing units by 1946.[45]

One result of this miserable state of affairs was that slum conditions abounded throughout many parts of Winnipeg in the 1930s and early 1940s. The city's Chief Inspector of Sanitation and Housing, F. C. Austin, reported the following conditions in the early 1940s:

> We frequently find large rooms, and rooms not so large, subdivided to make smaller rooms by lumber or beaver board partitions, regardless of the room area, or light and ventilation values; or, a half-height partition behind which we find dark cubby holes containing an old, and more often than not, foul, gas range; the room and the cubby hole being the homes . . . of a good many of the low income group; the combined odors of frowziness; products of combustion, cooking, soiled clothings, washing hung up to dry, and the indescribable odor of humanity packed into close quarters; conceive as many as a half dozen such set-ups or more, in the one house (and there are a great many of these in the city) and we have an unanswerable argument for rental type housing . . .[46]

Unfortunately for Winnipeg's poor, no relief in the way of adequate housing facilities came about until the late 1940s and early 1950s. The tradition of privatism, coupled with a conservative and financially squeezed private and public sector, overruled the compassionate arguments of health inspectors and social workers.

THE LEGACY OF STRIKE: POLITICS IN WINNIPEG, 1919-1945.

The trauma of the Winnipeg General Strike carried over into federal, provincial and, most significantly, municipal politics. At the civic level, two opposing groups emerged in the months following the strike. On one side stood the anti-labour Citizens' League which was in fact a continuation of the Citizens' Committee of One Thousand formed in the early days of the strike (Appendix, Table XV). On the other was a precariously unified labour group, first organized under the banner of the Dominion Labour Party.* Although each side was to undergo several name changes and some variations in their attitudes and positions in subsequent years, the alienation between the two groups remained quite consistent.

The contest between the two groups began in the civic election of 1919.[47] In the months following the bitter end of the strike, fear of the One Big Union still gripped the Citizens' Committee and labour's deep sense of injury made it almost inevitable that the struggle that had begun with the strike would be transferred to the arena of civic politics. Organization of the Citizens' League got underway in August 1919 with a meeting attended by over three thousand held at the Board of Trade building. In September an executive of six officers and fifty members-at-large was chosen and it is apparent from the persons who served in this capacity that the Citizens' League was comprised almost exclusively of business and professional men who lived in the high and middle income areas of the city, for the most part in the South End. Soon after these initial meetings ward committees were established, a women's auxiliary was formed and a mass rally planned.

Labour was also organizing in the late summer and early fall of

*In later years the labour groups organized themselves around the Cooperative Commonwealth Federation (CCF) and New Democratic Party (NDP).

1919. In October a platform was drawn up and approved and a central campaign committee, with headquarters in the city's Labour Temple, was established. The labour supporters also organized a finance and literature committee and a Women's Labour League. By the time the campaign began, the political polarization of the city was most apparent and was neatly symbolized by the opposing headquarters used by the two parties — the Board of Trade offices and the Labour Temple.[48]

The campaign was fought in all seven wards in the shadow of the strike. In the mayoralty contest, it was a straight two-way fight between the League and labour. Supporters of the League defined the issue at stake in this crucial issue as "people versus class rule", "red or white", "the law of Canada versus the O.B.U."[49] Despite the attempt of the labour group, particularly their mayoralty candidate S. J. Farmer, to engage in rational debate, the emotionally charged post-strike atmosphere made this election the most bitter municipal contest in the history of the city. Thus labour's platform calling for such things as union rights for civic workers, public ownership of utilities, a municipal dairy, and a progressive property tax policy exempting all homes assessed at under $3,500, were soon lost in inflamed rhetoric. It soon seemed as if the second round of the strike was underway.

The election, held on November 28, was close. The incumbent mayor, Charles F. Gray, defeated S. J. Farmer by only three thousand votes but it was the contest for council seats that most clearly revealed the divisions in the city. The Citizens' League won Wards 1 through 4 while Labour managed to win Wards 5, 6 and 7. The new aldermen, combined with seven carried over from 1918, formed a city council of fourteen, evenly divided between the two groups.

Both sides were disappointed with the results. Labour was particularly bitter because it felt that the property qualifications, the plural vote, and the non-resident vote (based on property ownership and estimated at 10,000 in 1919), all worked against the expression of true public opinion. The League, on the other hand, was shaken by the fact that labour had done so well and in December 1919 this group was reorganized. Financial support was sought by a levy on members of the business community and a very neat gerrymander of the city's electoral system was secured. The latter involved two amendments to the city's charter: one replaced the fourteen-member council based on seven wards with an eighteen-member council based on three wards; the other set the boundaries of the wards. The labour strongholds — Wards 5, 6 and 7 — were split off into a new Ward 3. These changes, together with the aforementioned voting regulations, ensured that in subsequent elections the League and its supporters had a better than even chance of victory. Even in the new Ward 3, for example, approximately ten per cent of the voters were non-resident property owners likely to support the goals of the League.[50]

In the years that followed, the patterns established in the first post-strike election held firm, although the virulence and strident ideological overtones of the 1919 election did not often reappear. In subsequent elections the basic issue that divided the two groups was whether public funds, raised through taxes on the wealthier citizens, should be used to increase services which largely benefited the working classes. Labour continually sought increased extension of social services and public responsibilities while the Citizens' League was opposed to almost everything that might increase business and property taxes. They were content to leave such stewardship to private initiative and personal fortune.

The 1922 civic election was fought against a backdrop of long-standing grievances by the people of Winnipeg against the Winnipeg Electric Company. The company had been formed in 1892 with a thirty-five-year franchise to operate an electric street railway system; later, by the absorption of other companies, it acquired rights to generate and distribute power.[51] From the outset, however, the Winnipeg Electric Company was little concerned about good public relations. Controversy concerning the company's labour relations, service, prices, and monopoly aspirations was always present. By 1922 the list of grievances by various groups in the city against the company was a long one. The specific issue in the campaign, however, was the request by the company to extend its charter for ten years, from 1927 to 1937.

During the election campaign, the competing labour and citizens' groups took opposite sides in regard to the franchise extension. While the Citizens' Campaign Committee's candidate, J. K. Sparling, supported the application of the company, Farmer and the labour group did not. More important, however, was the fact that

Farmer and his supporters used the opportunity to call for municipal ownership of the utility and to raise questions regarding the cozy relationship of Sparling with the Winnipeg Electric Company. When the results were in and Farmer had defeated Sparling by almost four thousand votes there could be no doubt that the city's unaligned voters had perceived the private company's demands for an extension of their franchise as a threat and had supported the candidate who promised to protect the community's interests. There is abundant evidence that Farmer's victory reflected a rejection of the Winnipeg Electric Company rather than acceptance of Farmer and labour. "It was the political bungling of the W. E. C. and its spokesmen within city council that revitalized the labour challenge and once more brought Farmer . . . back into the arena."[52] Had it not been for a gerrymandered ward system, Farmer might have been able to bring with him to city council a labour majority; as it turned out, only three labour aldermen were elected out of a total of nine seats.[53]

Farmer came to the mayor's chair with a background of involvement in labour affairs. An immigrant from Wales, he worked in various jobs, including a stint with the CPR, before moving to Winnipeg in 1909. He quickly became involved in labour politics in the city and although not prominent in the 1919 General Strike, he was closely associated with the labour side. After the strike, Farmer was labour's candidate for mayor in 1919 and again in 1920.

Following his victory in the 1922 campaign, Farmer proved himself to be an able mayor but he had the misfortune to come to office during the recession. In the election of 1924, he faced a formidable opponent in the person of Colonel R. H. Webb. Webb ran on a booster platform, "charging that the past divisions had served to depress the local economy," and won a substantial victory.[54]

A popular mayor, Lieutenant-Colonel Ralph Humphreys Webb, D.S.O., M.C., held office for eight terms (1925-27, 1930-34). Webb had come to Winnipeg following service in World War I and his war record, wooden leg, and gift for publicity and politics won him many supporters. He was a firm advocate of free enterprise, the British Empire, and the eradication of the "Communist menace." His initiative and business acumen had made him manager of the Marlborough Hotel, a member of the Board of Trade, a successful investor in real estate and securities, an executive member of the

Rotary Club and an organizer of the local tourist bureau. Winnipeg's best salesman until the arrival of Stephen Juba in 1957, Webb did a great deal to publicize the city in an effort to encourage tourism. Although successful as a promoter and politician, Webb's provocative statements while in office often rubbed salt in the wounds of 1919. Once he advocated deportation for the "radical agitators" of the 1919 strike, publicly urging that "the whole gang be dumped in the Red River."[55]

Another longtime mayor was John Queen who held office in 1935-36, and again from 1938 to 1942. A former alderman and member of the provincial legislature, Queen had been defeated by Webb in the election of 1933 before finally gaining the office in a closely fought race with the Citizens' League candidate in 1934, winning by only two hundred votes. Queen was British-born, a cooper by trade, and had come to Canada in 1906, where he quickly became involved with labour. One of the leaders of the 1919 strike and a committed social democrat, he continually insisted during his years in office that human welfare meant more than the city's fiscal reputation. His years in office, however, were marked by a split council and the massive problems of the Depression. A reformer rather than a radical, Queen concentrated on getting relief projects for the city and was successful in negotiating with Ottawa for the building of the Winnipeg Sewage Disposal System which provided enough jobs to alleviate the unemployment problem. He also helped promote municipal conferences and became an important spokesman for cities at the Union of Canadian Municipalities.[56]

Although labour occasionally captured the mayor's chair, the Citizens' League continued to dominate city hall. The reasons for the League's success over the years are easily pinpointed. The programs and philosophy of the League were the continuation, in a much more organized and formalized form, of the policies pursued by the city's commercial elite in the prewar period. In the postwar period, as before, they had superior funds, organizational skills and a homogeneity of purpose, all of which contributed to their success at the polls. Throughout, they were backed both by the influential Board of Trade (Chamber of Commerce after 1948) and the city's major newspapers. Despite statements to the contrary, the Citizens' League, by whatever name it was currently known, was in reality a Liberal-Conservative coalition and received support from these

Counting the votes for the Winnipeg proportional representation election, 1920.

major political parties. Furthermore, the League's straightforward platform of fiscal restraint for the most part appealed to the conservative nature of Winnipeg's middle and upper classes. And, perhaps, most important of all, they were constantly aided in their effort to control civic politics by a gerrymandered ward system, the plural vote, and a franchise based on property ownership. Together, these factors made the election of a labour majority on council a virtual impossibility.

The League was further assisted by fluctuations in labour unity throughout the years. While the businessmen of the city had few, if any, differences over policy, the same cannot be said of the labour groups. Plagued by internal dissension and a decline in union membership after the General Strike, the labour group only occasionally put up a united front. When they did they were usually able to win an even split of the seats on council, as the elections of 1919 and 1934-1935 illustrate. Yet for all its internal squabbling, labour did emerge in Winnipeg during this period as a strong and permanent element in civic life. And as the labour politicians matured under the influence of office, and their opponents learned to practice tolerance, Winnipeg slowly began to move toward a reconciliation between its various divisions.

Unlike many Canadian cities, Winnipeg had class-based party politics at the civic level from 1919. Despite all that has been written opposing such a system, the clash of values accompanying the city's explicit bipartisan conflict resulted in Winnipeg's having a much more effective city government in the postwar period than it had had before. Not only did the sharp divisions of political opinion on city council and on its committees help keep the civic administration in Winnipeg honest, but it also attracted to municipal politics a type of committed candidate who, in a less competitive system, would probably not have been interested in politics at all. Even more important, however, was the fact that city council was both more responsible to the community at large and more sensitive than it had been in the previous era. The mutual antipathy of the two factions led to a depth of understanding and compassion that was rare in politics.

Through the give and take of impassioned, though usually rational, debate, civic policy during this period was tempered by sincere humanitarian concern. The vigilance with which both groups on council examined each other's proposals not only stimulated its members, it clearly contributed to the generally high level of administration which Winnipeg attained during the most trying period of its history.[57]

The labour-business division that dominated municipal politics was also present in both provincial and federal politics. There was, however, one important distinction: at the senior levels the labour group was far more successful. The city had elected its first labour Member of Parliament, Arthur W. Puttee, in 1900 but it was not until after 1914 that labour members were elected with any degree of consistency. In 1914, Winnipeg elected its first labour member of the provincial legislature when Fred Dixon, an engraver who had arrived from England in 1904, won in Winnipeg Centre. The following year R.A. Riggs joined Dixon as a labour MLA. The election of both men signified the firm establishment of a tradition of nonconformity in provincial and federal politics that was symbolic of the large and restless working class of the city.[58] For while Winnipeg continued in the years after World War I to return Liberal and Conservative members to both provincial and federal houses, it also returned a growing number of labour and CCF representatives. Generally, the city's south end remained loyal to the major parties. The lower class, however, was divided into British workers prepared to vote against established norms and non-Anglo-Saxon workers who, in their search for acceptance, usually supported the Liberals or Conservatives.[59] Yet, in spite of the ethnic divisions in the working class, there was a remarkable pattern of success established by this group in the years following World War I and the Strike.

In 1920 a minor revolution occurred in the provincial election when the provincial labour party elected four out of a possible ten MLA's in Winnipeg and received 42.5 per cent of the votes cast. Of the four labour representatives returned — Fred Dixon, George Armstrong, John Queen, and Seymour Farmer — three were still in jail as a result of their strike activities.[60] In subsequent years this number declined but through to World War II, the city's workers continued to elect significant numbers of labour and — after 1933 — CCF members to the provincial house.

At the federal level, Winnipeg also returned a regular contingent of labour and CCF members. J. S. Woodsworth was elected in Win-

Winnipeggers enjoyed celebrating the city's fiftieth anniversary in 1924.

A police station on Rupert Avenue, c. 1930.

Major fires that occur during Winnipeg's cold winters are often spectacular events that produce amazing ice sculptures. But winter fires are also exceedingly dangerous. The conflagration that destroyed the Winnipeg Theatre on December 23, 1926, also took the lives of four firemen.

Interurban trains such as this ran in and out of Winnipeg from 1902-1939. The
Suburban Rapid Transit company had its Winnipeg terminus near the CPR station.
From there it ran down to Portage Avenue and then westward through St. James and
Charleswood, ending at the village of Headingly.

Winnipeg mosquito control, 1927.

The construction of the bridge over the Assiniboine River in 1912 facilitated the growth of south Winnipeg during this period. The concrete superstructures on the Osborne Street Bridge, which concealed counter-balances for raising it for river traffic, were removed in 1937.

nipeg's North End in 1921 and continued to hold his seat until his death in May 1942. In a by-election in November, Stanley H. Knowles, also a member of the CCF, retained the seat. In 1925, Woodsworth was joined in the House of Commons by A.A. Heaps, another labour-CCF member. Heaps was subsequently re-elected in the riding of Winnipeg North in 1926, 1930, and 1935. The other areas of the city, of course, continued throughout to elect Liberals and Conservatives, returning such men as Robert Rogers (Conservative), Leslie A. Mutch (Liberal), William W. Kennedy (Conservative) and Ralph Maybank (Liberal).[61]

THE URBAN COMMUNITY: SOCIAL AND CULTURAL DEVELOPMENT

World War I and its aftermath did much to alter Winnipeg's cultural conformity and provincialism and to bring about a significant change in the relationship between the city and its rural hinterland. During the prewar period, the relationship between Winnipeg and the rest of the province had been very close. The city's leaders during this period were entrepreneurs who made their living almost exclusively in dealing with the farmers of the surrounding countryside and Winnipeg was considered first and foremost as a service centre to the outlying rural areas. In the period after 1920, however, with the growing diversity of Winnipeg's commercial and industrial base, the increasing influence of multi-national and eastern-based corporations, and the expansion of labour organizations and the working class, this view changed. Although Winnipeg would rarely be as unmindful of its rural hinterland as other urban centres — the Grain Exchange prevented that — it did begin to consider itself exploited for the benefit of the countryside and often vented these feelings with verbal attacks on the rural-based provincial government. Indeed, the division between the city and the rest of the province reached its height during the twenties and thirties.

The growing distinction between city and its hinterland was apparent in other areas as well. The increasing size of Winnipeg and the influence of large numbers of British and European newcomers helped dilute the rural prejudices of the city's older Ontario residents. Even the old sharp division between worker and employer began slowly to close as unions won increased — though

certainly not total — acceptance, and as manners and dress became less formal. The old ways, with their emphasis on such things as temperance and a strong respect for the Lord's Day, were slowly eroded. With the widespread relaxation of traditional values that occurred during the "Roaring Twenties," Winnipeggers became more sophisticated and rejected the rural puritanism of earlier generations.

The shift that occurred is perhaps best typified by the changing attitude towards liquor. The city, along with the rest of the province, had known a form of prohibition since 1916. In 1923, however, the legislature passed a Government Liquor Control Act that allowed a government commission to import, buy and sell liquor. This beginning to a more reasonable approach to temperance was extended in 1928 when another act provided for direct retail sales from liquor stores and the sale of malt beverages — to men only — in hotels. Although the new system permitted only restricted public drinking, and was surrounded by countless niggling regulations, it was nonetheless a major change from earlier prohibition days.[62]

While Winnipeg society swept into the twenties with changed attitudes, habits of dress, and individual conduct, new patterns of mass entertainment emerged. In 1900 Winnipeg had only three operating theatres; by 1920 there were fourteen, capable of presenting live theatre, vaudeville, grand opera or motion pictures. There was something for almost every taste. The Walker, Winnipeg's most prestigious theatre, presented such productions as *Ivanhoe*, *Dracula*, *Hamlet*, *Madame Butterfly*, *Ben Hur* (complete with live horses and chariot race), *Peter Pan*, and *The Second Mrs. Tanqueray*, to name but a few. Vaudeville was also popular and to keep up with the demand the Orpheum played two shows a day, the Pantages three, and the Strand four. The city's stages were a parade of colour and activity.[63]

Throughout the 1920s, however, the motion picture provided more and more competition to live theatre. Gaudy signs and flamboyant portals dotted streets from Portage and Main to the remotest suburbs. Soon thousands of Winnipeggers were addicted to the screen's hypnotic flicker, anxiously awaiting the release of their idols' next picture. Harold Lloyd, Gloria Swanson, Rudolf Valentino, Charlie Chaplin and many other stars became, in Winnipeg, as

MAY. 14. 1921.
FOOTE.
7228.

The Manitoba Club belongs to the ranks of Canada's most exclusive clubs. The first of its kind in western Canada, the club is surrounded by history since it is located next to the site of the old Upper Fort Garry. The simple facade of the exterior belies the solid oak pillars and impressive oak staircase of the interior. At the top of the stairs is a fourteen by eighteen foot stained glass window created in 1898 to commemorate the Diamond Jubilee of Queen Victoria.

Winter Carnival, 1924.

Elk's Jazz Band.

elsewhere in North America, the favorites of moviegoers.

The popularity of the movies and the increasing use of radio gradually forced live theatre into decline in Winnipeg. Going to the movies was cheaper, quicker and not as much bother as the theatre: evening dress and carriages were not required. Increasingly, throughout the twenties, it became less profitable to bring in touring companies and the crash of 1929 further sealed the fate of professional theatre in Winnipeg. Although the Winnipeg Little Theatre company stoically kept the footlights burning, it was not until 1963, with the creation of the Manitoba Theatre Centre, that Winnipeggers once again had theatre of the same variety and high calibre they had enjoyed during the first two decades of the century.[64]

Elsewhere in the city other activities, such as music and ballet, fared better than did theatre. Music rested on firm bases in the churches, schools and ethnic organizations and was further stimulated by radio and the founding of the Manitoba Music Festival in 1919. In ensuing years the Festival became the pride of the city and the province. The security of the Festival was reinforced by the interest and talent of the city's many ethnic groups. Efforts to establish a symphony orchestra, begun in 1923, achieved only partial success, however; and the musical life of the city did not reach full stature until 1948. In that year the Winnipeg Musicians' Association, with the help of the CBC, sponsored the first concert of the Winnipeg Symphony Orchestra. The organization of the symphony was preceded in 1937 by the establishment of the Winnipeg Ballet Company which soon commanded national and international praise. In 1953 it was honoured with a royal charter and undertook its first Canadian tour. Since then the Company has won several awards and received acclaim wherever it has performed.[65]

The pace of life in Winnipeg, already quickened by the movies, relaxed liquor laws, and radio was further stimulated by the all but complete displacement of the horse by the automobile. The mobility provided by the family car also increased the summer trek to resort areas and substantial cottage towns began to surround beaches on Lake Winnipeg and Lake Manitoba. Riding Mountain National Park and Whiteshell Provincial Park, west and east of the city respectively, became summer attractions.

The Depression that began in 1929 ended many of these activities, at least for a majority of Winnipeggers. At one time or another during the decade virtually half the families in Winnipeg were receiving some form of public assistance. Relief was neither generous nor cheerfully given despite the sincere efforts of labour representatives on city council and, after 1934, of Mayor John Queen. The problem was that the city of Winnipeg had an abnormally heavy relief burden to carry as many rural residents flocked to the city in search of non-existent jobs. When it was discovered that many rural municipalities would pay a family's fare to Winnipeg and sustain it until it satisfied resident requirements to be taken onto the city's relief rolls the city's resentment increased toward its hinterland and the rurally oriented provincial government.[66]

During this decade, soup kitchens, clothing depots, wood lots, make-work projects, winter works, drainage ditches, all were part of daily life for many in the city. For the unemployed, card games, checkers, and dominoes played in Central Park and in a thousand stuffy rooms were popular pastimes. Others soaked up heat in the Williams Avenue Library, listened to interminable soap operas on radio, watched box cars being shunted in the CPR yards, or gawked at the street drama provided by the eviction of numerous tenants unable to pay their rent. Reverend Craig of Grace Church formed the Canadian Goodwill Industries, "turning junk that people don't need into jobs people do need." The *Winnipeg Tribune*, reporting that "there are babies being born in Winnipeg whose mothers have to wrap them in newspapers," organized a Friendship League and along with service clubs and other groups collected and distributed clothing.[67] The *Tribune's* "Empty Stocking Fund," begun in earlier years, also helped many at Christmas.

Recovery from the Depression did not come until after the beginning of World War II. When Canada declared war in September 1939, thousands of young Canadians flocked to join the forces, finding in the services their first full-time jobs. Also, many found employment in war-related industries as military equipment and supplies were rapidly produced to meet the insatiable needs of the Allies. Soon after the beginning of hostilities the old established armouries — Minto, Tuxedo (Fort Osborne), and McGregor — were so crowded that such unlikely places as the Central Immigration Hall and Jerry Robinson's Department Store were taken over by the military. But while the war virtually wiped out unemployment, it did not end hardship. There were shortages, rationing stamps, coupons, and the ever present fear for loved ones.

563

FOOTE.

Knox Presbyterian Church.

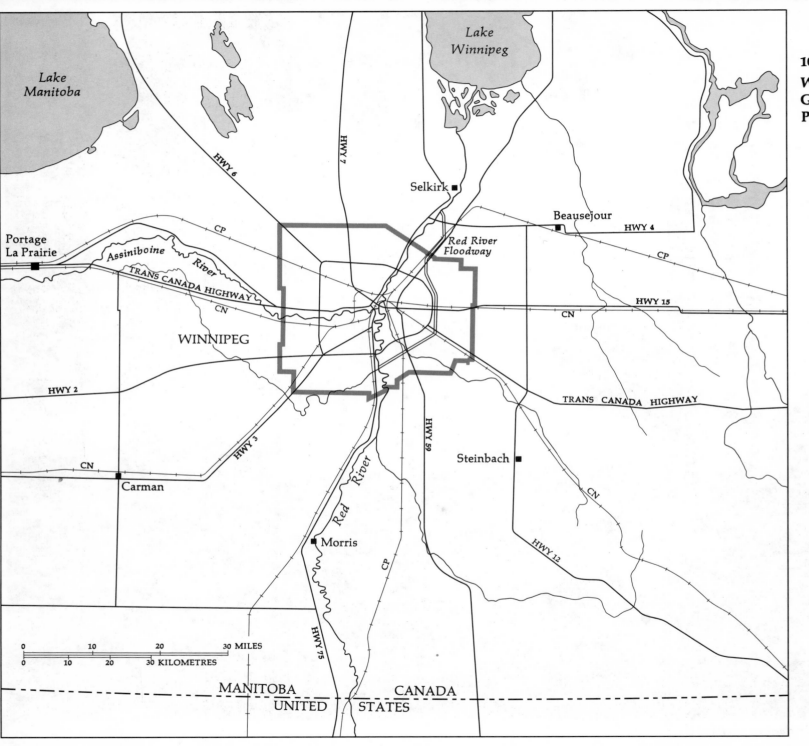

Lake
Manitoba

Lake
Winnipeg

HWY 6

HWY 7

Selkirk ■

Beausejour ■

HWY 4

CP

Portage
La Prairie ■

Assiniboine River

CP

Red River
Floodway

TRANS CANADA HIGHWAY

CN

HWY 15

CN

WINNIPEG

HWY 2

TRANS CANADA HIGHWAY

HWY 3

HWY 59

CN

Carman ■

Steinbach ■

Red River

HWY 12

Morris ■

CP

0   10   20   30 MILES
0   10   20   30 KILOMETRES

HWY 75

MANITOBA   CANADA
UNITED   STATES

Visit of George VI and Queen Elizabeth, 1939.

Office workers at the Western Canada Insurance Underwriters offices, 1940.

War industry in Winnipeg, 1941.

The T. Eaton Company building on Portage Avenue decked out for V.E. Day celebrations.

162   Winnipeg: An Illustrated History

Chapter Three

Transformation and Challenge 1946-1970

It was the era of bureaucratic competence, of the heir succeeding to the established business. The dreams of 1911 were no longer dreamed, and the vision was lacking to see that the continuance of Communism in the North End was a challenge to civic democracy, that local industry was necessary to offset the effects of head office controls and a transient managerial class, that a new concept of the city's future was needed, and that in the cultivation of the inner resources of mind and spirit by education and the arts was a civic enterprise which could both add to the well-being of the city and transcend any limitation of material resources. Only, on the whole, among the non-Anglo-Saxons of Winnipeg . . . [was] there at once that enterprise which made two industries flourish where none was before, and the capacity to live a whole and vigorous life.

W.L. Morton,
Manitoba: A History, 1957.

A LACK OF VISION

Winnipeg emerged from World War II in an optimistic mood, intent on fully experiencing the prosperity the postwar years promised. Six austere war years following on the Ten Lost Years of the Depression had generated an immense appetite for things long denied. A backlog of unfulfilled desires confronted empty inventories, not only in the field of domestic and luxury commodities, but also in essential things such as housing. Every train, bus, and plane brought returning soldiers with money in their pockets and high hopes for the future. On the home front wartime savings, long tied up in war savings stamps and victory bonds, were waiting to be spent.

The optimism of the immediate postwar years was not, however, based on reality, and in 1946 Winnipeggers faced a long, uphill struggle in their search for renewed progress and growth. With the end of the war, Winnipeg began a long campaign to overcome the cautious mood the Depression had inspired and the loss of confidence the retarded growth of the city had caused. The drain of energy and talent from the community during the Depression and war had severe repercussions. Immediately after war ended people were too preoccupied with jobs and catching up to worry much about the long-term future of the city. Pragmatism was the order of the day. Indeed, for more than a decade following the war, Winnipeggers lacked a concept of the city's future that might have instilled new energy into the community. The dreams of the early part of the century had been too brutally smashed to be so soon revived. Even the city's Anglo-Saxon business community, weakened by the Depression, the effects of head-office controls, and the transience of the managerial class, was unable to produce the leadership it had provided before. It was only in the late 1950s, with the establishment of metropolitan government, that Winnipeg really began to deal with its many problems.

The 1950 Flood

With the outbreak of war in 1914, Winnipeg entered a long period of almost continual crisis, including the 1919 strike, the depression, and two world wars. But in many respects the city's worst year was 1950. Although the site on which Winnipeg stood was known to be prone to flooding, the city was ill-prepared for the events of May 1950. By May 14th the Red River was 13 feet above flood stage and by the time the river began to recede the following week, the city had suffered tremendous damage: 100,000 Winnipeggers were forced to flee the city; 10,500 homes were flooded; business and provision of most services were disrupted or completely halted. Estimates of loss ran as high as $115,000,000. The cost in time, effort, and suffering was incalculable.

375

ECONOMIC GROWTH AND METROPOLITAN DEVELOPMENT

In contrast to the previous three decades, the forties and fifties were generally devoid of major economic crises and of a long series of crop failures. The result was that Winnipeg was able to stabilize its economic position. The major element in this maturation process was the fact that Winnipeg reached the stage of self-sustaining growth during this period. As other prairie cities grew, they gradually became more and more like Winnipeg and the city increasingly lost its specialized function in the western economy. The result was an increasing attention to serving the needs of the city and its immediate hinterland rather than those of the entire west. These needs, of course, grew as Winnipeg did and generated service, manufacturing and retail enterprises. The city's own market became more and more able to support various small industries and specialized public service. Also, since Winnipeg was the provincial capital, it secured a large part of the administrative expansion connected with the growth of the welfare state in the postwar period. In other words, while Winnipeg could not have thrived in earlier periods simply "by taking in its own washing," it was increasingly able to do so in the 1950s.[1]

Yet the fact that a large part of Winnipeg's growth impetus since 1945 was self-sustaining did not mean that historic functions as the transportation, financial, and wholesale metropolis of the west were completely negated (see Map 11).[2] What happened was that Winnipeg changed from a "gateway city" to a "central place city." While Winnipeg's once vast western hinterland was severely and permanently reduced in size, the city remained the largest metropolitan center in the prairie region. And although Edmonton and Calgary became major metropolitan areas in their own right, Winnipeg still had within its effective sphere of influence Manitoba, northwestern Ontario, and most of Saskatchewan. Furthermore, despite the encroachments on its metropolitan status by such cities as Vancouver and Edmonton, Winnipeg still remained a major national and international financial centre.[3]

Winnipeg's continued importance in Canada as a city performing metropolitan functions, providing financial, commercial and business services for a hinterland, was apparent in an analysis of seventeen metropolitan areas made in 1961. Winnipeg showed the

CPR Telegraph office.

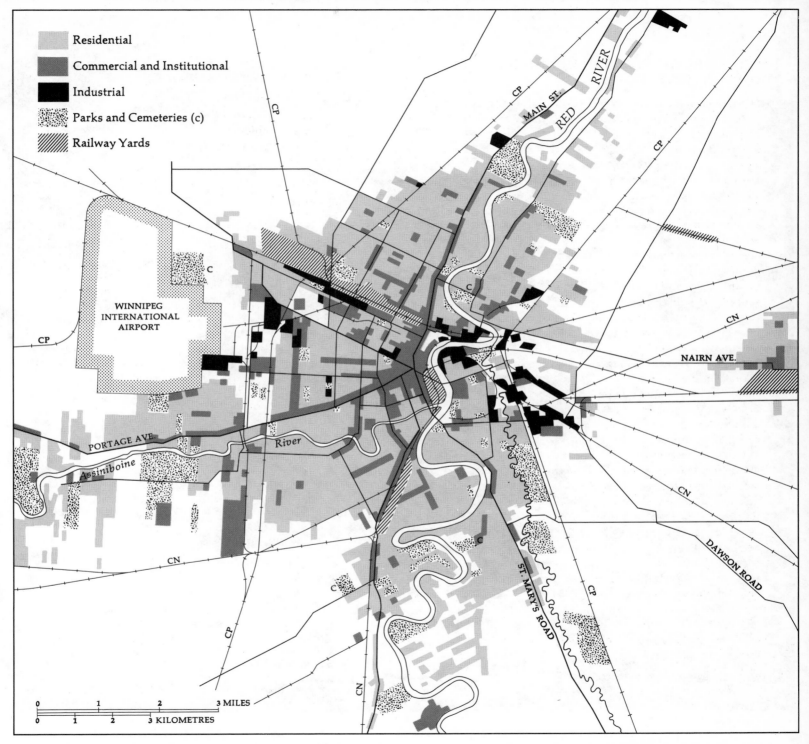

11

**Land Use in
Winnipeg 1955**

Residential

Commercial and Institutional

Industrial

Parks and Cemeteries (c)

Railway Yards

WINNIPEG
INTERNATIONAL
AIRPORT

RED RIVER

MAIN ST.

CP

CN

NAIRN AVE.

PORTAGE AVE.

Assiniboine River

ST. MARY'S ROAD

DAWSON ROAD

CN

CP

C

0   1   2   3 MILES

0 1 2 3 KILOMETRES

Portage and Main, 1957.

Motor Coach Industries.

highest value of wholesale sales per capita. Also, in the hierarchy of metropolitan areas regarding specialization in the performance of metropolitan functions, Winnipeg stood in the top or first level in company with such cities as Toronto, Montreal, Vancouver and Calgary, a position that put Winnipeg in front of such centres as Edmonton, London, Hamilton, Ottawa, St. John's and Victoria.[4]

Thus while there is no doubt that other western cities — particularly Calgary and Vancouver — made inroads upon Winnipeg's domination of the west, it is also clear that these inroads were limited. The reason for this is that the main advantage of rival western cities was their closer proximity to segments of the hinterland and this factor affected only a few economic activities such as retail trade and some branches of the wholesale trade. Winnipeg's superior resources and access to the hinterland as a whole were decisive advantages in respect to finance, transportation, administrative control, specialized services, manufacturing, and those branches of the wholesale trade in which large, diversified stocks and superior financial resources were of greater significance than freight rate advantages.[5] After the war, for example, Winnipeg continued to have the most diversified manufacturing industry in the prairie provinces. Despite the rapid growth of Edmonton and Calgary after 1950, Winnipeg's manufacturing employment remained larger (Appendix, Table I) than the combined total of these other two metropolitan centres.[6]

Some idea of the economic evolution of Winnipeg to 1961 can be gained by examining the changing proportion of the total labour force that was engaged in various industries. The changes outlined in Table XIII (Appendix) clearly show that the work forces of the small community of 1881, the large, complex city of 1921, and the metropolis of 1961 were markedly different. The basic and most significant changes occurred in agriculture and transportation. The sharp decline in the former, from 23.5 per cent involved in primary activities in 1881 to 1.7 per cent in 1921, is not surprising when it is realized that Winnipeg had grown by 1921 into a major urban area. The old Red River Settlement, with its river lot farms, was almost totally engulfed by a thriving commercial centre. The sharp increase in the transportation category, from 3.6 per cent to 15.8 per cent, points to Winnipeg's growth as the distribution centre for Manitoba and western Canada, while the decline between 1921 and 1961, from 15.8 per cent to 13.2 per cent, indicates the losses the city sustained to other western centres during these years. This same pattern prevailed in the trade category. Together, the high percentages in the transportation, trade, and service areas all pointed to Winnipeg's continuing importance as a regional distribution and service centre. It was primarily in these areas, and in the area of finance, that Winnipeg continued to act as a metropolitan centre for areas outside Manitoba.

Within the province itself, Winnipeg's economic importance was unchallenged. By 1970, 54 per cent of the people of Manitoba lived in the Winnipeg metropolitan area. This area also had 65.7 per cent of all the employees of the province, including 83.5 per cent of all manufacturing employees, 73.4 per cent of all trade employees and 63.3 per cent of all service industry employees. The Winnipeg urban area accounted for 62 per cent of all retail sales in Manitoba in terms of dollar value, and 95.4 per cent of the value of all wholesale sales. It also produced 83.2 per cent of all manufactured goods. Finally, metropolitan Winnipeg accounted for 74 per cent of Manitoba's share of individual income tax, 62 per cent of its sales tax revenues, and 59 per cent of its gasoline tax revenues.[7]

The relatively positive record of economic development in Winnipeg in postwar years was balanced by several less positive factors. Chief among these was the prairies' continued colonial status within the national economy: the region and its cities were to be the producers and shippers of primary products for sale on the competitive international market and were to purchase the bulk of their manufactured goods from the tariff-protected industries of central Canada. For over forty years Winnipeg prospered by doing just that, operating as the key shipping and trading point in the west; but in later years, when Winnipeg itself attempted to diversify its economic structure and become a manufacturing centre of some national importance, it found its opportunities severely limited. The persistence of a high concentration of industry in central Canada was the result of the concentration of Canada's major consumer market, coupled with the maintenance of high tariffs and other specific trade agreements that favoured the east. In short, the west and Winnipeg were relegated to specializing in regional manufacturing and service functions.

This domination of the Canadian economy by eastern Canada

When this residence was first built in 1900, it was one of Winnipeg's middle-class residences. Conversion of former residences to commercial uses is a common feature of Winnipeg's landscape. This photograph was taken in 1961.

also affected the quality of leadership and entrepreneurial skills available to the city. After 1913 an ever growing proportion of Canadian business enterprise became characterized by large firms operating nationally or internationally. The virtual stagnation of the west during this period, compared with the rapidly developing and more populous east, ensured the location in eastern Canada of the head offices and main production plants of these major corporations. The result was an increased number of branch offices and plants of both American and Canadian companies in Winnipeg.[8] The particular significance of these developments was that the individuals who managed the local branches of national and international firms were typically newcomers to Winnipeg. These aggressive individuals rarely sank roots in the community since they were almost certain to be transferred in due course to eastern Canada or the United States. The consequence was a reduced effort on the part of the Winnipeg business community to fight national policies that relegated the city to, at best, a secondary role in the Canadian economy.

All this meant for Winnipeg a period of only moderate growth, a time when its economic hinterland was restricted rather than expanded. In the process, Winnipeg attempted to consolidate its hold over a much smaller area and to diversify its narrow economic base. While the prairies remained a major market for the goods and services offered by the city, it was clear that more dynamic growth in the future could be achieved only to the extent that Winnipeg succeeded in opening up new markets in the north, in northwestern Ontario, and in the midwestern United States.

Winnipeg's economic development in the postwar period was also dependent, in a way it had never been before, on its relationship with the rest of the province. But the relationship remained poor in the 1940s and 1950s. Indicative of the old rivalry of city and country was continual bickering over the issues of daylight saving time and the colouring of margarine. Winnipeg supported both policies, the rest of the province did not. These trivial differences pointed to a far more important problem. Despite the fact that Manitoba was no longer an agricultural province with a largely rural population, the procedures, concepts, practices and legislation of the provincial government remained, for the most part, rural in nature. In this, as in so many other matters, the inability to confront the real problems of the period was in large part due to the failure of Winnipeg's establishment to articulate or support new and forward looking policies. As a result, successive provincial governments developed and pursued policies which virtually ignored the city.[9]

The relative unimportance of urban affairs in the eyes of the province was apparent in the comparative emphasis placed upon the various programmes and expenditures of provincial government departments. Despite Metropolitan Winnipeg's disproportionately large contribution to provincial revenue from taxation, it received less than ten per cent of all provincial expenditures on highways and less than forty per cent of capital expenditures.[10]

This unbalanced treatment of Metropolitan Winnipeg might have been acceptable if the city's problems could have been solved within the legislative powers and financial resources available to the urban government. But this was not the case. Winnipeg and the surrounding suburbs faced during the 1950s an increasingly desperate situation in which the intensity and extent of their difficulties increased annually while their powers and financial resources remained fixed.

The failure to make adequate provision for the needs of the metropolitan centre certainly damaged Winnipeg, but what was not generally recognized was the extent to which it damaged the rest of the province as well. In the postwar economy of Manitoba, Metropolitan Winnipeg played a critical role as a generator of economic activity; it was the economic hub of the entire province. Damage to the city therefore damaged Manitoba as a whole since the economic fate of the province was inextricably and powerfully bound up with the economic fate of the metropolis.

The challenge faced by Winnipeg in 1960 was to develop the full potential of its economic capacity, a challenge that was beyond its financial and legislative capacity. One solution to the problem lay in the formation of the Metropolitan Corporation of Greater Winnipeg, a move inspired more by the province than the city. But the opportunities presented by metro government would by themselves not solve all problems. What was also needed was an increased degree of urban empathy on the part of the rest of the province, and particularly the provincial government, so that the development of Winnipeg and Manitoba could proceed together.

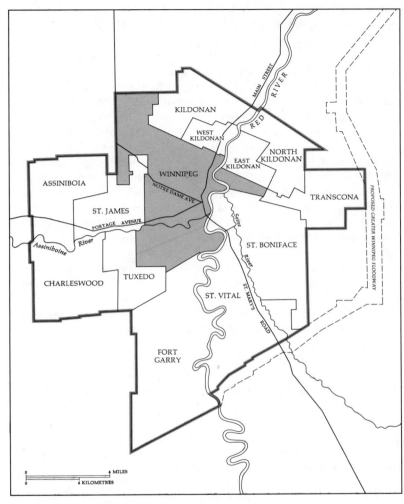

12   Metropolitan Winnipeg 1963

POPULATION GROWTH AND ETHNIC RELATIONSHIPS

Winnipeg's population growth rate between 1946 and 1960 was slower than it had ever been since incorporation in 1874. The city, for example, had had an average five year growth rate of 45.4 per cent between 1901 and 1921, and 8.3 per cent between 1921 and 1946. Between 1946 and 1961 it dropped to a low of 4.6 per cent (Appendix, Table V). Winnipeg's growth rate during this period also compared unfavourably with that of other western centres, particularly Calgary and Edmonton, which surged forward during these years (Appendix, Table IV). Even in terms of Winnipeg's domination of the province, the city declined in relation to its population as a percentage of the province's total population, and as a percentage of the total urban population (Appendix, Table III).

There were at least three reasons for this sharply reduced growth rate. First, Winnipeg was by the 1950s no longer the dynamic and predominant western metropolis it had once been. Second, immigration to the city, while steady, never reached the proportions it had in earlier periods, such as 1901-1913 and 1926-1929. The proportion of foreign-born in Winnipeg declined, while native-born — especially those born within the province of Manitoba — increased (Appendix, Tables VI and VII). The third and most important reason for Winnipeg's declining growth rate was that the population of Winnipeg was moving out of the city in significant numbers to the surrounding suburbs. By the decade of the 1960s this movement would result in Winnipeg experiencing a population loss.[11] Moreover, many newcomers to Winnipeg tended to settle in the municipalities surrounding the city rather than in the city itself. These areas of Metropolitan Winnipeg grew at the expense of the city of Winnipeg primarily because it no longer had much land available for development and, until the formation of metropolitan government in 1960, had a much higher tax structure. Families seeking residential accommodation and companies seeking industrial locations were forced or attracted to the surrounding municipalities (Appendix, Table XI and Map 12).

The more even dispersal of population over the wider area of Metropolitan Winnipeg helped further to alleviate in the 1940s and 1950s the tensions among ethnic groups within the city of Winnipeg. What happened was that although ethnic groups continued to exhibit a high degree of residential segregation, there was as well a marked dispersal of ethnic groups in terms of their movement towards the periphery of the urban area. In other words, ethnic groups in postwar Winnipeg were no longer confined to densely populated ghettos as they had once been in earlier periods. While the overall degree of residential segregation remained fairly stable, the tension it had often caused in previous years when groups were in close proximity to each other was significantly relieved. Part of the reason for this was that while patterns of ethnic grouping in the pre-1945 period had much to do with economics, continuing segregation in the postwar era was more a matter of choice.

This generalization is clearly revealed in an examination of three of Winnipeg's major ethnic groups. The major group in Winnipeg, those whose origins were given as British, continued in the post-1945 period to reveal a marked pattern of residential preference for the area south of the CPR tracks. Although there was considerable movement by this group between 1951 and 1961, generally from older residential areas to newer ones, this movement was directed towards residential sections within the southern half of the metropolitan area. Thus, while central and west Winnipeg lost persons of British origin, southern and western municipalities such as Charleswood, Assiniboia, St. James and Fort Garry experienced considerable growth due to an influx of Anglo-Saxons. There was also some movement to northern and eastern suburbs, such as North Kildonan and Transcona, since between 1951 and 1961 the percentage of the total British group residing south of the CPR tracks declined from 79.4 per cent to 72.8 per cent. It can also be noted, however, that despite this marked imbalance between northern and southern sections of the Winnipeg urban area, the British were distributed throughout the city in considerable numbers, a reflection of the large size of the group and its dominant status.[12]

The second most important ethnic group in postwar Winnipeg, the Ukrainians, continued to reveal a highly selective preference for the northern half of the metropolitan area. During the decade 1951-1961, the percentage of Ukrainians in the northern half of the metropolitan area declined from 66.6 per cent to 63.9 per cent, a loss of only 2.7 per cent. Yet the percentage of the total Ukrainian group in the old core area of settlement, the North End, decreased during the 1950s by 9.6 per cent. There was thus a significant amount of intra-urban migration confined largely to the northern half of the metro-

politan area. The main movement was out of North Winnipeg into the adjacent municipalities of East and West Kildonan.

The most highly segregated group in Winnipeg was the Jewish community. The first area of settlement for this group in Winnipeg was the North End. In the post-war period, however, Jews moved out of this area in large numbers and in two quite different directions. Between 1951 and 1961, the total Jewish population in the North End decreased by almost half, from 12,389 to 6,536. A considerable portion of this out-migration was absorbed by West Kildonan, the suburb adjoining Winnipeg's North End. The Jewish population of the municipality increased during the decade from 2,141 to 6,133. The second receiving area was in the municipality of River Heights, south of the city of Winnipeg. In 1951 the area contained only about two thousand Jews or twelve per cent of the total Jewish population. By 1961 the situation had changed considerably; there were then over five thousand Jews or twenty-seven per cent of the total.

These generalizations suggest that residential segregation of ethnic groups in the metropolitan area of Winnipeg continued, with few exceptions, to follow general patterns established in the pre-World War I period. Moreover, if residential segregation is taken as a viable indicator of assimiliation, it is clear that by 1961 very little change had taken place.[13]

Intra-urban migration patterns were, however, only one factor affecting ethnic relationships in Winnipeg in the postwar period. Another was that during the 1950s large numbers of non-Anglo-Saxons acquired a relative degree of affluence and were accorded by the charter group increasing degrees of respect and tolerance. Remembering the fear and insecurity of earlier times, the New Canadians, as they were now called, were determined to enter the mainstream of Winnipeg society even if it meant abandoning their culture.

The increasing acceptance of New Canadians in Winnipeg during the 1950s was apparent on many fronts. Status occupations, such as law and medicine, which had long been closed to non-Anglo-Saxons, were opened and were quickly filled. For the first time in the city's history a non-Anglo-Saxon mayor came to office. The election in 1956 of Stephen Juba, a Ukrainian, was an indication of the increasing influence of former "aliens" in Winnipeg life.

This was no isolated incident or accident. Not only was Juba returned in every subsequent election, he was joined by increasing numbers of other non-Anglo-Saxons on city council and in other public positions.[14] By the 1950s there were growing signs that the discrimination against foreigners which had for so long been a part of Winnipeg's social environment was moderating.

In almost every respect, then, the postwar development of Winnipeg fit into the pattern that the city had experienced since before 1900. Since that time Winnipeg had become more cosmopolitan in character with each succeeding decade, until by 1961 the non-British population of the city had reached almost sixty per cent of the total population. Winnipeg thus had one of the most pronounced ethnic mixes of any urban area in Canada and, with the exception of the French and Italian groups, had a larger percentage of all ethnic groups represented in the metropolitan area than in the country itself (Appendix, XIV). These figures present a somewhat distorted picture of the nature of Winnipeg, however, since they establish the cosmopolitan nature of the city on the basis of statistics only. The visitor to Winnipeg in 1960 would have found less evidence of its cosmopolitan character then than in previous decades before the absorption of ethnic groups into the mainstream.

There is other evidence, however, that suggests that absorption of the ethnic minorities into the dominant Anglo-Saxon group is far from complete. For while political and economic integration of the ethnic groups had taken place, these groups retained a strong feeling of ethnicity. The ethnic groups in the city maintained their own networks of clubs, organizations, and institutions which tended to confine many of their contacts within their own groups. Inter-ethnic contacts took place in considerable part only at the level of employment and the political and civic processes. The city's groups remained separated by the invisible but powerful barriers of ethnic identification.

Intra-ethnic relationships were centred around a wide variety of clubs and associations. The city's Ukrainians, to give but one example, had a thriving array of ethnic organizations. There were a large number of distinctively designed churches in North Winnipeg and in other areas of the city. These were large, imposing, and costly structures and most were built after 1945. The church, probably more than any other institution, served as a centre for cultural as well as religious activity. Other associations, clubs, and businesses were, however, also important. They included: the Brotherhood of Ukrainian Catholics; the Ukrainian Self-Reliance League; the Ukrainian Canadian Committee; the Prosvita Reading Society; the Ukrainian People's Home; the People's Cooperative Dairy; and innumerable Ukrainian stores, bookshops, workshops, and restaurants. Among the largest was the Ukrainian Labor Temple built in 1919. It housed a theatre with a seating capacity of one thousand which was used regularly for plays, concerts, and community meetings. There were also numerous rooms and offices for various organizational activities.[15]

Furthermore, during the 1960s and 1970s there was an increase in the awareness of the city's various ethnic groups. Such events as the celebration of Canada's, Manitoba's, and Winnipeg's centennials and the publication of the *Report of the Royal Commission on Bilingualism and Biculturalism*, which included a volume on "The Cultural Contributions of Other Ethnic Groups," made people more aware than at any other time of the contributions the various ethnic groups had made to the city. This increased awareness fostered new interest among young members of ethnic groups in their language and culture and genuine support for the idea of a cultural mosaic was forthcoming for the first time in Winnipeg's history. An enthusiastic affirmation of Winnipeg's cosmopolitan nature has, since 1970, been present in an annual week-long ethnic festival called Folklorama.

Recent trends in Winnipeg thus suggest the continued evolution of a cosmopolitan community. But overriding the decrease in ethnic discrimination and the increase in political and economic integration, was the continued dominance of an Anglo-Saxon culture. This, of course, was largely a result of the fact that the British were by far the largest ethnic group in Winnipeg. Yet it was also a result of that group's continued determination to meet the challenge of immigration. What evolved in Winnipeg by the 1960s was a culture which was more diverse but not fundamentally different from that established in the city in 1900. The premises of the city's charter group, and the social institutions which they planted, generally remained intact.

THE URBAN LANDSCAPE

Winnipeg emerged from the long winter of depression and war with a lot of catching up to do. The pressure on housing, for example, was severe since except for a few wartime houses construction had long been stagnant. Although the city's developers and builders got off to a slow start, it was not long after 1945 before they were reshaping the city with their housing projects (Appendix, Table XII). Entire streets were hastily constructed as the empty spaces of the city and its suburbs began to fill up like squares on a bingo card. This growth meant provision of new streets and sidewalks, sewers, water, electricity, and telephones — a mammoth task for city and private enterprise utilities. In short, there was a general air of prosperity: factories hummed, new industries and head offices located in the city, business was generally good, and housing construction exploded. One of the many areas built on in the immediate postwar period was in South Winnipeg on land formerly occupied by River Park. Sold in 1941 by the Winnipeg Electric Railway Company to developer C.E. Simonite, the forty acres of land were quickly filled with 250 homes.[16] One former resident of the area recalled the type of homes built:

> The houses were white stucco bungalows in the New American ranch style or the Cape Cod design. The contractor was careful to avoid sameness; he altered small details on each house, here varying the colour of the trim, the entrances, the roofs, there adding shutters to one picture window and leaving them off another. The houses were of three basic designs: a peaked roof bungalow of one and a half storeys with an acute peak over the front door and a picture window on one side; a one-storey bungalow with a low roof and a picture window; and a two-storey box with two windows downstairs and two upstairs. All three designs had slab doors with one of several window patterns cut into them, the most common being three descending upright triangles. [17]

An abrupt, though short, halt was brought to all building activity by a major flood in the spring of 1950. Flood stage in Winnipeg is eighteen feet above datum. In 1950 the Red River rose to 30.3 feet and caused enormous damage and dislocation.

Flood warnings were first issued to the residents of Winnipeg on April 7 when city engineer W. D. Hurst warned that flooding was "highly probable." This initial warning was followed during the next week by others from Mayor Garnet Coulter and officials of the provincial government. Plans were hurriedly made to strengthen and add to the inadequate dikes of the greater Winnipeg area, particularly when it was noted that a $1.1 million program of diking and other flood protection works proposed in 1949 had never been carried out.[18]

On April 22 began two weeks during which a vast volume of water from the United States, swollen by Canadian tributaries of the Red River and by heavy snow and rain, spread out over the farmlands, into towns and villages, and came within an inch or two of forcing the complete evacuation of Winnipeg. By May 6 the provincial government had placed full control of the flood-threatened area in the hands of the military, commanded by Brig. R.E.A. Morton. And from May 6 to 27, this flood control committee, given extraordinary powers, was the nerve centre of the battle. Men and equipment of the regular army, navy, and air force played vital roles in transportation, control and supply duties, while reserve units of all three services were called up on active service and manned dikes, pumps, and communications facilities.

The Red Cross and the Salvation Army were among the many organizations which provided much needed assistance in the long fight. There were as well thousands of volunteers, from teenagers to grandparents, who manned round-the-clock canteens, answered phones, housed the homeless, and above all carried millions of sandbags to shore up the sagging dikes.

By May 10, about seventy thousand women and children had been evacuated from the city, easing the strain on many of the municipal services. Brig. Morton had, meanwhile, prepared a plan called "Operation Blackboy" for the military control of the metropolitan area and the evacuation of all but about seventy-five thousand people from the city and the suburbs. By May 22, the river was definitely going down and five days later the flood control committee was disbanded. The job of rehabilitation — aided by a Flood Relief Fund which drew contributions from all over the world — was carried out in the ensuing months. It was an enormous task since over ten thousand homes had been flooded, one hundred thousand residents had been evacuated, and business had

An example of the single-storey industrial buildings, usually in suburban locations, which provided new quarters for most of Winnipeg's industries and wholesale businesses in the post-war period.

been severely disrupted or completely halted. Estimates of loss ran as high as $115 million. Ironically, the flood should not have come as any surprise to Winnipeggers since the Red River had flooded before, most notably in 1948. In 1950, however, the city was determined to ensure it would not happen again.

Efforts to protect Winnipeg and the surrounding suburbs from future flooding began immediately and by 1952 some progress had been made. A system of permanent dikes along the Red River and part of the Assiniboine River within the greater Winnipeg area was completed giving flood protection to a level of 26.5 feet in most areas and 30.3 feet in the downtown and Riverview areas.[19] But this did not satisfy Winnipeg and a long and often bitter campaign was waged with the federal and provincial governments to aid in the construction of a massive twenty-nine-mile-long floodway to divert water around the city in difficult years. The floodway was finally begun by the government of Premier Duff Roblin following his 1958 election victory and, with a grant of $31.5 million from Ottawa was completed in the early 1960s. The construction of the floodway was a huge task, comparable to scooping out a river almost thirty miles long from St. Norbert to Selkirk. An earth-moving job greater than the digging of the Suez Canal, Panama Canal, or the St. Lawrence Seaway, the Red River Floodway also involved the accommodation or relocation of aqueducts, highways, power lines, and Canadian National and Canadian Pacific railway lines. When finally completed, however, the floodway ensured that never again would flood threaten the city.[20]

Following the flood, Winnipeggers rapidly returned to their building activities. The most notable commercial building of the decade was the construction of Winnipeg's first major shopping centre at Polo Park which opened in 1959. In terms of public buildings, several new and important structures were completed during the 1950s. A new Winnipeg Stadium was opened in 1953 followed by the opening of the Winnipeg Baseball Stadium in 1954 and the Winnipeg Arena in 1955. These structures gave Winnipeg's famed football team, the Blue Bombers, a home and furnished a centre for other sports and spectacles, notably track, hockey, and the Red River Exhibition. In 1950 and 1955 two new additions to the Winnipeg General Hospital were completed. And between 1950 and 1960, sixteen new schools were opened and improvements and additions were made to several of the city's libraries and parks.

One of the more noteworthy additions was the construction of an outdoor theatre, known as Rainbow Stage, in Kildonan Park. Plans for such a facility were first put forward by the Civic Music League early in 1950. After a study was completed and plans drawn, construction began late in 1951 on the stage and, in 1953, on an amphitheatre. On September 22, 1953, the first concert was presented. Construction of pergola wings, fixed seats, and landscaping was completed in 1954 and the official opening was held on July 7, 1954, with a Variety Concert of city artists. During 1959, total attendance at all events at Rainbow Stage was approximately 62,500.

During the decade of the fifties, the municipalities surrounding Winnipeg grew far more quickly than did the city itself as Winnipeg workers moved into homes as far away as Transcona. And with this suburban growth, urban sprawl became as evident in Greater Winnipeg as it was elsewhere in North America. The division of work and home became ever more common as the dispersal of the population which had first been facilitated by the street railway was completed by the automobile. In the postwar years the road system that had been imposed on the city by the rivers and railroads was expanded by additional routes. Old bridges were replaced, new crossings were added, and a major impediment to free traffic flow was removed when the streetcar tracks were covered after 1955 as the last streetcars bowed out of operation and were replaced by an ever expanding fleet of trolley and diesel buses. The movement of freight by road through the city was also eased — allowing more room for passenger cars — by the construction of a perimeter highway around the city (see Map 13).

Prior to 1960 most physical growth took place without the benefit of long-term planning. Planning activities had been stagnant in the city since the appointment of a City Planning Commission in 1911. These initial efforts had led, by 1914, to the creation of a Greater Winnipeg Plan Commission but, shortly after the outbreak of World War I, its appropriation had been cancelled. Although there was some scattered activity between 1915 and World War II, the idea of planning for the future development of the city began to receive official attention only in 1943. In that year, a Metropolitan Planning Committee was established consisting of four members representing the provincial government and two representatives

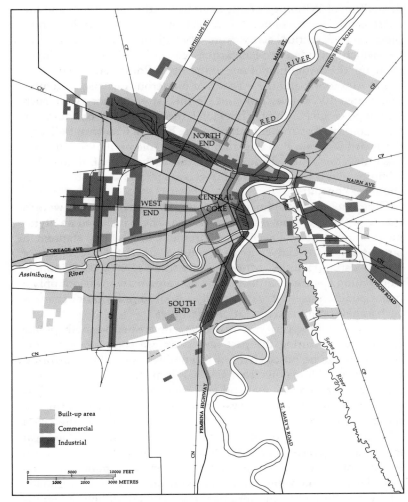

13 Land Use and Spatial Growth 1966

Legend:
- Built-up area
- Commercial
- Industrial

from each of the twelve participating municipalities. Mayor Garnet Coulter of Winnipeg appointed Aldermen H. C. Morrison and Jacob Penner as representatives. A year later, in 1944, Winnipeg City Council appointed its own Town Planning Commission. The two bodies then united under the cumbersome title of the Joint Executive Committee on Metropolitan Planning for Greater Winnipeg and set to work.[21]

Between 1944 and 1949 the committee worked toward the development of a comprehensive plan for Greater Winnipeg. Nine reports were published during these years dealing with such matters as major thoroughfares, zoning, residential areas, and the city's appearance.[22] But the reports had little effect beyond an informational role. Although the master plan reports were approved in principle they were applied only in a haphazard way by some of the member cities and municipalities. There was no compulsion in the form of legislation to set about implementing the master plan. Instead, Greater Winnipeg followed the familiar North American pattern of making plans and recommendations but not implementing them.

There was some forward-looking action taken, however, when in April 1949 a Metropolitan Planning Commission was created by the provincial legislature. The responsibility of the Commission was twofold: to plan for the future development and growth of Metropolitan Winnipeg; and to give technical planning advice and assistance to the member municipalities. During the 1950s the Metropolitan Planning Commission continued to function and did achieve a certain measure of success in establishing an understanding of metropolitan problems throughout the Greater Winnipeg area. It attained a higher degree of success, however, in the provision of technical advice and assistance to member municipalities. In matters of metropolitan concern, action on proposals was more difficult to attain since there was no government which could act or make decisions. Thus the experience of the Commission during the 1950s helped create a demand for metropolitan government, a goal that was finally achieved in 1960. But during the 1950s the work of the Metropolitan Planning Commission did not influence physical growth in any major way.[23]

While private construction, and the public services supportive of it, surged ahead, some efforts were also made to provide units of low-cost public housing for those families unable to compete for shelter on the private market. In July 1958, Winnipeg City Council established the Urban Renewal and Rehabilitation Board and during 1959 and 1960 several studies were made of the central part of the city with a view to establishing the areas that required redevelopment, rehabilitation, or conservation.[24] Considerable discussion followed the completion of the studies until, finally, in 1963 a small start in public housing was made with the construction of 165 units in the Burrows-Keewatin area of northwest Winnipeg. Another 328 units in the Jarvis Avenue district, renamed the Lord Selkirk Park development, were soon added. Other developments followed these, including successful efforts in the area of co-operative housing and in urban renewal on the old Midland Railway property in north central Winnipeg.[25] None of these efforts was initiated or completed without a great deal of public controversy, both over funding and the issue of citizen participation in the planning process, but they all eventually added much needed physical facilities.

By the end of the 1950s, then, Winnipeg had done much in the way of building to fill the backlog of demands that had accumulated between 1929 and 1945. Planning was beginning to be recognized as an essential ingredient in modern urban growth and there was a grudging recognition of the need for the public sector to involve itself directly in the building process. These trends, together with a prosperous economic situation and the growing demands on government, led to a building boom of major proportions in the 1960s and early 1970s. In the areas of commercial, educational, recreational, and governmental building there were countless new developments. Indeed, almost the entire urban landscape of Greater Winnipeg was altered as new zones were created and the character of old areas changed. Several new industrial parks, such as McGillvary Boulevard Industrial Area and Inkster Industrial Park, were developed to house both new and relocated industry. Several large shopping centre complexes sprang up. There were transformations in the educational sphere with the physical expansion of the centrally located University of Winnipeg and the construction of a new series of buildings to house the Manitoba Institute of Technology. The latter, built in West Winnipeg, opened in 1969 and was renamed Red River Community College. In the centre of the city, changes included such developments as the demolition of Winnipeg's famed city hall in the early 1960s and the construction on the same Main Street site of a new city hall complex; the construction, across from city hall, of the Centennial Centre, which included a planetarium, concert hall, and provincial museum; the demolition of one of the city's oldest hotels, the CPR's Royal Alexandra; and the erection of numerous highrise structures that changed Winnipeg's skyline. In this latter category were such buildings as the North Star Inn Hotel, the Royal Bank Building, the Place Louis Riel apartment building, the Bank of Montreal Building, the Board of Grain Building and, most notable of all, the Lombard Place development, which includes the Richardson Building, the Winnipeg Inn, the Lombard Street garage and an underground shopping concourse.

Other notable additions to the physical environment were a legacy of the 1967 Pan-American Games. These included an olympic swimming pool, a cycling velodrome, a high school stadium, a tartan track at the University of Manitoba, and the improvement of many existing facilities. More recently, the $15,000,000 Winnipeg Convention Centre Complex in the downtown area was not only a major addition itself, it was partially responsible for other changes such as new hotels and recreational facilities.

The reasons for this vast real estate investment — both public and private — during the past few years are complex, but some comments can be posed that put recent developments in historical perspective. The massive changes in Winnipeg's web of commercial, industrial, educational and governmental buildings and complexes indicated that the city was reversing — or at least halting — the trend of decline that had set in during the 1920s. By the 1950s Winnipeg had lost ground to Calgary and Edmonton as the great metropolis of western Canada. Winnipeg's image had deteriorated because of its relatively modest rate of growth of population and new development when compared with other centres in Canada where growth had been more dynamic. The rebuilding of significant sections of Winnipeg's non-residential sector thus reflects an attempt to overcome these long-term trends. And although it was clear that Winnipeg would not become the "Chicago of the North," one of the most dramatic building booms in its history did indicate that Winnipeg would continue to occupy a major place in hierarchy of Canadian cities.

CIVIC POLITICS

Postwar politics generally followed the pattern established in the inter-war period in which the business-oriented "citizens'" group continued to control city council while opposed by an articulate labour group. Politics in the late 1940s and 1950s were anything but dull, however, since several issues caused more than an average degree of interest in municipal affairs. Moreover, the 1950s witnessed the election of Winnipeg's most notable mayor, Steve Juba, a man who has dominated municipal politics in the city ever since.

The Winnipeg Electric Company had been a continual source of dispute between the citizens' and labour groups for several decades. In the 1920s it had for a time dominated civic politics and in later years conflict over its influence and business practices was always near the surface of political debate. The editor of the *Winnipeg Tribune*, Tom Green, noted that during the 1940s he "had the impression that some of the city aldermen were more the candidates of the Street Railway Company than the Citizens' Election Committee."[26] The issues over which the two groups clashed included such matters as line extensions, fare increases, extensions of the company's franchise, and bylaws regarding taxes and other regulations affecting the Winnipeg Electric Company. In 1948, however, a series of events began that ultimately removed the perennial issue of the Winnipeg Electric Company from civic politics.

The postwar industrial expansion of Winnipeg and Manitoba had by the late 1940s resulted in an acute power shortage. The problem was a common one in North America but in Manitoba there was no obvious solution. Activity in the electrical power field was divided among three authorities: the provincially controlled Manitoba Power Commission, the municipally owned Winnipeg City Hydro, and the privately owned Winnipeg Electric Company. The latter two companies were jointly responsible for the distribution of electricity in greater Winnipeg. They competed for customers in Winnipeg and each held monopoly franchises in different suburbs. In addition, the Winnipeg Electric Company owned and operated a public transportation system and a gas utility in the city.[27]

To deal with the province's power problems the provincial government appointed, in 1948, Dr. Hogg of the Ontario Hydro Commission to make a study and provide recommendations. The Hogg Report presented a number of alternative plans but the one favoured and accepted by the provincial legislature was Plan C.[28] It called for a comprehensive reorganization of the hydro-electric industry in Manitoba. The province was to establish a single agency which could own and operate all electric generating facilities in the province. An appropriate inter-municipal agency would take over responsibility for distribution of electricity in greater Winnipeg and the operation of a transit system. Under this system high- and low-cost power would be automatically averaged and integration and interconnection of hydro plants could be achieved. In short, the plan called for the reorganization of the production and distribution of electrical power on a public monopoly basis.

In the ensuing months and years a vigorous and sometimes bitter debate over the merits of Plan C was waged, particularly in the city of Winnipeg. Several issues were at stake. One was the future of Winnipeg Hydro. Created as a municipally owned utility in 1906 and operated very successfully thereafter, it was a proud possession of the citizens of Winnipeg. Any talk of its takeover by a provincial authority was not welcome. A second, more complicated issue was the proposed takeover of the Winnipeg Electric and Street Railway Company. The various sides in this dispute are not easily sorted out but generally it can be said that the labour group supported the takeover of the company while many business aldermen felt it should be allowed to continue to exist as a private company.[29]

The sequence of events leading to the final resolution of the issue began in 1951. In that year the provincial government passed legislation giving itself the power to expropriate the Winnipeg Electric Company. Detailed and secret negotiations followed with Winnipeg City Council, the result of which was the acceptance of Plan C. Sudden and concerted opposition by the *Winnipeg Free Press* to a public power monopoly succeeded in arousing antagonism to the measure, especially among the Winnipeg business community, and led to a submission of the plan to a referendum by the voters of Winnipeg. Despite the pleadings of experts and the support of the *Winnipeg Tribune*, Plan C was defeated by over 16,000 votes. But the referendum turned out to have been a futile exercise since a modified version of Plan C was ultimately implemented. In 1953, the province purchased the plants and the distributing and street transport system of the Winnipeg Electric Company and then resold them to the city of Winnipeg after a complicated series of transactions completed in 1955. Three publicly owned systems then emerged. The Greater Winnipeg Transit Commission was created in April 1953, taking over the facilities and services of the former Street Railway Company. In terms of hydro, there were two separate systems established — the Manitoba Power Commission and Winnipeg City Hydro, both under the supervision of the Manitoba Hydro Electric Board. As part of the agreement, City Hydro's distribution properties and customers outside Winnipeg (mainly in Transcona, Brooklands, East and West Kildonan) were turned over to the Manitoba Power Commission. Within the city of Winnipeg, City Hydro took over properties valued in excess of $7 million and approximately 18,000 additional customers.[30]

There were two major results for the city of Winnipeg from these events. First, the continued existence of City Hydro allowed Winnipeggers to keep obtaining power at a rate significantly below that charged in the rest of Manitoba. Also, City Hydro, in addition to paying all municipal taxes, made substantial contributions to the city's general fund. Between 1948 and 1960, for example, the average annual contribution was almost $700,000.[31] Second, the removal of the perennial issue of the Winnipeg Electric Street Railway Company from civic politics led to a substantial decline in hostility between the factions on city council in the late 1950s.

There were, however, several other factors that contributed to a change in the nature of Winnipeg civic politics in the decade of the 1950s. One was the fact that the labour group on council, along with their CCF allies, became far less militant as the party and its supporters sought to achieve middle-class respectability. Changes also occurred on the other side — the long control of the council by the Winnipeg Election Committee brought about a decline in their organization and support. Also, petty jealousies and ambitions developed among Winnipeg Election Committee aldermen and it was increasingly difficult for that group to present the united front that had been their major advantage. In short, by the mid-1960s there ceased to be as many serious differences in political perspective between the Winnipeg Election Committee and the other, usually labour, aldermen. Yet the Citizens' group continued to dominate city hall and the views of the business community still received far more attention than those of any other group.[32]

The slow decline in partisan politics in Winnipeg in the 1950s and early 1960s was further encouraged by the fact that the mayor's chair was virtually removed from contention with the election in 1956 of Stephen Juba. Independent of either group on council, Juba has, nevertheless, served continuously as mayor since that time. Indeed, his popularity has grown rather than declined and he has won every contest he entered effortlessly. In the first election of the amalgamated Winnipeg in 1971, for example, he recorded a landslide victory when he received 139,714 votes to only 49,014 for his nearest opponent.

Stephen Juba is a native Winnipegger, the son of Ukrainian immigrants. Although he had planned to be a lawyer, like many others his plans were interrupted by the Depression. Throughout the thirties and forties he worked at various jobs, finally establishing a successful wholesale company in 1949. After several unsuccessful attempts at both federal and provincial politics, he was elected to the provincial legislature in 1953 and held that seat until he resigned it in 1959. Juba's most significant victory came in 1956, however, when he became Winnipeg's first non-Anglo-Saxon mayor, defeating the incumbent, Mayor George Sharpe, by a narrow margin.

Juba is a maverick, a populist mayor who possesses just the right combination of qualities to win election after election. His background ensures him working-class support and his policies have won the favour of middle-class and business interests. The mayor favours development, is concerned about taxation, and does much to improve not only the city's self-image but also its reputation outside the province. In 1967, for example, Mayor Juba fought for and obtained the Pan-American Games for Winnipeg. During Juba's years in office, Winnipeg once again began to reassert itself; the downtown core has become the centre of building activity; and a confidence and pride that the city has not known since before 1913 have reappeared among Winnipeggers.[33]

The decline in the level of partisan politics practised in Winnipeg formed the background to a unified government for the entire urban area. Most metropolitan cities were characterized by a fragmented structure of administrative areas, reflected most often in the existence of a central city surrounded by a number of separate municipalities or towns. The imposition of a second tier of urban

The era of Winnipeg's electric street cars, which began in 1891, ended in September 1955.

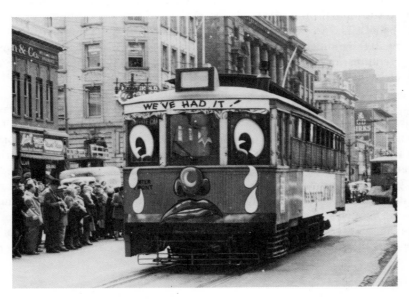

government fell short of solving problems of fragmentation and often introduced another element of conflict between the municipalities and the second-tier government, particularly over the allocation of limited financial resources. Typical examples of this two-tier approach are the municipality of Metropolitan Toronto, the Regional Municipality of Ottawa-Carleton, the Montreal Urban Community, and the regional districts established throughout British Columbia. Winnipeg, however, eventually moved from a fragmented metropolitan form of government to a unified, single level of urban government with the creation of Unicity in 1972. Even in Winnipeg, however, this ultimate step was implemented only after long years of struggle and controversy.

The division of what has always been a single economic community among a number of separate political jurisdictions had posed serious problems in regard to the provision of public services and the administration of community affairs. As early as 1883 the Government of Manitoba planned for the establishment of County Councils in each district of the province, including the greater Winnipeg area, to administer intermunicipal affairs. But the duration of this plan was brief. Poor communication and the expense of an additional level of government in the then sparsely settled province made the idea premature and impractical.[34]

Cooperative action became necessary in the years after 1910, however, as suburban populations grew to substantial proportions and major projects of community-wide benefit had to be undertaken and administered on a joint basis by all the municipalities in the Greater Winnipeg area. These joint ventures, many of which had to be initiated by the provincial government because of a lack of voluntary cooperation, took the form of single-purpose boards and commissions. Among these were the Greater Winnipeg Water District (established in 1913); the Greater Winnipeg Sanitary District (1935); the St. James-Winnipeg Airport Commission (1937); the Metropolitan Planning Commission (1949); the Greater Winnipeg Transit Commission (1953); and several others.[35]

Despite these agencies there was a growing awareness in the years between 1950 and 1960 of the need for better coordination of the services provided by these authorities. There was a widespread feeling that they could no longer provide the joint services essential to the municipalities, particularly those areas that were experiencing rapid postwar development. Increasingly the central city of Winnipeg came to resent the services it perforce provided the surrounding municipalities, community-wide services including hospitals, major parks, and recreational and cultural facilities. For their part, the satellite municipalities complained of their inability to raise revenues to match those of the central city, while at the same time they attracted Winnipeggers with the lure of lower taxes. Although the suburbs continually complained of the inadequacy and high cost of public transit, for example, they were unwilling to help underwrite the perpetual transit deficit.

As a result of these and other difficulties, a first step toward the formation of a second-tier government — Metropolitan Winnipeg — finally took place in 1951 when a provincial-municipal committee was formed to study the political and financial problems of Manitoba municipalities. In November 1952 a subcommittee, studying the special situation in Greater Winnipeg, recommended that a central board be established to handle the essential municipal services of the metropolitan area. After further exploratory discussions with the area municipalities the provincial government in 1955 appointed the Greater Winnipeg Investigating Commission to study more precisely all aspects of metropolitan problems. Following four years of investigation, including visits to a number of Canadian, American, and European cities, the Commission recommended the establishment of a strong central authority with responsiblity for a large number of inter-municipal services. After additional hearings, the Manitoba Government cut the Gordian knot and introduced to the legislature Bill 62, an Act to Establish the Metropolitan Corporation of Greater Winnipeg. It became law in March 1960.[36]

The new Metro Winnipeg encompassed the whole of the area from the junction of the Red and Assiniboine, north to St. Andrews, south to St. Norbert, west to Assiniboia, and east to Transcona. It was practically a recreation of the District of Assiniboia of the days of the fur trade. The area was composed of seven cities, five suburban municipalities, and one town: a total of thirteen municipalities, with the City of Winnipeg forming the centre. The Metropolitan Corporation was given jurisdiction over a number of services considered to be of joint concern throughout the urban area. The existing boards and commissions were dissolved and their

In the biggest upset in Winnipeg's election history Stephen Juba, a third generation Canadian of Ukrainian origin, defeated George E. Sharpe, the incumbent. Sharpe (on left) is shown here congratulating Juba who, by his victory in the mayoralty contest of 1956, became Winnipeg's first non-Anglo-Saxon mayor. Juba first ran unsuccessfully in the aldermanic elections of 1950 and 1951. In 1952 and 1954 he unsuccessfully contested the mayoralty, while winning a 1953 election to the provincial legislature. In 1956 he was finally successful, defeating mayor Sharpe, "a prosperous, Anglo-Saxon businessman," whose father had been mayor in 1904-1906. Juba won by about 2,000 votes in an election that was "fought with clear ethnic, class, and establishment overtones." Juba has not been seriously challenged since that election and has now held office for longer than any of his predecessors.

responsibilities were assumed by Metro Winnipeg, along with some other services previously administered by the municipalities themselves. The newly elected Metro Council was, for example, charged with the preparation of a development plan for the area as a whole. In addition, certain functions closely related to the plan became a direct responsibility of the Corporation. These included traffic control, zoning, transit, sewers and water, major streets and bridges, water supply, and the establishment and maintenance of major parks and garbage disposal. The Council was also charged to make a uniform assessment of all property for the purposes of local taxation and later assumed control of land along rivers and streams.

Almost from its commencement Metro Government in Greater Winnipeg was fraught with problems. In Winnipeg, the city's mayor, Stephen Juba, was offended at this blow to the primacy of Winnipeg which he and his council had hoped to expand to engulf the suburbs. Winnipeg city taxpayers came to believe Metro was designed for the benefit of the suburbs and was unnecessary because it replaced services already provided; besides, some Metro councillors were thought to be both arrogant and extravagant. At one point "Metrophobia" became so intense on Winnipeg city council that a motion to withdraw from Metro failed by only two votes. The suburbs, on the other hand, bewailed both their loss of power and the introduction of another taxing authority. The Metropolitan Corporation of Greater Winnipeg thus became the scapegoat for all the complaints of a confused citizenry and a whipping boy for ambitious politicians.[37]

Despite the lack of grace with which Metro government was received by the municipalities and the city, it did make positive contributions to the Greater Winnipeg area during the 1960s. In the field of planning it produced for the first time a master blueprint for the region called the Metropolitan Development Plan. In the area of transportation it laid out new thoroughfares, built several bridges, and upgraded the regional transit system. It coordinated the use and distribution of water and the disposal of sewage. It equalized land assessment throughout Greater Winnipeg, transferring some of the city's tax burden to the surrounding suburbs, and provided an overall building and zoning code. Metro even enhanced the appearance of the urban environment by enlarging the area's parks, landscaping its streets, building playgrounds, and by giving the long-neglected river banks needed attention.

The introduction of Metro Government in 1960 thus provided an improvement in the quality of certain services administered on a regional basis. But it also aggravated a more critical problem — the individual citizen's sense of frustration under a two-tier structure. This frustration stemmed from three main roots: fragmented authority, segmented financial capacity, and lack of citizen involvement. In seeking a solution to the problems of the area, the NDP provincial government that was elected in 1969 felt that any new structure had to provide easier access to government by the citizens. While it was considered necessary that all major services had to be unified, there also had to be developed a system whereby government could be brought closer to the people. These were felt to be parallel processes and one could not succeed without the other.[38]

After lengthy discussion and debate, the provincial government created on January 1, 1972, a unique form of government for Greater Winnipeg. On that day Winnipeg area municipalities, including the historic French-speaking city of St. Boniface, ceased to exist as distinct legal entities. Their local governments were replaced by a fifty-member Greater Winnipeg City Council which controlled an urban territory approximately seventeen miles in diameter with a population close to 550,000 (see Map 14). With the formation of Unicity in 1972, Winnipeg thus became the first major Canadian city to move beyond the stage of split-level metropolitan government to a single administration for its entire metropolitan area.

The concept of Unicity as it was spelled out in the legislation creating a new city embraced two fundamental principles. First, the new council had the power to unify all services under a single administration. Second, a system of thirteen community committees were created through which individuals could achieve a greater sense of involvement with the processes of urban government. It is still too early to tell whether this new form of government will provide a workable mechanism for resolving increasingly complex urban problems. In any case, the basic reorganizaton of municipalities into a single metropolitan-regional government does hold the potential of eliminating the fragmentation of services, insuring a

Opened in 1906, the Royal Alexandra served as one of Winnipeg's luxury hotels until it closed in 1967 and was demolished in 1971. When it first opened it was the most splendid hostelry in the CPR chain and for years it was the social centre of the city. Its huge rotunda, its impressive dining room graced with the Challenger murals, the tea room, the crystal ballroom, the vice-regal suite: all made the Royal Alexandra Hotel one of the city's best.

more equitable distribution of finances, reducing competition between municipalities for industry, and providing for area-wide planning. The fact is that many urban problems, particularly those dealing in matters of land use, environmental control and industrial development are of such a scale and encompass such a range of activities that regional government is required.

Structural changes, however, do not necessarily bring about better government. In the first two elections held under the new Unicity format in 1971 and 1974, there was a fairly strong resemblance to the pattern of politics long practised in the old city of Winnipeg. The business interests, now calling themselves the Independent Citizens Election Committee, used many of their old arguments regarding non-partisanship, the need for progress, and so on to capture thirty-seven of the fifty seats on council in 1971. Their labour rivals, running on the platform of a wider degree of civic democracy, extension of services, and a more equitable distribution of taxes, captured only seven seats. Significantly, however, by 1974 ten genuine independents had been elected to Unicity council, many from the former suburbs. This could suggest that in the future the old class polarization may be superseded by an alignment pitting the old city of Winnipeg against the former suburbs.[39]

The slow erosion of old patterns that occurred at the level of municipal and regional government was not duplicated in the provincial and federal arenas. In these areas, Winnipeg continued to be divided along class and ethnic lines, voting in a pattern established in the 1910s. Throughout the administrations of the Liberal-Progressives under both S.S. Garson (1942-1948) and Douglas Campbell (1948-1958), and the Conservatives under Duff Roblin (1958-1968), Winnipeg continued to provide strong support for the CCF-NDP. In 1945, under the leadership of a former mayor, S.J. Farmer, the CCF formed the official opposition in the province, led by a strong contingent of Winnipeg members — most notably Farmer himself and Lloyd Stinson. In subsequent provincial elections the city consistently elected several CCF-NDP members, usually from the north end, although Stinson managed to win elections regularly, though not consistently, in a south Winnipeg riding.[40] This pattern held firm until 1969 when the NDP, under the leadership of Edward R. Schreyer, formed the provincial government. It is notable that in the 1969 election the NDP owed a good deal of its

Royal tour entering the Royal Alex, 1951

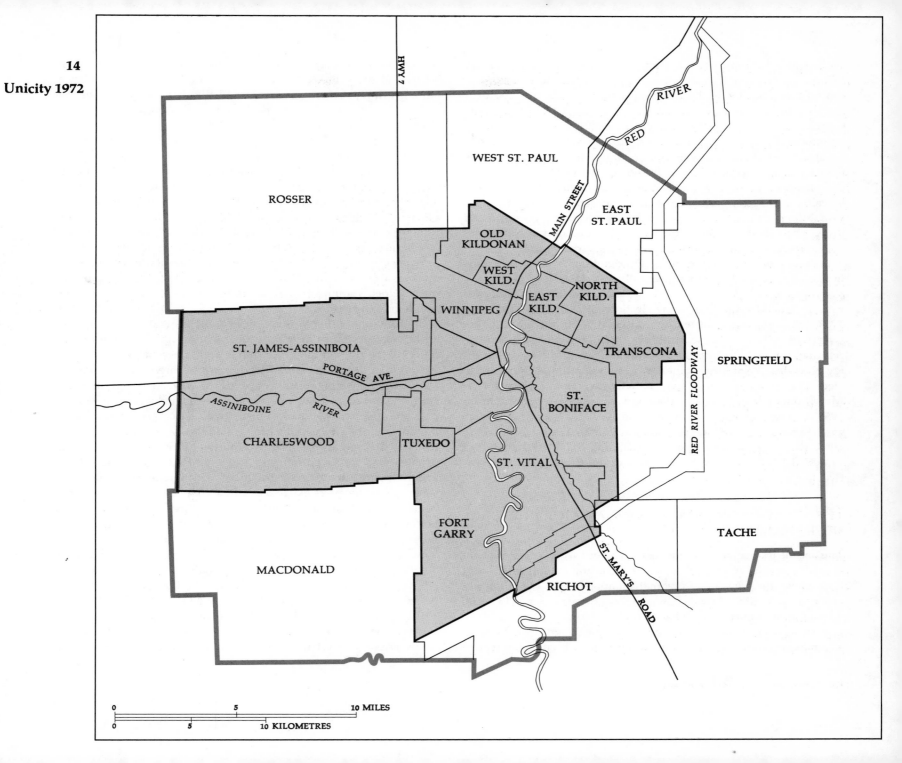

14
Unicity 1972

HWY 7

RED RIVER

WEST ST. PAUL

ROSSER

MAIN STREET

EAST ST. PAUL

OLD KILDONAN

WEST KILD.

NORTH KILD.

WINNIPEG

EAST KILD.

TRANSCONA

ST. JAMES-ASSINIBOIA

PORTAGE AVE.

SPRINGFIELD

ASSINIBOINE RIVER

CHARLESWOOD

TUXEDO

ST. BONIFACE

RED RIVER FLOODWAY

ST. VITAL

FORT GARRY

MACDONALD

TACHE

RICHOT

ST. MARY'S ROAD

| 0 | | 5 | | 10 MILES |
| 0 | | 5 | | 10 KILOMETRES |

success to urban support. Of twenty-seven seats in metropolitan Winnipeg, the party won seventeen, mainly in the poorer north and central districts. One of the reasons for the upsurge in support for the NDP in metropolitan Winnipeg in 1969 was a decline in ethnic consciousness. By the 1960s the old-line parties could no longer automatically count on strong support from the city's ethnic groups. The fact was that Winnipeg's non-Anglo-Saxons were sufficiently integrated that they no longer felt the need to vote Liberal or Conservative as a means of demonstrating their desire for acceptance by the charter group. Thus ethnic voting gave way to a more straightforward competition between those disposed to reform and those who called for restraint, and in this situation the NDP were able to increase their support in Winnipeg significantly.[41]

In federal elections, the CCF-NDP did not make any major gains in the city. In the two north end ridings — Winnipeg North and Winnipeg North Centre — A.M. Stewart and Stanley Knowles were returned for the CCF in the elections of 1945, 1949, 1953 and 1957, but both were defeated by Conservatives in the Diefenbaker sweep of 1958. In subsequent elections, however, the ridings returned to the NDP with the election of David Orlikow and Stanley Knowles. Winnipeg's other two federal ridings continued to elect Conservatives and Liberals. Winnipeg South elected L.A. Mutch (Liberal) in 1945 and 1949, O.C. Trainor (Conservative) in 1953, Gordon Chown (Conservative) in 1957, 1958, and 1962, Margaret Konantz (Liberal) in 1963, and L.R. Sherman (Conservative) in 1965. Winnipeg South Centre elected Ralph Maybank (Liberal) in 1945 and 1949, and then stuck with Gordon Churchill (Conservative).[42]

THE URBAN COMMUNITY: SOCIAL AND CULTURAL DEVELOPMENT

The decade immediately following the end of World War II was not a notable one in Winnipeg's social and cultural evolution. It was a time when "the grey pall of pragmatism hung heavy" over both city and provincial life.[43] In virtually all areas of endeavour — the arts, education, literature, and religious life — little progress was made toward securing a social order capable of fulfilling the needs of all Winnipeggers. Instead, the city and its leaders seemed content to rest on the accomplishments of previous decades. Then, in the late 1950s and early 1960s, there was a return of the old confidence among Winnipeg's Anglo-Saxons and this fact, coupled with the revitalized energy of Winnipeg's other ethnic groups, brought about renewed vigour in Winnipeg society.

One indicator of the advent of an era of rapid change was the election, in 1958, of a new provincial government led by Duff Roblin. The Roblin government, with a Winnipeg member at its helm, was more mindful of urban problems and needs than previous administrations. In its creation of the Metropolitan Corporation of Greater Winnipeg, its relaxation of liquor laws, its support for the floodway, its redistribution of seats in the provincial legislature (giving the city a substantially increased voice in the affairs of the province), its support through government grants to art galleries, museums, theatre groups, and historical societies, the new government helped Winnipeg develop and encouraged it to deal with old problems in new ways.

Spurred on both by these developments and the boundless energy and optimism of Mayor Juba, Winnipeg had begun by the late 1950s to reassert itself. But unlike earlier periods, when Anglo-Saxons had been almost exclusively in the forefront of initiative and change, this time other groups led the way. Although the pressure to adapt to a Canadian way of life remained strong in Winnipeg and the schools had shown great success in assimilating immigrants, the city's ethnic groups had lost neither their folk culture nor their enterprise. Fed by a postwar influx of educated and sophisticated displaced refugees, the city's Poles, Ukrainians, Jews and Germans pursued their traditions with a renewed dedication. The city's ethnic press expanded, ethnic clubs increased their membership, and ethnic dance, music and literature flourished. A member of Winnipeg's Jewish community, Maitland Steinkopf, chaired the Manitoba Centennial Commission. Steinkopf envisioned Winnipeg as a centre for the arts and his enthusiasm had much to do with the building of the Centennial Centre.

The centennial complex was only one of a host of developments completed, begun, or planned in the city in the late 1950s and 1960s. The Manitoba Theatre Centre moved into spacious new quarters on Market Street in 1970; the Winnipeg Art Gallery received a new and striking home on Memorial Boulevard; and the

Horse racing at Polo Park in the 1950s.

The Rainbow Stage, 1956.

The Royal Winnipeg Ballet on tour.

city of Winnipeg began construction of its own centennial project, a major library in the downtown core. Together with the creation of new parks, the expansion of facilities in several established ones, and increased government grants to a wide variety of cultural groups and agencies, these developments made the "good life" in the fullest sense available as never before.

It was during these years that Winnipeg's reputation as a thriving centre for literature, sport, and culture was made. In the field of literature, there was such an outpouring of novels either set in Winnipeg or written by novelists who had spent considerable parts of their lives in the city that one reviewer observed that "if CanLit is a genus, 'PegLit is a thriving species and novels about growing up in Winnipeg a distinct subspecies."[44] He was referring to works by such noted Canadian writers as Jack Ludwig, John Marlyn, Dorothy Livesay, Adele Wiseman, Margaret Laurence, and Patricia Blondal, to name but a few. Culturally, it was said of Winnipeg that it had "the most vitally alive and well balanced range of musical, artistic and cultural activities of any Canadian city."[45] Reference here was to the accomplishments of the Royal Winnipeg Ballet, the Winnipeg Symphony Orchestra, Rainbow Stage, the Winnipeg Art Gallery, and the Manitoba Theatre Centre. What was perhaps most noteworthy was that these activities far outdrew, in total attendance, professional sports. In sports, Winnipeg became noted especially for curling and football. Between 1947 and 1970, a Winnipeg rink won the Canadian curling championship no fewer than seven times. In football, the Winnipeg Blue Bombers gained fame by playing in the Grey Cup final ten times between 1946 and 1965, winning the coveted prize five times.

These accomplishments did not mean that some sort of utopia had been reached in Winnipeg, but they signified the creation of a genuine community life for all Winnipeggers, which had been forged from the social, economic and political divisions of the past. As Winnipeg prepared to enter its second century, there were a growing number in the community who realized that only with continued concern, involvement and effort could the city look forward with confidence to the future.

This 1960 photograph of the junction of the Red and Assiniboine Rivers presents a frequently forgotten aspect of Winnipeg's geography. In the days of exploration, and for several decades after settlement commenced, the junction of the two rivers was designated "The Forks," a name that included more than the immediate vicinity. In these early years the two rivers were essential and prominent features of the prairie settlement since they served as vital transportation links. But from the coming of the railroad in the 1880s Winnipeg generally ignored her rivers and allowed the once bustling riverfront to become "the forgotten backyard of a too-busy city." Since the early 1960s, however, efforts have been made to utilize the miles of waterfront for recreational purposes.

The Winnipeg skyline, 1975.

North Main Street, viewed from the Richardson Building at Portage and Main.

L.B. Foote with his camera at the corner of Portage Avenue and Main Street, 1950.

Appendix
Statistical Tables

TABLE I
The Growth of Manufacturing in
Winnipeg, 1881-1971

Year	Population	Number of Firms*	Number of Employees	Payroll $(000)	Value of Products $(000)
1881	7,985	106	950	411	1,700
1891	25,639	307	2,359	1,177	5,611
1901	42,340	103	3,155	1,811	8,616
1911	136,035	177	11,705	7,614	32,699
1921	179,087	419	11,406	15,500	75,200
1926	191,998	446	15,474	20,087	87,696
1931	218,785	543	17,693	22,293	73,723
1936	215,814	594	16,673	18,061	73,316
1941	221,960	677	23,831	30,169	127,913
1946	229,045	756	26,730	42,355	206,381
1951	235,710	849	27,704	65,742	292,497
1956	255,093	869	26,629	80,892	309,520
1961	265,429	736	23,694	86,394	326,881
1971	246,270	633	22,667	133,361	465,804

*The discrepancy between the figures in this category is accounted for by the fact that the figures for 1881 and 1891 are based on *all* establishments, regardless of size, while the figures for 1901-1961 are based on firms with *five or more* employees.

Source: *Censuses of Canada, 1881-1961; The Manufacturing Industries of Canada, 1941*; and City of Winnipeg, *Municipal Manual, 1963*.

TABLE II
Number of Males Per 1,000
Females in Winnipeg, 1881-1971 *

Year	Ratio
1881	1393
1886	1100
1891	1095
1901	1075
1906	1271
1911	1207
1916	1018
1921	1004
1926	967
1931	1006
1936	960
1941	961
1946	939
1951	913
1956	946
1961	952
1966	928
1971	924

*Figures are not available for 1896.

Source: *Censuses of Canada, 1881-1971.*

TABLE III
Urban Population Growth and Distribution
in Manitoba, 1871-1971

Year	Population of Winnipeg	Population of Manitoba	Winnipeg's Population as Percentage of Total Population	Urban Population of Manitoba*	Winnipeg's Population as Percentage of Total Urban Population
1871	241	25,228	1.0	—	—
1881	7,985	62,260	12.8	9,276	86.1
1891	25,639	152,506	16.8	41,498	61.8
1901	42,340	255,211	16.6	70,436	60.1
1911	136,035	461,394	29.5	200,365	67.9
1916	163,000	553,860	29.4	241,014	67.6
1921	179,087	610,118	29.3	261,616	68.4
1926	191,998	639,056	30.4	278,858	68.8
1931	218,785	700,139	31.2	315,969	69.2
1936	215,814	711,216	30.3	310,927	69.4
1941	221,960	729,744	30.4	321,873	69.0
1946	229,045	726,923	31.5	337,331	67.9
1951	235,710	776,541	30.3	439,580	53.6
1956	255,093	850,040	30.0	510,583	50.0
1961	265,429	921,686	28.8	599,084	44.3
1971	246,270	988,250	24.9	686,445	35.9

*Includes all incorporated cities, towns and villages of 1,000 and over only.

Source: *Censuses of Canada, 1871-1971; Censuses of Prairie Provinces, 1916-1946.*

TABLE IV
Population Growth in Major Western Cities, 1901-1971

Year	Winnipeg	Regina	Saskatoon	Calgary	Edmonton	Vancouver
1901	42,340	2,249	113	4,392	4,176	27,010
1911	136,035	30,213	12,004	43,704	24,900	100,401
1921	179,087	34,432	25,739	63,305	58,821	163,200
1931	218,785	53,209	43,291	83,761	79,187	246,593
1941	221,960	58,245	43,027	88,904	93,817	275,353
1951	235,710	71,319	53,268	129,060	159,631	344,833
1956	255,093	89,755	72,858	181,780	226,002	368,844
1961	265,429	112,141	95,526	249,641	281,027	384,522
1966	257,005	131,127	115,892	330,575	376,925	410,375
1971	246,270	139,469	126,449	403,319	438,152	426,256

Source: *Censuses of Canada, 1901-1971*

TABLE V
Population Growth in Winnipeg,
1871 - 1971

Year	Population	Numerical Change	Per Cent Change
1871	241	—	—
1881	7,985	7,444	3,624.1
1886	20,238	12,253	153.4
1891	25,639	5,401	26.7
1896	31,649	6,010	23.4
1901	42,340	10,691	33.8
1906	90,153	47,813	113.0
1911	136,035	45,882	50.7
1916	163,000	26,965	19.8
1921	179,087	16,087	9.9
1926	191,998	12,911	7.2
1931	218,785	26,787	13.9
1936	215,814	-2,971	-1.4
1941	221,960	6,146	2.8
1946	229,045	7,085	3.2
1951	235,710	6,665	2.9
1956	255,093	19,383	8.2
1961	265,429	10,336	4.1
1966	257,005	-8,424	-3.2
1971	246,270	-10,735	-4.2

Source: *Censuses of Canada, 1871-1971; Census of Population and Agriculture of the Northwest Provinces, 1906;* and *Censuses of the Prairie Provinces, 1916-1946.*

TABLE VI
Birthplace of Winnipeg's Canadian-Born Population, 1881-1961

Birthplace	1881 No.	1881 %	1891 No.	1891 %	1901 No.	1901 %	1911 No.	1911 %	1921 No.	1921 %	1931 No.	1931 %	1941 No.	1941 %	1951 No.	1951 %	1961 No.	1961 %
Maritimes*	354	4.4	733	2.9	888	2.0	2775	2.0	3075	1.7	2855	1.3	2509	1.1	2554	1.0	3365	1.3
Quebec	576	7.1	1146	4.5	1365	3.2	2799	2.1	3083	1.7	2818	1.3	2540	1.1	2302	1.0	2580	1.0
Ontario	3395	42.5	7242	28.2	10419	24.6	20564	15.1	21402	11.9	19301	8.8	16415	7.4	14002	5.9	13859	5.2
Saskatchewan	—	—	—	—	—	—	587	.4	1969	1.1	4245	1.9	7643	3.4	10196	4.3	11907	4.5
Alberta	—	—	—	—	—	—	221	.2	618	.3	1150	.5	1833	.8	2162	.9	3008	1.1
B.C.	8	.1	25	.1	32	.1	175	.1	450	.2	579	.3	828	.4	1539	.7	2328	.8
Yukon & Territories	31	.4	57	.2	325	.8	52	.1	20	.1	14	.1	20	.1	36	.1	98	.1
Manitoba	1032	12.9	5510	21.4	13322	31.5	31849	23.4	62961	35.2	92524	42.3	112649	50.7	131667	55.8	152569	57.5
Total Canadian-Born	5387	67.5	14713	57.3	26351	62.2	59967	44.1	93584	52.4	123634	56.5	144437	65.0	164458	69.7	189714	71.5
Total Population	7985	100	25639	100	42340	100	136035	100	179087	100	218785	100	221960	100	235710	100	265429	100

* Includes Newfoundland in 1951 and 1961.

Source: *Censuses of Canada, 1881-1961.*

TABLE VII
Birthplace of Winnipeg's Foreign-Born Population, 1881-1971

Birthplace	1881 No.	1881 %	1891 No.	1891 %	1901 No.	1901 %	1911 No.	1911 %	1921 No.	1921 %	1931 No.	1931 %	1941 No.	1941 %	1951 No.	1951 %	1961 No.	1961 %	1971 No.	1971 %
Great Britain	1697	21.2	7196	28.1	8202	19.4	39999	29.4	49970	28.0	47644	21.8	38244	17.2	28574	12.1	21945	8.3	15170	6.2
United States	365	4.6	877	3.4	1405	3.3	5798	4.3	7052	3.9	5902	2.7	5242	2.4	4272	1.8	3717	1.4	3180	1.3
Scandinavia	32	.4	1193	4.6	2199	5.2	3669	1.4	2857	1.6	4008	1.8	2896	1.3	2263	1.0	1923	.7	—	—
Germany	37	.5	339	1.3	699	1.6	1866	1.4	641	.3	1241	.6	767	.4	1540	.6	7599	2.9	4545	1.8
Russia*	—	—	477	1.9	1445	3.4	19478	14.3	18429	10.3	15895	7.3	15054	6.8	14577	6.2	12240	4.6	8940	3.6
Poland	—	—	23	.1	—	—	—	—	2776	1.6	16164	7.4	11971	5.4	11584	5.0	10133	3.8	7975	3.2
Italy	10	.1	13	.1	99	.3	517	.4	689	.3	685	.3	569	.2	591	.2	2461	.9	4000	1.6
Asia	—	—	16	.1	119	.3	757	.5	919	.5	1136	.5	783	.4	853	.4	1145	.4	2715	1.1
Other	457	5.7	805	3.1	1821	4.3	3984	2.9	1900	1.1	2476	1.1	1997	.9	6998	3.0	14552	5.5	14765	6.0
Total Foreign-Born	2598	32.5	10926	42.7	15989	37.8	76068	55.9	85233	47.6	95151	43.5	77523	35.0	71252	30.3	75715	28.5	61290	24.9
Total	7985	100	25639	100	42340	100	136035	100	179087	100	218785	100	221960	100	235710	100	265429	100	246270	100

*Russia includes the following: 1901-Romania; 1911-Bukovina, Galicia, Bulgaria, Romania, Austria, Bohemia, and Hungary; 1921-Ukraine, Galicia, Bulgaria, Romania, Austria, Czechoslovakia, Hungary, and Yugoslavia; 1931-Ukraine, Romania, Austria, Czechoslovakia, Hungary, and Yugoslavia; 1941-Bulgaria, Romania, Austria, Czechoslovakia, Hungary, and Yugoslavia; 1951, 1961, 1971-U.S.S.R.

Source: *Censuses of Canada, 1881-1971.*

TABLE VIII
Ethnic Origins of Winnipeg's Population, 1881-1971

Ethnic Group	1881 No.	1881 %	1901(a) No.	1901(a) %	1911 No.	1911 %	1921 No.	1921 %	1931 No.	1931 %	1941 No.	1941 %	1951 No.	1951 %	1961 No.	1961 %	1971 No.	1971 %
Asian	2	.1	121	.3	597	.5	849	.5	1060	.5	1029	.5	1653	.7	2325	.9	4485	1.8
British	6679	83.6	31230	73.8	84552	62.1	120569	67.3	132416	60.5	130394	58.7	119367	50.6	113615	42.8	100420	40.8
French	450	5.6	1379	3.3	3695	2.0	3944	2.2	4970	2.3	6969	3.1	9898	4.2	13945	5.2	13850	5.6
German	186	2.3	2283	5.4	8912	6.5	4762	2.7	13209	6.0	12170	5.5	17461	7.4	30249	11.4	26710	10.8
Italian	26	.3	147	.3	769	.6	1311	.7	1664	.8	1609	.7	1743	.7	4216	1.6	6770	2.7
Jewish	4	.1	1156	2.7	9023	6.6	14449	8.0	17236	7.9	17027	7.7	15552	6.6	11690	4.4	10815	4.4
Netherlands	5	.1	92	.2	535	.4	1236	.7	1641	.8	2644	1.2	4146	1.8	6814	2.6	5080	2.1
Polish	—	—	—	—	4743	3.5	5696	3.2	11228	5.1	11024	5.0	13889	5.9	16573	6.2	14335	5.8
Russian (b)	6	.1	1771	4.2	5016	3.7	11714	6.5	5792	2.6	5170	2.3	5105	2.2	9812	3.7	1160	.5
Scandinavian	409	5.1	3322	7.8	4956	3.6	6147	3.4	8945	4.0	9177	4.1	9261	3.9	10093	3.8	7790	3.2
Ukrainian	—	—	—	—	3599	2.6	6381	3.6	18358	8.4	22578	10.2	32272	13.7	35975	13.6	33200	13.5
Indian & Eskimo	9	.1	8	.1	30	.1	44	.1	51	.1	24	.1	210	.1	1082	.4	4945	2.0
Others	209	2.6	831	1.9	10608	7.8	1985	1.1	2215	1.0	2145	.9	5153	2.2	9040	3.4	16710	6.8
Totals	7985	100	42340	100	136035	100	179081	100	218785	100	211960	100	235710	100	265429	100	246270	100

Notes: a) No figures are available for 1891.

b) Russian includes the following :1901-Austro-Hungarian; 1911-Austrian, Hungarian, Bulgarian and Romanian; 1921, 1931, 1941-Austrian, Czech, Slovak, Hungarian, and Romanian; 1951 - Austrian, Czech, Slovak and Hungarian; 1961, 1971 — U.S.S.R.

Source: *Censuses of Canada, 1881-1971.*

TABLE IX
Major Religious Affiliations of Winnipeg's Population, 1881-1971

Religion	1881 No.	1881 %	1891 No.	1891 %	1901 No.	1901 %	1911 No.	1911 %	1921 No.	1921 %	1931 No.	1931 %	1941 No.	1941 %	1951 No.	1951 %	1961 No.	1961 %	1971 No.	1971 %
Anglican	2373	29.7	6854	26.7	10175	24.0	31338	23.0	44359	24.8	45539	20.8	47405	21.4	40639	17.2	37043	14.0	30270	12.3
Baptist	349	4.4	1046	4.1	2055	4.9	5062	3.7	5092	2.8	5157	2.4	4857	2.2	4620	2.0	5966	2.2	4650	1.9
Greek Orthodox	—	—	—	—	—	—	—	—	—	—	2736	1.2	4615	2.1	6142	2.6	9515	3.6	8085	3.3
Jewish	21	.2	645	2.5	1145	2.7	8934	6.6	14390	8.0	17153	7.8	16917	7.6	15959	6.8	12582	4.7	10255	4.2
Lutheran	292	3.7	2291	8.9	4253	10.0	11151	8.2	9931	5.5	14829	6.8	14434	6.5	15408	6.5	22424	8.5	17430	7.0
Presbyterian	2365	29.6	5952	23.2	10172	24.0	30367	22.3	44533	24.9	22210	10.2	17931	8.1	13058	5.5	9086	3.4	7825	3.2
Roman Catholic	1020	12.8	2470	9.6	5143	12.2	19729	14.5	24118	13.5	46990	21.5	32462	14.6	39467	16.7	58239	22.0	63300	25.7
Ukrainian Catholic (a)	—	—	—	—	230	.5	3411	2.5	9195	5.1	—	—	16310	7.3	21936	9.3	19746	7.4	17555	7.1
United Church (b)	1491	18.7	5360	21.0	8041	19.0	17473	12.9	19328	10.8	50608	23.1	59917	27.0	65562	27.8	71330	26.9	53985	21.9
Other & No Religion	74	.9	1021	4.0	1126	2.7	8570	6.3	8148	4.6	13563	6.2	7112	3.2	12929	5.5	19498	7.3	32915	13.4
Totals	7985	100	25639	100	42340	100	136035	100	179087	100	218785	100	221960	100	235710	100	265429	100	246270	100

Notes: a) Included with Roman Catholics in 1931.

b) Includes Congregationalists and Methodists until 1931.

Source: *Censuses of Canada, 1881-1971.*

TABLE X
Age Composition of Winnipeg's Population, 1886-1971

Year	0 - 14	15 - 44	45 - 64	65 +	Total Population
1886	7,018(34.7%)	11,375(56.2%)	1,647 (8.1%)	194 (0.9%)	20,238
1891	8,734(34.1%)	14,348(56.0%)	2,252 (8.8%)	305 (1.1%)	25,639
1901	13,999(33.1%)	22,602(53.4%)	4,702(11.1%)	871 (2.0%)	42,340
1911	38,002(27.9%)	80,303(59.9%)	13,698(10.1%)	2,057 (1.5%)	136,035
1921	56,031(31.3%)	94,102(52.5%)	24,244(13.5%)	4,457 (2.5%)	179,087
1931	53,226(24.3%)	115,470(52.8%)	41,394(18.9%)	8,625 (3.9%)	218,785
1941	41,027(18.5%)	114,168(51.4%)	52,623(23.7%)	14,142 (6.4%)	221,960
1951	50,084(21.2%)	109,818(46.6%)	52,266(22.2%)	23,542(10.0%)	235,710
1961	69,014(26.0%)	112,650(42.4%)	55,436(20.9%)	29,329(11.0%)	265,429
1971	54,695(22.1%)	104,940(42.6%)	54,830(22.3%)	31,785(12.9%)	246,270

Source: *Censuses of Manitoba, 1885-86; Censuses of Canada, 1891-1971.*

TABLE XI
Population Growth in Winnipeg and Suburbs, 1901-1971

Suburbs	1901	1911	1921	1931	1941	1951	1961	1971
Assiniboia	357	681	1,024	2,032	1,968	2,663	6,088	— (e)
Charleswood	450	701	869	1,226	1,934	3,680	6,243	12,185
East Kildonan	563	1,488	6,379	9,047	8,350	13,144	27,305	30,150
Fort Garry	730	1,333	2,401	3,926	4,453	8,193	17,528	26,135
North Kildonan (a)	—	—	—	—	1,946	3,222	8,888	17,715
Old Kildonan (b)	—	—	—	—	704	869	1,327	1,865
St. Boniface	2,019	7,483	12,821	16,305	18,157	26,342	37,600	46,750
St. James	257	4,535	11,745	13,903	13,892	19,569	33,977	71,385
St. Vital	585	1,540	3,771	10,402	11,993	18,637	27,269	32,940
Transcona(c)	—	—	4,185	5,747	5,495	6,752	14,248	22,745
Tuxedo(d)	—	—	277	559	777	1,627	1,627	3,260
West Kildonan	668	1,767	4,641	6,132	6,110	10,754	20,077	24,080
Winnipeg	42,340	136,035	179,087	218,785	221,960	235,710	265,429	246,270

Notes:
a) Included with East Kildonan until 1941.
b) Included with West Kildonan until 1941.
c) Transcona incorporated in 1921.
d) Tuxedo incorporated in 1913.
e) Included with St. James.

Source: *The Metropolitan Development Plan* (Winnipeg, 1968); *Census of Canada, 1971.*

TABLE XII
Value of Building Permits Issued in Winnipeg, 1900-1970

Year	Value of Permits	Year	Value of Permits
	(in millions of dollars)		(in millions of dollars)
1900	1.4	1936	1.4
1902	2.4	1938	2.0
1904	9.7	1940	3.3
1906	12.6	1942	2.9
1908	5.5	1944	4.4
1910	15.1	1946	11.9
1912	20.6	1948	18.6
1914	1.9	1950	19.5
1916	2.3	1952	19.3
1918	2.0	1954	35.8
1920	8.1	1956	29.5
1922	6.6	1958	28.5
1924	3.1	1960	36.4
1926	10.4	1962	34.2
1928	10.5	1964	27.9
1930	6.6	1966	33.7
1932	2.1	1968	46.3
1934	.7	1970	41.5

Source: City of Winnipeg, Engineering Department; and City of Winnipeg, *Municipal Manuals.*

TABLE XIII
The Labour Force of Winnipeg by Industry, 1881-1961

Industry	1881	1921	1951	1961
Primary: agriculture, forestry, fishing, trapping & mining	23.5	1.7	1.1	.7
Manufacturing	24.2	16.9	25.2	20.2
Construction	4.8	7.3	6.0	6.3
Transportation and communication	3.6	15.8	12.4	13.2
Trade	14.9	21.7	23.4	20.5
Finance, insurance, real estate	2.2	6.0	4.9	5.2
Community, business and personal service	20.6	20.6	18.2	23.1
Government employees; all levels	1.2	4.8	6.6	8.2
Other or unspecified	5.0	5.2	2.3	2.6
	100%	100%	100%	100%
Total classified	5,029	74,067	109,227	116,077

Source: *Censuses of Canada, 1881-1961.*

TABLE XIV
Ethnic Origins of the Metropolitan Winnipeg Population, 1901-1971

Ethnic Group	1901	1911	1921	1931	1941	1951	1961	1971
Asian	.3	.4	.5	.4	.4	.6	.7	1.4
British	71.2	61.0	67.4	61.4	59.2	51.4	45.0	43.0
French	6.5	4.3	4.9	5.0	5.8	9.3	8.3	8.6
German	5.2	6.3	6.2	5.1	5.4	7.7	10.6	11.5
Italian	.3	.5	.7	.7	.7	.6	1.2	1.7
Jewish	2.6	6.2	6.5	6.0	6.0	5.1	3.9	3.4
Netherlands	.2	.4	.9	1.0	1.5	2.4	3.1	2.8
Polish	—	3.3	2.7	5.0	4.5	5.0	5.2	4.8
Russian	1.4	1.1	1.9	1.0	.9	.9	.9	.4
Scandinavian	7.5	3.5	3.3	3.8	4.0	3.7	3.8	3.2
Ukrainian	—	2.5	3.1	7.3	9.1	11.2	11.3	11.9
Others	4.8	10.5	1.9	3.3	2.5	2.1	6.0	7.3
Totals	100.0%	100.0%	100.0%	100.0%	100.0%	100.0%	100.0%	100.0%

Source: *Censuses of Canada, 1901-1971.*

TABLE XV
Class Politics in Winnipeg: Citizens' Groups

1919	Citizens' Committee of One Thousand
1919-1921	The Citizens' League of Winnipeg
1922	Citizens' Campaign Committee
1923-1924	The Winnipeg Better Civic Government Association (Winnipeg Civics Association)
1925-1928	No overt organization
1929-1932	Civic Progress Association
1932-1935	No overt organization
1936-1959	Winnipeg Election Committee
1960-1965	Civic Election Committee
1966-1971	Greater Winnipeg Election Committee
1971-	Independent Citizens' Election Committee

Notes
INTRODUCTION

[1]The history of Manitoba during the years prior to 1870 has been the subject of numerous books and articles. The standard work is W. L. Morton, *Manitoba: A History* (Toronto, 1957). Some of the more important specialized studies are: A. S. Morton, *A History of the Canadian West to 1870-71* (Toronto, 1939); J. M. Gray, *Lord Selkirk of Red River* (Toronto, 1963); E. E. Rich, *The Fur Trade and the Northwest to 1857* (Toronto, 1967); A. C. Gluek, *Minnesota and the Manifest Destiny of the Canadian Northwest* (Toronto, 1965); and G.F.G. Stanley, *The Birth of Western Canada* (Toronto, 1960), pp. 1-74. See also H. C. Klassen, "The Red River Settlement and the St. Paul Route, 1859-1870," unpublished M.A. thesis, University of Manitoba, 1963; A. M. Henderson, "From Fort Douglas to the Forks," *Historical and Scientific Society of Manitoba Transactions*, Series III, No. 23 (1966-67), pp. 15-32; and Alan F. J. Artibise, "The Crucial Decade: Red River at the Outbreak of the American Civil War," *ibid.*, pp. 59-66. To avoid confusion in the following pages the use of several terms must be explained. Prior to 1862 there were two distinct groups of buildings within the borders of present-day Winnipeg. The homes and farms of a few original Selkirk settlers were located on Point Douglas. To the south, at the confluence of the Red and Assiniboine Rivers, was located the Hudson's Bay Company post of Upper Fort Garry. See the map and account of the establishment of Fort Douglas and Upper Fort Garry in G. Bryce, "The Five Forts of Winnipeg," *Transactions of the Royal Society of Canada*, Volume III, Section II, 1885, pp. 135-145. These two "settlements," however, made up only a part of the larger "Red River Colony." Up and down the Red River and along the banks of the Assiniboine were located the river lot farms of Scottish, French, and Métis settlers. A good map of the entire Red River Colony is contained in Morton, *Manitoba*, p. 89. Thus, when reference is made to the Red River Colony, it is meant to include more than just Upper Fort Garry and Point Douglas.

[2]For general accounts of the Seven Oaks Massacre see Morton, *Manitoba*, pp. 53-55; and James A. Jackson, *The Centennial History of Manitoba* (Toronto, 1970), pp. 49-51. A more detailed account can be found in Mar-

garet MacLeod and W. L. Morton, *Cuthbert Grant of Grantown: Warden of the Plains of Red River* (Toronto, 1974), pp. 38-72.

[3]For accounts of the 1826 flood see Edith Patterson, *Tales of Early Manitoba* (Winnipeg, 1970), pp. 19-20; J. W. Chafe, *Extraordinary Tales from Manitoba History* (Toronto, 1973), pp. 54-55; and S. P. Matheson, "Floods at Red River: Some Tales of the Great Inundations of 1826, 1852, and 1861," *Historical and Scientific Society of Manitoba Transactions*, Series III, No. 3 (1947), pp. 5-13.

[4]Robert B. Hill, *Manitoba: History of Its Early Settlement, Development and Resources* (Toronto, 1890), pp. 98-99.

[5]Morton, *Manitoba*, Chapter 4. See also Frits Pannekoek, "A Probe Into the Demographic Structure of Nineteenth Century Red River," in Lewis H. Thomas, ed., *Essays on Western History* (Edmonton, 1976), pp. 83-95.

[6]J. P. Prichett, *The Red River Valley* (Toronto, 1942), pp. 254-255.

[7]Morton, *Manitoba*, pp. 77-78.

[8]Artibise, "The Crucial Decade."

[9]Joseph Howard, *Strange Empire: Louis Riel and the Métis People* (Toronto, 1974), pp. 39-45.

[10]J. Steen and W. Bryce, *Winnipeg, Manitoba and Her Industries* (Winnipeg, 1882), pp. 8-10; and William Douglas, "The Forks Becomes a City," *Historical and Scientific Society of Manitoba Transactions*, Series III, No. 1 (1944-45), pp. 73-75.

[11]G. F. Reynolds, "The Man Who Created the Corner of Portage and Main (Henry McKenney)," *Historical and Scientific Society of Manitoba Transactions*, Series III, No. 26 (1969-1970), pp. 5-40.

[12]Margaret McWilliams, *Manitoba Milestones* (Toronto, 1928), pp. 88-89.

[13]There is little record of the growth of Winnipeg between 1863 and 1870. See, however, Steen and Bryce, *Winnipeg and Her Industries*; Douglas, "The Forks Becomes a City," pp. 73-75; Reynolds, "The Man Who Created the Corner of Portage and Main"; and George Bryce, "The Illustrated History of Winnipeg," Chapter XIII. The latter source is a series of forty arti-

cles that were run in the Saturday editions of the *Manitoba Free Press* during 1905. Also useful, particularly for the maps of Winnipeg in 1869 and 1872, is H. A. Hosse, "The Areal Growth and Functional Development of Winnipeg from 1870 to 1913," unpublished M.A. thesis, University of Manitoba, 1956.

[14]W. J. Healy, *Winnipeg's Early Days: A Short Historical Sketch* (Winnipeg, 1927), pp. 14-15.

[15]George Young, *Manitoba Memories* (Toronto, 1897), pp. 63-64.

[16]Morton, *Manitoba*, p. 166.

[17]*Ibid.,*pp. 165-173. See also A. Begg and W. R. Nursey, *Ten Years in Winnipeg* (Winnipeg, 1879), Chapters I to IV; R. C. Bellan, "The Development of Winnipeg as a Metropolitan Centre," unpublished Ph. D. thesis, Columbia University, 1958, pp. 19-22; and *Manitoba Free Press*, 9 Nov. 1872 and 30 Nov. 1872.

[18]A short history of almost all merchants in Winnipeg in 1880 is contained in both Steen and Bryce, *Winnipeg and Her Industries*; and W. T. Thompson and E. E. Boyer, *The City of Winnipeg* (Winnipeg, 1886).

[19]*Ibid,*; and Morton, *Manitoba*, pp. 167-168.

[20]Bryce, "History of Winnipeg," Chapter XXII; Steen and Boyce, *Winnipeg and Her Industries*, pp. 17-42; and Morton, *Manitoba*, p. 168. The stories of Winnipeggers who made fortunes in real estate are numerous. For one example see Thompson and Boyer, *The City of Winnipeg*, pp. 26-28.

[21]A. D. Phillips, "The Development of Municipal Institutions in Manitoba to 1886", unpublished M.A. thesis, University of Manitoba, 1948, Part II, Chapter I.

[22]Begg and Nursey, *Ten Years in Winnipeg*, p. 52. See also, Bryce, "History of Winnipeg," Chapter XX.

[23]Begg and Nursey, *Ten Years in Winnipeg*, p. 53.

[24]*Ibid.*, pp. 55-56. See also J. H. O'Donnell, *Manitoba As I Saw It* (Winnipeg, 1909), pp. 73-76.

[25]There is no evidence available to suggest that this view was a mistaken one for there is no reason why the Legislature should have refused Winnipeg's request. Unless, of course, members representing other incipient "commercial emporia" felt, as Begg did, that incorporation was the key to rapid progress.

[26]Bryce, "History of Winnipeg," Chapter XX; Begg and Nursey, *Ten Years in Winnipeg*, p. 53; *The Manitoba Gazette and Trade Review*, 4 May 1872; Healy, *Winnipeg's Early Days*, p. 25; *Manitoba Free Press*, 14 Dec. 1872; and Hill, *Manitoba*, p. 517.

The Hudson's Bay Company and the four other property owners had good reason to oppose incorporation. In 1874 the assessment on these properties was as follows: H.B.C. - $595,312; Bannatyne - $84,225; McDer-

mott - $78,876; Macaulay - $44,500; and Alexander Logan - $53,000. See Thompson and Boyer, *The City of Winnipeg*, p. 19.

[27]See, for example, *The Manitoban*, 8 April 1872.

[28]*Ibid.*, 15 March 1873; Bryce, "History of Winnipeg," Chapter XX.

[29]*Manitoba Free Press*, 8 March 1873. Manitoba at this time had an appointed Upper House of seven members and an elected assembly of twenty-four.

[30]Begg and Nursey, *Ten Years in Winnipeg*, pp. 80-81.

[31]*The Manitoban*, 8 March 1873; *Statutes of Manitoba*, 1873, Chapter 7; and *Manitoba Free Press*, 15 November 1873.

[32]*Manitoba Free Press*, 25 Oct. 1873. See also *ibid.*, 22 July 1874 in which Winnipeg's incorporation is referred to as "an event of importance and will be hereafter looked upon as a noteworthy landmark in the path of British American progress."

[33]For a more detailed discussion of Ontario influences on Manitoba's municipal development see Phillips, "The Development of Municipal Institutions." It should be noted that the Bill of Incorporation was framed by Francis Evan Cornish, Winnipeg's first mayor. Cornish was a lawyer who received his training in Ontario.

[34]From the date of incorporation in November 1873 until 1886 the government of Winnipeg was carried on under the powers of a special charter of incorporation granted by the provincial legislature. In the latter year this special charter was repealed, and from that time until 1902 the city's affairs were administered under the provisions of the Manitoba Municipal and Assessment Acts. In practice this change signified no reduction in the city's powers. In 1902 the city again obtained a special charter, which arrangement lasted until the present day.

[35]*The Manitoban*, 7 Feb. 1874 and 14 Feb. 1874.

[36]Begg and Nursey, *Ten Years in Winnipeg*, pp. 110-111.

[37]*Ibid.*, p. 101; *The Manitoban*, 28 Feb. 1874.

CHAPTER ONE

[1]Healy, *Winnipeg's Early Days*, p. 21.

[2]Good accounts of the difficulties encountered on the Dawson Road and the American route can be found in Pierre Berton, *The National Dream: The Great Railway, 1871-1881* (Toronto, 1970), pp. 52-58; and M. Fitzgibbon, *A Trip to Manitoba* (Toronto, 1880). See also C. M. Studness, "Economic Opportunity and the Westward Migration of Canadians During the Late Nineteenth Century," *Canadian Journal of Economics and Political Science*, Vol. XXX (1964), pp. 570-584.

[3]For detailed accounts of Winnipeg's efforts to obtain railways see R.

Bellan, "Rails Across the Red: Selkirk or Winnipeg," *Historical and Scientific Society of Manitoba Transactions*, Series III, No. 18 (1961-62), pp. 69-77. See also Alan F. J. Artibise, *Winnipeg: A Social History of Urban Growth, 1874-1914* (Montreal, 1975), Chapter 4.

[4]Although Morris was not elected, he did receive a majority of the votes cast in Winnipeg. See *ibid*, p. 330.

[5]Good accounts of the boom can be found in J. Macoun, *Manitoba and the Great Northwest* (Guelph, 1882), Chapter 27; Healy, *Winnipeg's Early Days*, pp. 22-25; Pierre Berton, *The Last Spike: The Great Railway, 1881-1885* (Toronto, 1971), pp. 52-58; and J. Gray, *Booze* (Toronto 1972), pp. 3-19.

[6]Thompson and Boyer, *The City of Winnipeg*, pp. 26-28.

[7]Chafe, *Tales from Manitoba History*, p. 117.

[8]*Ibid.*, p. 118; Healy, *Winnipeg's Early Days*, p. 23.

[9]A. V. Thomas, "The Weight of a New Broom," *Canada Monthly*, Vol. XVI, No. 2 (June 1914), p. 91.

[10]K. H. Norrie, "The Rate of Settlement of the Canadian Prairies, 1870-1911," *Journal of Economic History*, Vol. XXXV (June 1975), pp. 410-427.

[11]During this period of development in western Canada, urban centres were service centres for the agricultural sector. See P. A. Phillips, "Structural Change and Population Distribution in the Prairie Region: 1911 to 1961," unpublished M.A. thesis, University of Saskatchewan, 1963, pp. 11-13.

[12]J. M. S. Careless, "The Development of the Winnipeg Business Community," *Transactions of the Royal Society of Canada*, 1970, 4th Series, pp. 239-254.

[13]For a complete listing of railways built through, from, or to Winnipeg up to 1931, see M. L. Bladen, "Construction of Railways in Canada to the Year 1885," *Contributions to Canadian Economics*, Vol. V. (1932), pp. 43-60; and Bladen, "Construction of Railways in Canada From 1885 to 1931," *ibid.*, Vol. VII (1934), pp. 82-107.

[14]For a detailed discussion of these and other concessions see W. T. Jackman, *Economic Principles of Transportation* (Toronto, 1935).

[15]General discussions of Winnipeg's economic development in this period can be found in the following: Bellan, "The Development of Winnipeg"; J.M.S. Careless, "Aspects of Urban Life in the West — 1870-1914," in Gilbert A. Stelter and Alan F. J. Artibise, eds., *The Canadian City: Essays in Urban History* (Toronto, 1977), pp. 125-141; R. Schmidt, "Winnipeg as a Transportation Centre," in T. Kuz, ed., *Winnipeg, 1874-1974: Progress and Prospects* (Winnipeg, 1974), pp. 211-225. The annual reports of the Winnipeg Board of Trade, found in the Provincial Archives of Manitoba, also contain a great wealth of material.

[16]G. F. Parsons, "Winnipeg As a Financial Centre," in Kuz, *Winnipeg*, pp. 189-210.

[17]Peter C. Newman, *The Canadian Establishment*, Vol. 1 (Toronto, 1975), p. 210. See also *The Financial Post*, Dec. 4 and 11, 1976.

[18]Bellan, "The Development of Winnipeg," pp. 142-143; C. W. Parker, ed., *Who's Who in Western Canada, 1911* (Vancouver 1911), p. 103.

[19]Bellan, "The Development of Winnipeg," Chapters 4-7; and Parsons, "Winnipeg As a Financial Centre."

[20]Alan F. J. Artibise, "Advertising Winnipeg: The Campaign for Immigrants and Industry, 1874-1914," *Historical and Scientific Society of Manitoba Transactions*, Series III, No. 27 (1970-71), pp. 75-106.

[21]Artibise, *Winnipeg*, p. 123.

[22]*Ibid.*, p. 124.

[23]*Ibid.*

[24]R. C. Bellan, "Relief in Winnipeg: The Economic Background," unpublished M.A. thesis, University of Toronto, 1941, pp. 46-47.

[25]K. McNaught and D. J. Bercuson, *The Winnipeg Strike: 1919* (Don Mills, 1974), p. 6.

[26]*Ibid.*, See also D. J. Bercuson, *Confrontation at Winnipeg: Labour, Industrial Relations and the General Strike* (Montreal, 1974), Chapter I.

[27]G. MacInnis, *J. S. Woodsworth: A Man to Remember* (Toronto, 1953), pp. 81-83. See also *Manitoba Free Press*, 23 Oct. 1911; and Bercuson, *Confrontation at Winnipeg*, pp. 19-20.

[28]P. Voisey, "The Urbanization of the Canadian Prairies, 1871-1916," *Histoire sociale/Social History*, Vol. VIII, No. 15 (May 1975), pp. 77-101.

[29]It must be noted that not all Winnipeggers consistently or enthusiastically supported immigration. Organized labour tended to look upon immigrants as cheap labour and their recruitment as a plot by the commercial elite to reduce wages. See, for example, *The Voice*, 24 Jan. 1902 and 23 April 1903.

[30]The word "foreign" refers to those residents of Winnipeg who were not born in either Canada or Great Britain and whose origin was other than British. While this usage is not strictly accurate — persons born in Britain are also "foreigners" — it does correspond to the manner in which the word was used in Winnipeg until the 1960s.

[31]A detailed discussion of natural increase, infant mortality, and health facilities in Winnipeg can be found in Artibise, *Winnipeg*.

[32]Between 1881 and 1911, Manitoba grew at an average rate of 98 per cent per decade. Winnipeg grew at an average rate of 169 per cent per decade.

[33]A table showing the population of Canadian cities and their rank by size for the period 1871-1921 can be found in Artibise, *Winnipeg*, p. 132.

[34]Artibise, "Advertising Winnipeg." See also H. Troper, *Only Farmers Need Apply: Official Canadian Government Encouragement of Immigration from the*

United States, 1896-1911 (Toronto, 1972).

[35]A useful analysis of the Manitoba experience that follows the model put forward by Louis Hartz in *The Founding of New Societies* (New York, 1964) is J. E. Rea, "The Roots of Prairie Society," in D. P. Gagan, ed., *Prairie Perspectives* (Toronto, 1970), pp. 46-55.

[36]A. Smith, "Metaphor and Nationality in North America", *Canadian Historical Review*, Vol. LI, No. 3 (September 1970), pp. 247-275.

[37]John Marlyn, *Under the Ribs of Death* (Toronto, 1957), p. 24.

[38]Rea, "Roots of Prairie Society," p. 51. See also G. F. Chapman, "Winnipeg: The Melting Pot," *The Canadian Magazine*, Vol. XXXIII, No. 5 (September 1909), pp. 409-416; and Chapman, "Winnipeg: The Refining Process," *ibid.*, No. 6 (October 1909), pp. 548-554.

[39]*Town Topics*, 17 July 1899.

[40]See Bellan, "Relief in Winnipeg," pp. 46-62.

[41]The cities with which Winnipeg was compared were: Halifax, Saint John, Quebec, Montreal, Toronto, London, Hamilton, Ottawa, Regina, Saskatoon, Edmonton, Calgary, Vancouver and Victoria.

[42]Rea, "Roots of Prairie Society," pp. 51-52. See also John H. Thompson, "The Prohibition Question in Manitoba, 1892-1928," unpublished M.A. thesis, University of Manitoba, 1969.

[43]*Manitoba Free Press*, 1 March 1913; and Chapman, "Winnipeg: The Melting Pot," p. 413.

[44]*Winnipeg Telegram*, 13 May 1901.

[45]*Manitoba Free Press*, 7 December 1912.

[46]"Public School Education in Winnipeg," *Souvenir of Winnipeg's Diamond Jubilee, 1874-1924* (Winnipeg, 1924), p. 65. See also F. Gonick, "Manitoba Public Educational Institution as an Inculcator of Social Values, 1910-1930," unpublished paper in possession of author.

[47]Enrolment jumped from 7,500 in 1900 to 25,814 by 1914. See Artibise, *Winnipeg*, p. 200.

[48]W. J. Sisler, *Peaceful Invasion* (Winnipeg, 1944), pp. 19-20.

[49]*Ibid.*, pp. 69-70. See also W. G. Pearce, *Winnipeg School Days* (Manitoba Archives, 1951), pp. 24-25; and J. W. Chafe, *An Apple for the Teacher: A Centennial History of the Winnipeg School Division* (Winnipeg, 1967), pp. 65-66.

[50]See, for example, H. Herstein, "The Growth of the Winnipeg Jewish Community and the Evolution of its Educational Institutions," *Historical and Scientific Society of Manitoba Transactions*, Series III, No. 22 (1966-67), pp. 27-66; V. Turek, *The Poles in Manitoba* (Toronto, 1967), Chapters VII-IX; and M. H. Marunchak, *The Ukrainian Canadians: A History* (Winnipeg, 1970), pp. 151-153 and *passim*.

[51]Unfortunately, the Manitoba School Question is far too complicated to detail here. See L. Clark, ed., *The Manitoba School Question* (Toronto, 1968).

It contains a good bibliography.

[52]The Compromise of 1897 provided that "when pupils in any school spoke French or any language other than English, the teaching of this was to be in French, or other such language, and English upon the bilingual system." Morton, *Manitoba*, p. 271. It is important to note that Manitoba's school system had originally been bilingual but the "British had succeeded in 1890 in replacing existing legislation with an act that called for unilingual (English) schools. It was this 1890 legislation that was changed by the Compromise of 1897. See Artibise, *Winnipeg*, Chapter II.

[53]M. Donnelly, *Dafoe of the Free Press* (Toronto, 1968), p. 57 and *passim*. In the period 1911-1915, Dafoe published a series of sixty-four articles on the education question in the pages of the *Manitoba Free Press*.

[54]Turek, *Poles in Manitoba*, p. 220. See also J. H. Syrnick, "Community Builders: Early Ukrainian Teachers," *Historical and Scientific Society of Manitoba Transactions*, Series III, No. 21 (1965), pp. 25-34.

[55]*Winnipeg Tribune*, 22 August 1908. For other representative opinions on behalf of the charter group see *ibid.*, 27 June 1912; and *Manitoba Free Press*, 20 May 1909 and 8 December 1913.

[56]*Ibid.*, 12 June 1909.

[57]*Winnipeg Tribune*, 20 May 1909.

[58]See L. Orlikow, "A Survey of the Reform Movement in Manitoba, 1910-1920," unpublished M.A. thesis, University of Manitoba, 1958, for a detailed discussion of Manitoba politics during this period.

[59]See T. Petersen, "Ethnic and Class Politics in Manitoba," in M. Robin, ed., *Canadian Provincial Politics: The Party Systems of the Ten Provinces* (Scarborough, 1972), pp. 69-115.

[60]Jackson, *Centennial History of Manitoba*, p. 173. The Children's Act had some serious shortcomings. No child could be forced to attend school unless he was a "neglected child" whose parents ignored their "moral duties" in raising him. Only parents who contributed to "juvenile delinquency" could be prosecuted. Finally, any child apprehended had to be treated, under the provisions of the law, in the same manner as criminals, thus tempting the truant officers to ignore rather than arrest young offenders. In short, despite Premier Roblin's statements that the act was an effective alternative to a compulsory attendance law, it was only barely enforced in Winnipeg and not at all in rural areas.

[61]Morton, *Manitoba*, pp. 311-312. The ethnic minorities, particularly the Ukrainians and French, were opposed not only to the abolition of the bilingual clause but also to compulsory attendance legislation. The former were used to having sons and daughters help earn the family living, while the French were afraid such legislation would lead to "godless" institutions. Moreover, the lack of an attendance law meant that any changes in

the school laws that were obnoxious could be resisted, at the expense of the children, by refusing to allow them to attend school.

[62]See R. D. Fromson, "Acculturation or Assimilation: A Geographic Analysis of Residential Segregation of Selected Ethnic Groups: Metropolitan Winnipeg, 1951-1961," unpublished M.A. thesis, University of Manitoba, 1965.

[63]Bellan, "The Development of Winnipeg," pp. 71-227.

[64]Artibise, *Winnipeg*, Appendix D, pp. 308-319.

[65]*Ibid.*, Chapters 10-13.

[66]*Ibid.*, Chapter 7 and *passim*.

[67]In 1911, for example, when Winnipeg had only 1.5 per cent of its population in the 65 and over age group, only Calgary, Regina, and Edmonton had a lower percentage. The percentages for other cities are as follows: Montreal, 3.2 per cent; Toronto, 3.3 per cent; Vancouver 1.7 per cent; Ottawa, 3.9 per cent; Hamilton, 4.0 per cent; Quebec, 5.0 per cent; Halifax, 4.9 per cent; London, 5.7 per cent; Calgary, 1.1 per cent; Saint John, 5.7 per cent; Victoria, 3.2 per cent; Regina, 0.7 per cent; and Edmonton, 1.2 per cent. Figures are not available for Saskatoon. A good discussion of the implications of the age distribution of the population can be found in C. B. Davidson, H. C. Grant, and F. Shefrin, *The Population of Manitoba* (Winnipeg, 1938), pp. 78-92 and *passim*.

[68]Between 1901 and 1911, for example, the age group 0-14 grew by 58.3 per cent, while the age group 15-44 grew by only 39.1 per cent. The other age groups, 45-64 and 65+ also grew at a faster rate than did the 15-44 group. The increase for the 45-64 group was 52.7 per cent over the period 1901-1911; for the 65 and over group it was 73.4 per cent. In short, all three groups that were in some sense more dependent on the community than the 15-44 group increased during this crucial period at a faster rate, causing severe strains on Winnipeg's already inadequate social and educational facilities.

[69]Artibise, *Winnipeg*, Chapters 10 and 11. A good survey of the various ethnic newspapers in Winnipeg during this period is Canada Press Club, *The Multilingual Press in Manitoba* (Winnipeg, 1974).

[70]See, for example, H. Herstein, "The Growth of the Winnipeg Jewish Community"; Turek, *Poles in Manitoba*; and S. Belkin, *Through Narrow Gates: A Review of Jewish Immigration, Colonization and Immigrant Aid Work in Canada, 1849-1940* (Montreal, 1966).

[71]D. McArton, "75 Years in Winnipeg's Social History," *Canadian Welfare*, Volume 25 (October, 1949), pp. 11-19.

[72]For discussions of the work of the Margaret Scott Nursing Mission see Artibise, *Winnipeg*, Chapter 10; H. Macvicar, *The Story of the Mission* (Winnipeg, 1939); and K. Pettipas, "Margaret Scott and the Margaret Scott Nursing Mission, 1904-1943" (Manitoba Archives, unpublished paper, 1970).

[73]For discussions of All People's Mission see Artibise, *Winnipeg*, Chapter 10; K. McNaught, *A Prophet in Politics: A Biography of J. S. Woodsworth* (Toronto, 1959); and G. N. Emery, "The Methodist Church and the 'European Foreigners' of Winnipeg: The All Peoples Mission, 1889-1914", *Historical and Scientific Society of Manitoba Transactions*, Series III, No. 28 (1971-1972), pp. 85-100.

[74]These factors are very apparent when early maps of the Winnipeg area are compared to later ones. See Alan F. J. Artibise and Edward H. Dahl, *Winnipeg in Maps/Winnipeg par les cartes, 1816-1972* (Ottowa, 1975).

[75]Reynolds, "Man Who Created the Corner of Portage and Main," pp. 21-22.

[76]Henderson, "From Fort Douglas to the Forks," pp. 15-32.

[77]Begg and Nursey, *Ten Years in Winnipeg*, p. 118.

[78]Chafe, *Tales From Manitoba History*, pp. 105-107.

[79]Begg and Nursey, *Ten Years in Winnipeg*, p. 77.

[80]H. A. Hosse, "The Areal Growth and Functional Development of Winnipeg, 1870-1913," pp. 85-86.

[81]*Ibid.*, p. 118.

[82]*Henderson's Directory of Winnipeg*, 1901. See also R. Rostecki, "The Rise and Fall of Winnipeg's Old Business District," *Heritage Canada*, Vol. 2, No. 3 (Summer 1976), pp. 28-31.

[83]*Manitoba Free Press*, 20 Dec. 1910.

[84]Rostecki, "Winnipeg's Old Business District," pp. 29-30.

[85]Gray, *Boy From Winnipeg*; and Gray, *Booze*.

[86]George H. Ham, *Reminiscences of a Raconteur* (Toronto, 1921), pp. 53-55.

[87]Artibise, *Winnipeg*, Chapter 9.

[88]Marlyn, *Under the Ribs of Death*, p.11.

[89]"Tide of Winnipeg's Population Pouring Northward," *The Dominion*, Vol. 4, No. 1 (October 1912), pp. 13-14.

[90]See, for example, City of Winnipeg Urban Renewal and Rehabilitation Board, *Urban Renewal Study No. 5: Selkirk Avenue-CPR Yards-Salter Street-Main Street* (Winnipeg, n.d.).

[91]Artibise, *Winnipeg*, Chapter 13.

[92]Sisler, *Peaceful Invasion*, p. 13.

[93]*Annual Reports* of the Winnipeg Electric Railway Company, 1910-1915. See also Blake, *The Era of Streetcars in Winnipeg, 1881-1955* (Winnipeg, 1971).

[94]The development of Winnipeg's street railway system was particularly important in facilitating the dispersal of population into the municipalities surrounding Winnipeg. See Blake, *The Era of Streetcars in Winnipeg*; and Blake, *The Era Interurbans in Winnipeg, 1902-1939* (Winnipeg, 1971).

[95]*Manitoba Free Press*, 20 June 1903.

[96]Gray, *Boy From Winnipeg*, pp. 119-120.

[97]Artibise, *Winnipeg*, Chapter 9.

[98]*Manitoba Free Press*, 6 Nov. 1909.

[99]Artibise, *Winnipeg*, Chapter 9.

[100]For a fuller account of St. James' Development see M. M. Ferguson, *A History of St. James* (Winnipeg, 1967).

[101]Paterson, *Tales of Early Manitoba*, pp. 72-74.

[102]*Pioneers and Early Citizens of Manitoba* (Winnipeg, 1971), pp. 56-57.

[103]Chafe, *Tales From Manitoba History*, p. 107.

[104]Paterson, *Tales of Early Manitoba*, pp. 78-79.

[105]*Ibid.*, p. 78; Begg and Nursey, *Ten Years in Winnipeg*, pp. 127-128, 137. See also Alan F. J. Artibise, "Winnipeg's City Halls, 1876-1965," *Manitoba Pageant*, Vol. XXII, No. 3 (Spring 1977), pp. 5-10.

[106]G. B. Brooks, *Plain Facts About the New City Hall* (Winnipeg, 1884), p. 3.

[107]See, for example, Charles R. Tuttle, *A History of the Corporation of Winnipeg Giving An Account of the Present Civic Crisis . . .* (Winnipeg, 1883).

[108]John W. Graham, *Winnipeg Architecture, 1831-1960* (Winnipeg, 1960), p. 12.

[109]Hill, *Manitoba*, pp. 527-528.

[110]Paul H. T. Thorlakson, "A Chapter of Manitoba's History," *The Winnipeg Clinic Quarterly*, Vol. XXIII (1970), pp. 45-47.

[111]Morton, *Manitoba*, p. 173.

[112]Careless, "Winnipeg Business Community."

[113]Artibise, *Winnipeg*, p. 200.

[114]Careless, "Winnipeg Business Community"; Artibise, *Winnipeg*, Chapters 2 and 3.

[115]*Winnipeg Times*, 16 April 1883.

[116]*Manitoba Free Press*, 12 Nov. 1884. See also Artibise, *Winnipeg*, Chapter 3; and Alan F. J. Artibise, "Mayor Alexander Logan of Winnipeg," *Beaver*, Outfit 304: 4 (Spring 1974), pp. 4-12.

[117]*Manitoba Free Press*, 12 Dec. 1884.

[118]*Ibid.*, 10 Nov. 1884.

[119]See, for example, Guy Bourassa, "The Political Elite of Montreal: From Aristocracy to Democracy," in L. D. Feldman and M. D. Goldrick, eds., *Politics and Government of Urban Canada* (Toronto, 1969), pp. 124-133.

[120]Artibise, *Winnipeg*, Chapter 2.

[121]Artibise, *Ibid.*, p. 124.

[122]*The Clubs, Societies and Associations of Winnipeg* (Winnipeg, 1908), *passim*.

[123]Artibise, *Winnipeg*, pp. 30-31.

[124]See, for example, Bercuson, *Confrontation at Winnipeg*, Chapter 1.

[125]*Winnipeg Telegram*, 28 January 1914.

[126]Morton, *Manitoba*, p. 304.

[127]For detailed accounts of Winnipeg's health problems see Artibise, *Winnipeg*, Chapters 10, 12 and 13.

[128]Province of Manitoba, *Sessional Papers*, 1905, No. 10, pp. 368-371.

[129]*Winnipeg Times*, 6 April 1883. The clergy did get wind of the arrangement in 1910. One result was the appointment of a "Royal Commission on Charges Re: Vice and of Graft Against the Police." This report contains details of the segregation arrangement. The report, along with ten volumes of evidence, is in the Provincial Library of Manitoba, Winnipeg.

[130]*Toronto Globe*, 12 November 1910.

[131]L. Orlikow, "Reform Movement in Manitoba, p. 30. See also Joy Cooper, "Red Lights of Winnipeg," *Historical and Scientific Society of Manitoba Transactions*, Series III, No. 27 (1970-1971), pp. 61-74.

[132]See Richard Allen, *The Social Passion: Religion and Social Reform in Canada, 1914-28* (Toronto, 1971).

[133]Frederick Beal DuVal was born in Maryland and educated at Princeton University and the Princeton Theological Seminary. After serving as a minister in the United States from 1875 to 1888 he came to Winnipeg to become pastor of Knox Presbyterian Church. He served in this capacity for over twenty years and in 1908 had become moderator of the Presbyterian Church of Canada. This was preceded by his chairmanship of the Winnipeg Ministerial Association in 1902. Prior to his authorship of this pamphlet, he had been deeply involved in previous campaigns to rid Winnipeg of prostitution. See Parker, *Who's Who in Western Canada*, p. 167; and Gray, *Red Lights on the Prairies* (Toronto, 1971), p. 35.

[134]*Manitoba Free Press*, 12 November 1910.

[135]*Winnipeg Telegram*, 17 and 18 November 1910.

[136]*Manitoba Free Press*, 5 December 1910.

[137]*Ibid.* See also *Winnipeg Telegram*, 13 December 1910.

[138]Gray, *Red Lights on the Prairies*, pp. 56-57.

CHAPTER TWO

[1]Phillips, "Prairie Region," pp. 26-27 and *passim*.

[2]The best account of the background to the strike can be found in Bercuson, *Confrontation at Winnipeg*. On the strike itself see *ibid.*; D. C. Masters, *The Winnipeg General Strike* (Toronto, 1957); Norman Penner, ed., *Winnipeg 1919: The Strikers' Own History of the Winnipeg General Strike* (Toronto, 1973); J. E. Rea, ed., *The Winnipeg General Strike:* (Toronto, 1973); and K. McNaught and D. J. Bercuson, *The Winnipeg Strike: 1919* (Don Mills, 1974). The McNaught and Bercuson study has a very good chapter dealing with "pivotal interpretations of the Winnipeg General Strike." The account of

the strike given here relies heavily on these sources.

³D. J. Bercuson, *1919: A Year of Strikes* (Ottawa, 1974), p. 2.

⁴Bercuson, *Confrontation at Winnipeg*, p. 62.

⁵Rea, *The Winnipeg General Strike*, pp. 5-6.

⁶Lloyd Stinson, *Political Warriors: Recollections of a Social Democrat* (Winnipeg, 1975), p. 224.

⁷H. C. Pentland, "Fifty Years After," *Canadian Dimension*, Vol. 6, No. 2 (July 1969), p. 16.

⁸D. J. Bercuson, "The Winnipeg General Strike," in I. Abella, ed., *On Strike: Six Key Labour Struggles in Canada, 1919-1949* (Toronto, 1974), p. 21 and *passim*.

⁹Bellan, "The Development of Winnipeg," Chapters 11 and 12; and T. C. Knight, *Economic Survey of Manitoba: Report to Provincial Legislature*, Volumes I and II (Winnipeg, 1938).

¹⁰During this period Winnipeg was by far the most important manufacturing centre in the prairie region. See Phillips, "Prairie Region," pp. 61 and *passim*.

¹¹*Royal Commission on Municipal Finances and Administration of the City of Winnipeg* (Winnipeg, 1939), pp. 3-10. See also Morton, *Manitoba*, Chapter 16.

¹²See Greater Winnipeg Board of Trade, *Annual Report for 1925*; J.N.T. Bulman, *The Industrial Development Board of Manitoba, 1925-1943* (Winnipeg, 1944).

¹³Morton, *Manitoba*, pp. 394, 465; Chafe, *Tales From Manitoba History*, pp. 158-159.

¹⁴For a detailed discussion see W. T. Jackman, *Economic Principles of Transportation* (Toronto, 1935).

¹⁵Bellan, "The Development of Winnipeg," p. 349.

¹⁶R. B. Short, "The Wholesale Function in Winnipeg," unpublished M.A. thesis, University of Manitoba, 1973, pp. 54-64.

¹⁷For discussions of the problems of retailers see Bellan, "The Development of Winnipeg," pp. 366-367; and Knight, *Economic Survey of Manitoba*, Volume II, pp. 192-199.

¹⁸R. C. Bellan, "Relief in Winnipeg;" and City of Winnipeg, *Report of the Joint Special Committee on Housing Conditions and Special Committee on Unemployment and Relief Works* (Winnipeg, 1938).

¹⁹City of Winnipeg, *Submission to Royal Commission on Dominion-Provincial Relations* (Winnipeg, 1937).

²⁰*Royal Commission on Municipal Finances and Administration of City of Winnipeg*, pp. 3-10.

²¹See, for example, J. McLennan, "Greater Winnipeg Industrial Expansion," *The Winnipeg Actimist*, June 1948, pp. 10, 42-43.

²²Industrial Development Board of Manitoba, *Annual Report for 1936*.

²³See "Winnipeg's Growing Clothing Industry," *The Winnipeg Actimist*, March 1936, pp.3-4.

²⁴The defeat of the provincial Conservative government of Premier R. Roblin in 1915 by the Liberals also added to the problem. Roblin had long relied on the ethnic vote for support while the Liberals, led by T. C. Norris, promised to accelerate assimilation of non-British groups. See Peterson, "Ethnic and Class Politics in Manitoba," pp. 69-115. Furthermore, in the years after 1916, both the Liberal and Conservative parties began to decline as effective forces. Since both had acted in their quest for political power "as bonds of society and agents of assimilation," their decline added to the general sense of malaise during this period. See Morton, *Manitoba*, p. 361.

²⁵For the period 1914-1920 see especially Morris K. Mott, "The 'Foreign Peril': Nativism in Winnipeg, 1916-1923," unpublished M.A. thesis, University of Manitoba, 1970. I want to acknowledge my debt to this piece of work for much of the material in this section.

²⁶*Winnipeg Telegram*, 10 June 1919. On the question of anti-German propaganda see Mott, "The 'Foreign Peril'," pp. 15-17.

²⁷*Winnipeg Tribune*, 29 January 1915.

²⁸Mott, "The 'Foreign Peril'," pp. 15-18.

²⁹*Ibid*. See also J. E. Rea, "The Politics of Conscience: Winnipeg After the Strike," Canadian Historical Association, *Historical Papers 1971*, pp. 276-288.

³⁰Mott, "The 'Foreign Peril'," p. 23. See also Masters, *Winnipeg General Strike*, pp. 29-30; and *Winnipeg Tribune*, 31 January 1919.

³¹See, for example, M. H. Marunchak, *The Ukrainian Canadians: A History* (Winnipeg, 1970), pp. 147-150.

³²Mott, "The 'Foreign Peril'," pp. 23-25.

³³Peter Krawchuk, *The Ukrainians in Winnipeg's First Century* (Toronto, 1974), p. 37.

³⁴See, for example, Turek, *Poles in Manitoba*, Chapter X.

³⁵Marlyn, *Under the Ribs of Death*, p. 117.

³⁶While economics and the efforts of real estate developers obviously had something to do with patterns of residential segregation in Winnipeg, voluntary segregation on the basis of ethnicity and class was far more important. See, for example, Fromson, "Acculturation or Assimilation"; and W. J. Carlyle, "Growth, Ethnic Groups and Socio-Economic Areas of Winnipeg," in Kuz, ed., *Winnipeg*, pp. 27-42.

³⁷It should be noted, however, that some of the new arrivals did cause disruptions within their own ethnic groups. See, for example, Krawchuk, *The Ukrainians in Winnipeg*, p. 46 and *passim*. Conflicts within ethnic groups had also occurred earlier. See, for example, H. H. Herstein, "The Growth of

the Winnipeg Jewish community and the Evolution of Its Educational Institutions," unpublished M.ED. thesis, University of Manitoba, 1964, pp. 28-33 and *passim.*

[38]The Depression did not bring an abrupt and complete end to discrimination. See, for example, L. Carpenter, "Deportation of Immigrants During the Depression," unpublished paper, Manitoba Archives, February 1973.

[39]Rea, "Roots of Prairie Society," p. 53.

[40]M. Davis and J. F. Krauter, *The Other Canadians: Profiles of Six Minorities* (Toronto, 1971), p. 128.

[41]W. L. Morton, *One University: A History of the University of Manitoba* (Toronto, 1957), pp. 17-147.

[42]For details of building activity during the 1920s see the following sources: Winnipeg Town Planning Commission, *Preliminary Reports,* Nos 1-9 (Winnipeg, 1946-1948); *Winnipeg Centennial Souvenir Book* (Winnipeg, 1974); Morton, *Manitoba;* and the *Winnipeg Free Press* and *Winnipeg Tribune.*

[43]City of Winnipeg, *Municipal Manuals.*

[44]City of Winnipeg, *Submission to Royal Commission on Dominion-Provincial Relations* (Winnipeg, 1937).

[45]City of Winnipeg Health Department, *Report of the Thirtieth Annual Survey of Vacant Houses . . .* (Winnipeg, 1947).

[46]*Ibid.,* pp. 15-16.

[47]The best account of this election is Rea, "Politics of Conscience." See also J. E. Rea, "The Politics of Class: Winnipeg City Council, 1919-1945," in C. Berger and R. Cook, eds., *The West and the Nation: Essays in Honour of W.L. Morton* (Toronto, 1976), pp. 232-249.

[48]Rea, "Politics of Conscience," p. 279.

[49]Paul Phillips, "'Power Politics': Municipal Affairs and Seymour James Farmer, 1909-1924," in A. R. McCormack and I. MacPherson, eds., *Cities in the West* (Ottawa, 1975), p. 162.

[50]Rea, "Politics of Conscience," *passim.*

[51]For a brief history of the company see Artibise, *Winnipeg,* pp. 93-94.

[52]Phillips, "Power Politics," p. 165.

[53]Phillips, *Ibid.,* p. 170.

[54]*Ibid.,* pp. 159-176.

[55]A. B. McKillop, "Citizen and Socialist: The Ethos of Political Winnipeg, 1919-1935," unpublished M.A. thesis, University of Manitoba, 1970, pp. 73-77. For an excellent article on Webb, see John H. Thompson, "The Political Career of Ralph H. Webb," *Red River Valley Historian,* Summer 1976, pp. 1-7.

[56]McKillop, "Citizen and Socialist," *passim.*

[57]*Ibid.,* p. 242.

[58]Jackson, *Centennial History of Manitoba,* p. 189.

[59]Peterson, "Ethnic and Class Politics in Manitoba," pp. 79-80.

[60]Martin Robin, *Radical Politics and Canadian Labour, 1880-1930* (Kingston, 1968), p. 207.

[61]For further information on Winnipeg's MP's see: McNaught, *A Prophet in Politics;* Leo Heaps, *The Rebel in the House: The Life and Times of A.A. Heaps, M.P.* (London, 1970); and J. K. Johnson, ed., *The Canadian Directory of Parliament, 1867-1967* (Ottawa, 1968).

[62]Jackson, *Manitoba,* p. 209. See also John H. Thompson, "The Prohibition Question in Manitoba, 1892-1928," unpublished M.A. thesis, University of Manitoba, 1969.

[63]Gray, *The Roar of the Twenties, passim;* Chafe, *Tales From Manitoba History,* pp. 156-166.

[64]Morton, *Manitoba,* pp. 415-417.

[65]H. Mardon, "The Arts in Winnipeg," *Westworld,* Vol. 2, No. 6 (Nov.-Dec. 1976), p. 7; D. Ahlgren, "A History of the Royal Winnipeg Ballet," unpublished paper, Manitoba Archives, 1973.

[66]Jackson, *Manitoba,* p. 225.

[67]Chafe, *Tales From Manitoba History,* p. 169.

CHAPTER THREE

[1]Kuz, ed., *Winnipeg, 1874-1974,* pp. 67-71.

[2]Winnipeg's prominence as a transportation centre was also bolstered during the post-World War II period by the development of air facilities. See, for example, L. O. Rowland, "Winnipeg: A Focal Aviation Point," *The Winnipeg Actimist,* August 1947, pp. 5, 18.

[3]T. J. Kuz, "Metropolitan Winnipeg: Inter-Urban Relationships", in Kuz, ed., *Winnipeg, 1874-1974,* pp. 7-20.

[4]L. O. Stone, *Urban Development in Canada* (Ottawa, 1967), pp. 187-196.

[5]Bellan, "The Development of Winnipeg," Chapter XIV.

[6]G. A. Nader, *Cities of Canada,* Volume I (Toronto, 1975), pp. 249-250.

[7]Metropolitan Corporation of Greater Winnipeg, *The Place of Winnipeg in the Economy of Manitoba* (1971), pp. 2-3.

[8]H. Mardon, "Winnipeg — HQ of Branch Offices," *Westworld,* Vol. 2, No. 4 (July-August 1976), p. 8.

[9]Morton, *Manitoba,* Chapter 20.

[10]*The Place of Greater Winnipeg in the Economy of Manitoba, passim.*

[11]A. F. J. Artibise, "Patterns of Population Growth and Ethnic Relationships in Winnipeg, 1874-1974," *Histoire sociale/Social History,* Vol. IX, No. 18 (November 1976) pp. 297-335.

[12]This analysis, and that of the Ukrainian and Jewish groups which follow, is based on Fromson, "Acculturation or Assimilation: A Geographic

Analysis of Residential Segregation of Selected Ethnic Groups: Metropolitan Winnipeg, 1951-1961."

[13]*Ibid.*, pp. 148-149.

[14]For an analysis of Juba's election see M. S. Donnelly, "Ethnic Participation in Municipal Government: Winnipeg, St. Boniface, and the Metropolitan Corporation of Greater Winnipeg," in Feldman and Goldrick, eds., *Politics and Government of Urban Canada* pp. 61-71. On the larger question of non-Anglo-Saxons' participation in public life see Krawchuk, *The Ukrainians in Winnipeg*; Stinson, *Political Warriors*; and Turek, *Poles in Manitoba*.

[15]Krawchuk, *The Ukrainians in Winnipeg*.

[16]Simonite was also a city alderman who was involved in several "conflict of interest" affairs. See Stinson, *Political Warriors*, pp. 258-260.

[17] M. McCracken, *Memories are Made of This* (Toronto, 1975), pp. 6-7.

[18]Good accounts of the flood can be found in the following sources: *Winnipeg Tribune*, 14 July 1970; *Winnipeg Centennial Souvenir Book*, pp. 92-97; Jackson, *Manitoba*, pp. 241-243.

[19]City of Winnipeg, *Municipal Manual 1962*, p. 25.

[20]Morton, *Manitoba*, pp. 488-489.

[21]The best account of planning activities in Winnipeg is R. D. Fromson, "Planning in a Metropolitan Area — The Experiment in Greater Winnipeg," unpublished M.C.P. thesis, University of Manitoba, 1970. I am indebted to this work for much of the material on planning in this section.

[22]See, *Summary of Recommendations, Comprehensive Plan for Greater Winnipeg* (Winnipeg, 1950).

[23]See, for example, S. G. Rich, "Metropolitan Winnipeg, 1943-1961," in McCormack and MacPherson, eds., *Cities in the West*, pp. 237-255.

[24]See, for example, *Urban Redevelopment Study No. 1 — South Point Douglas* (1959); and *Urban Renewal Study No. 5 — Selkirk-Avenue, CPR Yards, Salter Street, Main Street* (1960).

[25]Stinson, *Political Warriors*, pp. 322-326.

[26]P. Barber, "Class Conflict in Winnipeg Civic Politics: The Role of the Citizens' and Civic Election Organizations," unpublished paper, Manitoba Archives, March 1970, p. 10.

[27]P. Barber, "The Nationalization of the Winnipeg Electric Company: The Dispute Over Plan C," unpublished paper in possession of author, p. 1. I am indebted to Paul Barber for a copy of this paper.

[28]Morton, *Manitoba*, pp. 458-459.

[29]Barber, "Nationalization of the W.E.C.," *passim*.

[30]City of Winnipeg, *Municipal Manual 1961*, p. 191.

[31]*Ibid.*, p. 195.

[32]For discussions of post-1945 politics in Winnipeg, see J.E. Rea, *Parties and Power: An Analysis of Winnipeg City Council, 1919-1975* (Winnipeg, 1976); and "Reform Politics in Winnipeg: opening things up," *City Magazine*, Vol. 1, No. 3 (February-March 1975), pp. 29-36.

[33]Stinson, *Political Warriors*, pp. 280-291.

[34]P. H. Wichern, ed., *The Development of Urban Government in the Winnipeg Area* (Winnipeg, 1971), pp. 2-13.

[35]Rich, "Metropolitan Winnipeg."

[36]*Ibid.*

[37]See, for example, R. H. Kent, "The Dissonant Decade: A Study of Conflict Between the City of Winnipeg and the Metropolitan Corporation of Greater Winnipeg," unpublished M.B.A. thesis, University of Manitoba, 1970.

[38]*Winnipeg: An Explanation of its New Government* (Winnipeg, 1972).

[39]Rea, *Parties and Power*, pp. 20-23.

[40]Stinson served as a Winnipeg M.L.A. for fourteen years (1945-1959), and as leader of the CCF for eight (1953-1960). He was defeated in the 1959 election. See Stinson, *Political Warriors*, pp. 94-206.

[41]Peterson, "Ethnic and Class Politics in Manitoba," pp. 96-115.

[42]Johnson, *Canadian Directory of Parliament*.

[43]Morton, *Manitoba*, p. 466.

[44]Marvin Goody in *Books in Canada*, May, 1976, p. 23.

[45]H. Mardon, "Accounting for the Arts in Winnipeg," *Westworld*, Vol. 2, No. 6 (Nov.-Dec. 1976), p. 7.

Suggestions for Further Reading

The sources that are available to the reader who wishes to delve deeper into the history of Winnipeg are quite numerous. This brief section is meant only to highlight some of the material available; further information can be obtained from a recently published bibliography of materials relating to the city of Winnipeg and surrounding areas. This excellent source book is D.L. Sloane, J.M. Roseneder, M.J. Hernandez, eds., *Winnipeg: A Centennial Bibliography* (Winnipeg: Manitoba Library Association, 1974). It contains over 1400 separate listings of materials relating to the city. A more concise bibliography can be found in A.F.J. Artibise, "Canadian Urban Studies," *Communique: Canadian Studies*, Vol.3, No.3 (April 1977), pp. 96-101.

It should also be pointed out that much of the best material on Winnipeg is found in archives, city records, and newspapers. It cannot be too strongly stressed that anyone seriously interested in pursuing this subject must sooner or later refer to the records held by the City of Winnipeg, the Provincial Archives of Manitoba, and the Public Archives of Canada. The city's many newspapers must also be consulted, particularly the *Winnipeg Tribune* and the *Winnipeg Free Press*. Further, the *Transactions* of the Manitoba Historical and Scientific Society contain numerous specialized articles on Winnipeg. Rather than attempting to mention all of them here, it is recommended that the reader examine the entire series.

Finally, it must emphasized that the following listing of source materials is very selective; it represents the author's view of some of the better material available and has been included here only as a guide so that topics discussed in the book can be explored in more depth. The reader should also consult the "notes" section of this book and the bibliographies contained in many of the publications mentioned below as guides for further research into Winnipeg's history. Also useful is A.F.J. Artibise, "Researching Winnipeg," *Urban History Review*, No.2-72 (June 1972), pp. 14-18.

GENERAL SOURCES

Since the City of Winnipeg figures so prominently in the history of Manitoba, it is natural that W.L. Morton's, *Manitoba: A History* (Toronto: University of Toronto Press, 1957 [2nd edition, 1967]) contains much material on the city. This is an excellent introduction to the city since it places Winnipeg in a provincial context. The only detailed history published to date is Alan F.J. Artibise, *Winnipeg: A Social History of Urban Growth, 1874-1914* (Montreal: McGill-Queen's University Press, 1975). Although this book only takes the story to 1914, it does contain previews and forecasts as well. The reader should consult Alan F.J. Artibise and E.H. Dahl, *Winnipeg in Maps/Winnipeg par les cartes, 1816-1972* (Ottawa: Public Archives of Canada, 1975). This atlas consists of thirty-one facsimile reproductions of manuscript and printed maps of Winnipeg arranged in sequence to illustrate the city's history. Each map is accompanied by explanatory and interpretive comments. The maps are organized into four sections and each of these is introduced by a short essay.

Broader in scope than both these books is the *Winnipeg Centennial Souvenir Book* (Winnipeg: Provost Publications, 1974). Despite the fact that this publication is clearly in the class of promotional literature and is further marred by a large number of advertisements, it does contain a great deal of valuable material on the period 1874-1974. It is certainly the best publication to come out of Winnipeg's recent centennial celebrations. The most enjoyable introduction to Winnipeg's history, however, is *Winnipeg 100* (Winnipeg: Winnipeg Free Press, 1974). Compiled by Edith Paterson and other members of the *Free Press* staff, this volume is a photographic history

of the city. Although there is no accompanying text, the descriptions that go with the photographs tell a great deal about life in Winnipeg. Finally, the National Museum of Man and the National Film Board have published, as part of Canada's Visual History Series, a set of thirty slides with an accompanying essay and slide descriptions. This is A.F.J. Artibise, *Winnipeg: The Growth of a City, 1874-1914* (Ottawa, 1974).

SPECIFIC THEMES

The Origins and Incorporation of Winnipeg

The history of this early period of the city's history is covered in a number of books and articles. Besides Morton's *Manitoba*, some of the more important specialized studies are: A.S. Morton, *A History of the Canadian West to 1870-1871* (Toronto: University of Toronto Press, 1973); J.M. Gray, *Lord Selkirk of Red River* (Toronto: Macmillan Company of Canada, 1963); E.E. Rich, *The Fur Trade and the Northwest to 1857* (Toronto: McClelland and Stewart, 1967); A.C. Gluek, *Minnesota and the Manifest Destiny of the Canadian Northwest* (Toronto: University of Toronto Press, 1960); G.F.G. Stanley, *The Birth of Western Canada* (Toronto: University of Toronto Press, 1960); and Margaret McWilliams, *Manitoba Milestones* (Toronto: J.M. Dent and Sons, 1928). A specialized study of this early period is A.F.J. Artibise, "The Origins and Incorporation of Winnipeg," in A.R. McCormack and I. MacPherson, eds., *Cities in the West: Papers of the Western Canada Urban History Conference* (Ottawa: National Museum of Man, Mercury Series, 1975), pp. 5-25. The best contemporary accounts are: Alexander Begg and Walter R. Nursey, *Ten Years in Winnipeg* (Winnipeg: Times Publishing House, 1879); J.E. Steen and W. Boyce, *Winnipeg, Manitoba and Her Industries* (Chicago: Steen and Bouce, 1882); and W.T. Thompson and E.E. Boyer, *The City of Winnipeg* (Winnipeg: Thompson and Boyer, 1886).

Economic Growth and Metropolitan Development

The standard account of Winnipeg's economic development is Ruben C. Bellan, "The Development of Winnipeg as a Metropolitan Centre," unpublished Ph.D. thesis, Columbia University, 1958. Although this thesis has never been published, it is an excellent piece of work and is fully worth the effort of searching it out. It has not yet been superseded by anything of equal quality. Bellan's thesis should, however, be supplemented by a recently published volume that deals with Winnipeg for the entire period even while concentrating on more recent developments. This is Tony J. Kuz, ed., *Winnipeg, 1874-1974: Progress and Prospects* (Winnipeg: Manitoba Department of Industry and Commerce, 1974). Other useful works to consult are: J.M.S. Careless, "The Development of the Winnipeg Business Community, 1870-1890," *Transactions of the Royal Society of Canada*, 1970, 4th Series, pp. 239-254; R.C. Bellan, "Relief in Winnipeg: The Economic Background," unpublished M.A. thesis, University of Toronto, 1941; R.B. Short, "The Wholesale Function in Winnipeg," unpublished M.A. Thesis, University of Manitoba, 1973; and J.M.S. Careless, "Aspects of Urban Life in the West, 1870-1914," in Gilbert A. Stelter and Alan F.J. Artibise, eds., *The Canadian City: Essays in Urban History* (Toronto: McClelland and Stewart, 1977), pp. 125-141. Also useful is a slide set published by the Education Committee of the Canadian Association of Geographers entitled *Winnipeg: A Prairie Transportation Centre*. Compiled by M.S. Cowie as part of the Urban Profile Slide Series, this work contains twenty slides and a short explanatory booklet.

Population Growth and Ethnic Relationships

General discussions of population growth in Western Canada can be found in the following articles: L. Lenz, "Large Urban Places in the Prairie Provinces — Their Development and Location," in R.L. Gentlicore, ed., *Canada's Changing Geography* (Toronto: Prentice Hall Ltd., 1967), pp. 199-211; L.C. McCann, "Urban Growth in Western Canada, 1881-1961," *The Albertan Geographer*, No. 5 (1969), pp. 65-74; and Paul Voisey, "The Urbanization of the Canadian Prairies, 1871-1916," *Historie sociale/Social History*, Vol. VIII, No. 15 (May 1975), pp. 77-101. Two specialized studies that deal exclusively with Winnipeg are: W.J. Carlyle, "Growth, Ethnic Groups and Socio-Economic Areas of Winnipeg," in Kuz, ed., *Winnipeg, 1874-1974*, pp. 27-42; and A.F.J. Artibise, "Patterns of Population Growth and Ethnic Relationships in Winnipeg, 1874-1974," *Histoire sociale/Social History*, Vol. IX, No. 18 (November 1976), pp. 297-335.

The city's many ethnic groups have been examined in numerous studies. The best of these works is V. Turek, *The Poles in Manitoba* (Toronto: Polish Alliance Press, 1967). It contains several chapters devoted to this group's experiences in Winnipeg. The following also contain useful material on immigrants in Winnipeg, even though they are not as detailed as Turek's book: A. Chiel, *The Jews in Manitoba* (Toronto: Copp Clark, 1968); N. Kristjanson, *The Icelandic People in Manitoba* (Winnipeg: Wallingford Press, 1965); Peter Krawchuk, *The Ukrainians in Winnipeg's First Century* (Toronto: Kobzar Publishing Co., 1974); P. Yuzyk, *The Ukrainians in Manitoba: A Social History* (Toronto: University of Toronto Press, 1953); and Robert Painchaud, *Les francophones dans le monde des affaires de Winnipeg, 1870-1920* (Saint-Boniface: La Société Historique de Saint-Boniface, 1974). Considerable material on Winnipeg can also be found in M. H. Marunchak, *The Ukrainian Canadians: A History* (Winnipeg: Ukrainian Free Academy of Sciences, 1970). Winnipeg's vast ethnic press has also been the subject of a recent book published by the Canada Press Club. It is *The Multilingual Press in Manitoba* (Winnipeg, 1974).

The problems created by the city's large immigrant population have been examined in many books and articles. Two of these are reprints of contemporary works by J. S. Woodsworth, Superintendent of All Peoples' Mission. They are *My Neighbour* and *Strangers Within Our Gates* (Toronto: University of Toronto Press, 1972). Other important studies are: M. Mott, "The 'Foreign Peril': Nativism in Winnipeg, 1916-1923," unpublished M.A. thesis, University of Manitoba, 1970; W. J. Sisler, *Peaceful Invasion* (Winnipeg: Ketchen Printing Company, 1944); J. E. Rea, "The Roots of Prairie Society," in D. P. Gagan, ed., *Prairie Perspectives* (Toronto: Holt, Rinehart and Winston, 1970), pp. 46-57; and A.F.J. Artibise, "Divided City: The Immigrant in Winnipeg Society, 1874-1921," in G. A. Stelter and A.F.J. Artibise, eds., *The Canadian City: Essays in Urban History* (Toronto: McClelland and Stewart, 1977).

Winnipeg has also been the setting for several novels and some of these works give the reader an understanding of the city that cannot be gleaned from non-fictional work. The best is John Marlyn, *Under the Ribs of Death* (Toronto: McClelland and Stewart, 1957). Two penetrating discussions of the problems and attitudes of the Jewish community are: Adele Wiseman, *The Sacrifice* (Toronto: McClelland and Stewart, 1956); and Bess Kaplan, *Corner Store* (Winnipeg: Queenston House, 1975). Also noteworthy for its discussion of Winnipeg's Anglo-Saxon commercial class is D. Durkin, *The Magpie* (Toronto: University of Toronto Press, 1974 [Reprint of 1923 edition]).

The Winnipeg General Strike

The importance of this event in Winnipeg's history cannot be over emphasized. Fortunately, there is a wealth of literature on the subject. The most important works are: D. C. Masters, *The Winnipeg General Strike* (Toronto: University of Toronto Press, 1950); D. J. Bercuson, *Confrontation at Winnipeg: Labour, Industrial Relations and the General Strike* (Montreal: McGill-Queen's University Press, 1974); K. McNaught and D. J. Bercuson, *The Winnipeg Strike: 1919* (Don Mills, Longman Canada, 1974); J. E. Rea, ed., *The Winnipeg General Strike* (Toronto: Holt, Rinehart and Winston, 1973); and N. Penner, ed., *Winnipeg 1919: The Strikers' Own History of the Winnipeg General Strike* (Toronto: James Lorimer and Company, 1975). All these books contain good bibliographies for further reference.

The Urban Landscape

There is little good material dealing with Winnipeg's spatial growth during the past century with the exception of a thesis that deals with the period up to 1913. This is H. A. Hosse, "The Areal Growth and Functional Development of Winnipeg from 1870 to 1913," unpublished M.A. thesis, University of Manitoba, 1956. Another thesis that concentrates on a later period is also worth consulting. It is R. D. Fromson, "Acculturation or Assimilation: A Geographic Analysis of Residential Segregation of Selected Ethnic Groups: Metropolitan Winnipeg, 1951-1961," unpublished M.A. thesis, University of Manitoba, 1965. The city's street railway system is the subject of a short but interesting photographic study by H. W. Blake. *The Era of Streetcars in Winnipeg, 1881-1955* (Winnipeg: Highnell Printing Co., 1971) also contains a short essay about the early years of street car service in the city. A useful booklet on architecture in the city is W. P. Thompson, *Winnipeg Architecture: 100 Years* (Winnipeg: Queenston House, 1975). Also worth consulting are: R. R. Rostecki, *The Historic Architecture of Winnipeg, 1880-1920* (Winnipeg: privately published, 1972); and John W. Graham, *Winnipeg Architecture, 1831-1960* (Winnipeg: University of Manitoba Press, 1960). *The Metropolitan Development Plan* compiled by the Metropolitan Corporation of Greater Winnipeg in 1966 is a valuable aid to an understanding of the development of the city's landscape. It contains many helpful maps and charts. An excellent guide to the city's landscape is H. J. Selwood, *The Winnipeg Townscape: A Survey Guide* (Winnipeg: Manitoba Environmental Council, Study No. 7, 1976).

The material available on the formation of Metropolitan Winnipeg is abundant. In particular the following studies should be consulted: S. George Rich, "Metropolitan Winnipeg, 1943-1961," in McCormack and MacPherson, *Cities in the West*, pp. 237-268; P. H. Wichern, ed., *The Development of Urban Government in the Winnipeg Area* (Winnipeg: Department of Urban Affairs, Province of Manitoba, 1974); and Government of Manitoba, *Report and Recommendations of the Greater Winnipeg Investigating Commission* (Winnipeg: Queen's Printer, 1959).

The Urban Community: Society and Politics

There is little published material on society in Winnipeg. Perhaps the best available sources are the large number of novels set in Winnipeg, some of which have been mentioned above. Also, five of James Gray's recent books deal with social aspects of life in Winnipeg and all make for enjoyable reading. These books, all published by Macmillan of Canada, are: *The Winter Years* (1966): *The Boy from Winnipeg* (1970); *Red Lights on the Prairies* (1971); *Booze* (1972); and *The Roar of the Twenties* (1974). Another book that is worth consulting deals with the 1950s in Winnipeg. It is M. McCracken, *Memories Are Made of This* (Toronto: James Lorimer and Company, 1975). See also J. W. Chafe, *An Apple for the Teacher: A Centennial History of the Winnipeg School Division* (Winnipeg: Winnipeg School Division, 1967); and D. McArton, "75 Years in Winnipeg's Social History," *Canadian Welfare*, Vol. 25 (October 1949), pp. 11-19.

Studies of politics in Winnipeg are far more numerous. The best guide to the literature is P. H. Wichern, "Toward a History of Local Politics and Public Services in the Winnipeg Area: Research Notes and Sources," in P. H. Wichern, ed., *Studies in Winnipeg Politics* (Winnipeg: Department of Urban Affairs, Province of Manitoba, 1976), pp. 1-35. This volume also contains several other good essays on political subjects. Four other general studies are also worth consulting. They are: A.B. McKillop, "Citizen and Socialist: The Ethos of Political Winnipeg, 1919-1935," unpublished M.A. thesis, University of Manitoba, 1970; Paul Barber, "Class Conflict in Winnipeg Civic Politics: The Role of the Citizens and Civic Election Organizations," unpublished paper, Manitoba Archives, March 1970; Lloyd Stinson, *Political Warriors: Recollections of a Social Democrat* (Winnipeg: Queenston House, 1975); and J.E. Rea, *Politics and Power: An Analysis of Winnipeg City Council, 1919-1975* (Winnipeg: Department of Urban Affairs, Province of Manitoba, 1976). Several of Winnipeg's mayors have also been the objects of studies. These articles are: H. Huber, "Winnipeg's Age of Plutocracy: 1901-1914," unpublished paper, Manitoba Archives, 1970; Alan F.J. Artibise, "Mayor Alexander Logan of Winnipeg," *Beaver*, Outfit 304: 4 (Spring 1974), pp. 4-12; John H. Thompson, "The Political Career of Ralph H. Webb," *Red River Valley Historian*, Spring 1976, pp. 1-7; and Paul Phillips, " 'Power Politics': Municipal Affairs and Seymour James Farmer, 1909-1924," in A.R. McCormack and I. MacPherson, eds., *Cities in the West: Papers of the Western Canada History Conference* (Ottawa: National Museum of Man, Mercury Series, 1975), pp. 159-180.

Index

Acculturation, 52
Adanac Club, 88
Aitkins, J.A.M., 86
Alberta, 116
All People's Mission, 54-55
Alloway, Alderman, 84
Alloway and Champion Bank, 32, 36
American Fur Company, 13
American Party, 14
"Anti Social Evil Crusade", 104
Arbuthnot, John, 50
Architecture, 76, 78, 139
Armstrong, George, 111, 146
Armstrong's Point, 70
Ashdown, James H., 18, 46, 50, 55, 84, 98
Assimilation, of non-Anglo-Saxon immigrants, 44, 46, 50, 52, 54-55, 190; public school system as agent of, 46, 50, 52; social and structural, 52; cultural, 52; voluntary associations and private charities as agents of, 54-55
Assiniboia, 132; as suburb, 174; and Metropolitan Winnipeg, 184
Assiniboia, District of, 17, 184
Assiniboine River, 11; 1826 flood of, 12; dike system, 178
Assiniboine Park, 133, 138, 139
Austin, F. C., 142
Austro-Hungarian Society, 128

Bank of Montreal Building, 180
Bannatyne, A.G.B., 18, 84
Baptist Church, 105
Bawlf, Nicolas, 32
Begg, Alexander, 18, 20
Bird, C.J., 20

Blondal, Patricia, 194
Boer War, 42
The Boy from Winnipeg, 44
Boyer, E.E., 28
Bray, R.E., 114
Britain, 28; immigrants from, 40
British Columbia, municipal government in, 184
British North America, 24
Brooks, George B., 80
Brotherhood of Ukrainian Catholics, 175
Brown, George, 14
Brydges, C.J., 84
Builder's Exchange, 88
Burrows-Keewatin area, 180

Caledonia Curling Club, 84
Calgary, 46, 116, 122, 166, 170
Campbell, Douglas, 188
Campbell, George H., 86
Canadian Broadcasting Company (CBC), 156
Canadian Fire Insurance Company, 36
Canadian Goodwill Industries, 156
Canadian Imperial Bank of Commerce, 36, 62
Canadian Industrial Exhibition Association, 88
Canadian Manufacturers' Association, 88
Canadian National Railway (CNR), 70
Canadian Northern Railway, 36
Canadian Pacific Railway (CPR), Manitoba route proposals for, 24, 26; Winnipeg negotiations for main line of, 26; end of monopoly, 30, 32; effect of on Winnipeg, 56, 57; and North End, 64, 66
Carleton Club, 88
Carruthers, G.F., 86
Centennial Centre, 180, 190
Central Immigration Hall, 156

Charleswood, 132, 174
Chown, Gordon, 190
Churchill, Gordon, 190
Citizen's Committee of One Thousand, 111, 114
Citizen's Election Committee, 181
Citizen's League, 142, 144, 146
City Planning Commission, 178
The City of Winnipeg, The Capital of Manitoba, and The Commercial Railway & Financial Metropolis of the Northwest, 28
Civic Music League, 178
Cockshutt Plow Company, 58
Commercial Club, 88
Commercial elite, optimism of, 28, 30; growth ethic of, 30; and labour, 38; and municipal politics, 84, 86, 144, 146, 188; dominance of, 98, 99, 100, 102. See also Winnipeg Board of Trade
Congregationalist Church, 105
Coolican, Jim, 26, 28
Co-operative Commonwealth Federation (CCF), 142, 146, 182, 188, 190
Cornish, Francis Evans, 22, 78
Coulter, Garnet, 176, 179
Craig, Reverend, 156

Dafoe, John W., 50
Dawson Route, 23-24
Deacon, T.R., 106
Depression, 132; effects of, 122, 126; building demolition during, 139, 142; relief assistance during, 156
Diefenbaker, John G., 190
Dixon, Fred, 146
Dominion Labour Party, 142
DuVal, F., 105

East Kildonan, 132, 138, 174
Eaton Company, T., 138
Edelweiss Brewery, 128
Eden, Alderman, 84
Edmonton, 26, 116, 122, 166, 170
Education, language of instruction issue, 50, 52, 128; compulsory, 50, 52, 128. *See also* Public schools
Emerson, 18
Ethnic groups, German, 128, 132, 190; Ukrainian, 128, 130, 132, 174, 175, 190; British, 130, 174; Jewish, 132, 174, 190; Polish, 132, 190; Anglo-Saxon, 190. *See also* Ethnic relations; Immigrants
Ethnic relations, and dominance of Anglo-Protestant immigrants, 42, 98, 99, 100, 102; post-World War I, 126, 128, 130, 132; and ethnic and residential segregation, 68, 76, 132, 173, 174; and integration of "New Canadians", 174-175. *See also* Immigrants
Evans, William Sanford, 98, 99, 105, 106

Farmer, S.J., 143, 144, 146, 188
Film Exchange Building, 138
Folklorama, 175
Fonseca, W. G., 55
The Forks, 20
Fort Garry, Hotel, 62; as suburb, 132, 174
Fort Garry, Upper, 17, 42, 55, 57; as commercial centre, 14; Royal Hotel in, 14; McKenney's store in, 16
Fort Gibraltar, 11
Fort Osborne, 114
Fort Osborne Barracks, 17, 62
Fort Rouge, 68, 76
Forum Block, 142
Fur trade, 11, 13, 17-18

Garson, S.S., 188
Gault Company, 62
German Society, 54
The Globe, on annexation of Red River Colony, 14
Globe & Mail, on social vice in Winnipeg, 105
Grand Trunk Pacific Railway, 36
Grant, Cuthbert, 12
Gray, Charles F., 114, 143
Gray, James, 44
Great West Life Assurance Company, 36

Greater Winnipeg, plan for, 179
Greater Winnipeg Investigating Committee, 184
Greater Winnipeg Plan Commission, 178
Greater Winnipeg Sanitary District, 184
Greater Winnipeg Transit Commission, 182, 184
Greater Winnipeg Water District, 184
Green, Tom, 181
Gurney, Mary Irene, 98

Hamilton, Charles, 86
Heaps, A.A., 114, 152
Heubach, F.W., 133
Historical and Scientific Society of Manitoba, 80, 84
Hogg, Dr., 181
Housing, shortage, 142; public, 179-180
Hudson, Henry, 11
Hudson Bay, 13, 14
Hudson's Bay Company, 12, 138, 142; attitude of toward settlement of Northwest, 11, 13; effect of monopoly of on Red River Colony, 13-14; struggle against free traders, 13-14; opposition of to Winnipeg's incorporation, 20, 22; and land speculation in Winnipeg, 55-56
Hurst, W.D., 176
Hutchings, E.F., 38

Icelandic Lutheran Synod, 105
Icelandic (Progressive) Society, 54
Immigrants, influx of, 40; dominance of Anglo-Protestant, 42, 98, 99, 100, 102; assimilation of, 42, 44, 46, 50, 52, 54-55, 190; Jewish, 42, 46, 50, 64; Scandinavian, 42, 50, 64, 68, 74; German, 42, 50, 64, 68, 74; Ontario, 40, 42, 64; British, 40, 42, 64; Slavic, 46, 50, 64; Ukrainian, 50; Polish, 50; and language of instruction, 50, 52, 128; and compulsory education, 50, 52, 128; economic and social problems of, 52; and voluntary associations, 54-55
Imperial Home Reunion Movement, 36
Independent Citizen's Election Committee, 188
Independent Labour Party, 99
Industrial Development Board of Manitoba, 116
Inkster Industrial Park, 180
International Purity Federation, 104
Irish Association, 54
Ivens, William, 111

Joint Executive Committee on Metropolitan Planning for Greater Winnipeg, 179
Juba, Stephen, 144, 174-175, 181, 182, 186, 190

Kennedy, William N., 80, 152
Kildonan, 76. *See also* East Kildonan; North Kildonan; West Kildonan
Kildonan Park, 138, 139; Rainbow Stage in, 178, 194
Kirk, Jessie, 100
Kittson, Norman W., 13
Knights of Labor, 38, 99
Knowles, Stanley H., 152, 190
Konantz, Margaret, 190

Labour, and growth of the trade union movement, 36, 38; strikes, 38; organizations, 99, 100; internal unrest, 146; and City Council, 182; and municipal politics, 188. *See also* Winnipeg General Strike
Lake Manitoba, 24, 156
Lake Winnipeg, 12, 23, 156
Lake of the Woods, 23
Lake of the Woods Yacht Club, 98
Laurence, Margaret, 194
Lepine, Ambroise, 78
Livesay, Dorothy, 194
Logan, Alexander, 80, 86
Lombard Place, 180
Lord's Day Act, 105
Ludwig, Jack, 194
Luxton, William Fisher, 78
Lyon, W.H., 84

McCormick Harvesting Machine Company, 58
Macdonald, John A., 22, 24, 26
Macdonnell, Miles, 11
McGillvary Boulevard Industrial Area, 180
McGregor, Armory, 156
McKenney, Henry, 14, 16
Mackenzie, Alexander, 24, 26
McMillan, Daniel, 84, 142
McWilliams, Margaret, 100
Main Street Bridge, 70
Manitoba, 11, 166; and Confederation, 14, 16-17; influx of immigrants into, 42; bilingual schools issue in, 52; voting rights for women in, 100;

reorganization of hydro-electric industry in, 181-182
Manitoba Act, 17
Manitoba Centennial Commission, 190
Manitoba Children's Act, 52
Manitoba Club, 62, 84, 88
Manitoba College of Physicians and Surgeons, 84
Manitoba Free Press, 50; on population growth, 16-17; on necessity of railway service, 24; on the Dawson Route, 24; on the wholesale trade, 32; on bicycles as transportation, 70
Manitoba government, and Winnipeg's incorporation, 20; relations with Winnipeg, 170, 172; and intermunicipal affairs, 184, 186; Bill 62, 184; 1969 election, 186, 188
Manitoba Hydro Electric Board, 182
Manitoba Institute of Technology *see* Red River Community College
Manitoba Law Society, 84
Manitoba Liquor Control Act, 152
Manitoba Medical College, 132
Manitoba Music Festival, 156
Manitoba Power Commission, 181, 182
Manitoba Public Schools Act, 50
Manitoba Theatre Centre, 156, 190, 194
Manitoba Trade Review, 18
The Manitoban, on incorporation, 20
Marlborough (Olympia) Hotel, 138
Marlyn, John, 130, 194
Martin, E.D., 105, 106
Maryland Bridge, 70
Massey-Harris Co. Ltd., 58
Maybank, Ralph, 152, 190
Medical Arts Building, 138
Merchants' Bank, 62
Metis, and Seven Oaks Massacre, 12; and conflicts within Red River Colony, 14
Methodist Church, 105
Methodist-Episcopal Church, 62
Metropolitan Planning Commission, 179, 184
Metropolitan Planning Committee, 178, 179
Metropolitan Winnipeg, 172, 184; Council, 186
Midland Railway, 62
Minnesota, Territory of, 14
Minto Armory, 156
Mississippi Valley, 14
Montreal Urban Community, 184

Moral and Social Reform League, 104-105
Morris, Alexander, 26
Morrison, H.C., 179
Morton, R.E., 176
Mulvey, Robert, 55
Mulvey, Stewart, 55
Mutch, Leslie A., 152, 190

Nanton, Augustus, 142
National Association of Real Estate Exchanges, 88
"New Canadians", 174-175
New Democratic Party (NDP), 142, 188, 190
Norris, T.C., 52
North Kildonan, as suburb, 174
North Star Inn Hotel, 180
North West Company, attitude of toward settlement of Northwest, 11; hostility of toward Red River Colony, 12
Northern Trust Company, 32
Northwest Commercial Travellers' Association, 88
Northwest Territories, 17
Nor'Wester, 14, 16

Ogilvie Flour Mills, 66
One Big Union, 110, 128, 142
Ontario, immigrants from, 40
Orlikow, David, 190
Orpheum Theatre, 62, 152
Osborne Street Bridge, 70
Ottawa-Carleton, Regional Municipality of, 184

Pacific Scandal, 24
Panama Canal, 116
Pantages Theatre, 62, 152
Pembina, 13
Penner, Jacob, 179
The People's Voice (The Voice), 38
Place Louis Riel, 180
Plain Facts About the New City Hall, 80
Playhouse Theatre, 142
Point Douglas, 11, 16, 55, 56, 64, 66, 68, 105, 139
Polish National Catholic Church, 105
Polish Teachers' Training School, 50
Polo Park, 138, 178
Port Moody, 26
Portage la Prairie, 18

Prangman, Peter, 12
Presbyterian Church, 105
Prince Albert, 26
Prince Edward Island, 11
The Problem of Social Vice in Winnipeg, 105
Prosvita Reading Society, 175
Public schools, as agents of assimilation, 46, 50, 52. *See also* Education
Public Schools Act of Manitoba *see* Manitoba Public Schools Act
Puttee, Arthur W., 38, 146

Queen, John, 111, 144, 146, 156

Red Cross, 176
Red River, 11, 24, 26; 1826 flood of, 12; 1950 flood of, 176, 178; dike system, 178
Red River Colony, 20; founding of, 11-12; and North West Company, 12; economy of, 12; population growth of, 12-13; government of, 13; effect of Hudson's Bay Company monopoly on, 13; effect of free trade on, 14; and annexation proposals from Canada and United States, 14; internal conflicts in, 14; Winnipeg as part of, 16, 170; Wolseley expedition to, 23
Red River Community College, 180
Red River Exhibition, 178
Red River Floodway, 178
Red River Rebellion, 14, 16, 98
Red River Valley, 14
Regina, 116
Richardson, James H., 116
Riding Mountain National Park, 156
Riel, Louis, 98
Riggs, R.A., 146
Riley, Alderman, 50
River Heights, as suburb, 174
Robertson Block, 62
Robinson's Department Store, 142, 156
Roblin, Duff, 178, 188, 190
Roblin, R.P., 50, 52
Rogers, Robert, 142, 152
Roman Catholic Church, 74
Royal Alexandra, 180
Royal Bank Building, 180
Royal Caledonian Curling Association, 98
Royal Commission on Bilingualism and Bicul-

turalism, Report of, 175
Royal North West Mounted Police, 111, 114
Royal Winnipeg Ballet, 156, 194
Russell, R.B., 111
Russian Orthodox Greek Church, 105
Russian Revolution, 126, 128
Ruthenian Catholic Church, 105
Ruthenian National Society, 54
Ruthenian Training School for Teachers, 50
Ryan T., 50, 86

St. Andrews, and Metropolitan Winnipeg, 184
St. Andrew's Society, 54,80
St. Boniface, 74, 76, 132, 138
St. Charles Country Club, 98
St. George's Snowshoe Club, 98
St. George's Society, 80
St. James, 74, 76, 132, 139; as suburb, 174
St. James-Winnipeg Airport Commission, 184
St. John's College, 133
St. John's Park, 68
St. Norbert, and Metropolitan Winnipeg, 184
St. Paul, 14, 23, 26
St. Paul's College, 133
St. Peter and Paul Society, 54
St. Vital, 76, 132, 133, 138, 139
St. Vital Park, 139
Salvation Army, 54, 176
Saskatchewan, 116, 166
Saskatoon, 116
Sayer, Pierre G., 13
Scandinavian Anti-Saloon League, 105
Schreyer, Edward R., 188
Schultz, Dr., 55
Scott, Thomas, 78
Scott Nursing Mission, Margaret, 54
Selkirk, 26
Selkirk, Earl of, 11
Seven Oaks Massacre, 12
Sharpe, George, 182
Shearer, J.G., 104, 105, 106
Sherman, L.R., 190
Shoal Lake aqueduct, 102, 104
Simonite, C.E., 176
Sons of England, 54
Sparling, 143, 144
Steinkopf, Maitland, 190

Stewart, A.M., 190
Stinson, Lloyd, 188
Stovel's Printing Company, 62
Strand Theatre, 152

Thompson, W.T., 28
Toronto, Metropolitan, 184
Town Planning Commission, plan for Greater Winnipeg, 179
Town Topics on Boer War, 42
Trainor, O.C., 190
Trans Canada Airline, 139
Transcona, 76, 132; as suburb, 174; and Metropolitan Winnipeg, 184
Tuxedo, 132
Tuxedo Armory, 156

Ukrainian Canadian Committee, 175
Ukrainian Co-operative Dairy, 175
Ukrainian Labor Temple, 175
Ukrainian People's Home, 175
Ukrainian Self-Reliance League, 175
Under the Ribs of Death, 130
Unicity, 133, 182, 184, 186, 188
Union Bank, 62
Union of Canadian Municipalities, 144
Union Club, 88
Unitarian Conference, 105
United Grain Growers, 32
United States, proposal to annex Red River Colony, 14; and trade tariffs, 30
University of Manitoba, 62, 133, 180
University of Winnipeg, 138, 180
Urban Renewal and Rehabilitation Board, 180

Vancouver, 40, 130; as rival trade centre, 116
Victoria, 46
The Voice see The People's Voice
Voluntary associations, as agents of assimilation, 54-55
Vulcan Iron and Engineering Works, 38, 66

Walker Theatre, 62, 142, 152
Webb, R.H., 116, 144
West Kildonan, 76, 132, 174
Western Canadian Immigration Association, 42, 88

Western Canadian Real Estate Association, 88
White, William, 142
Whiteshell Provincial Park, 156
Whittier Park, 138
Winnipeg, as part of Red River Colony, 16; origin of name, 16; growth of (1870-1874), 16-17, 23; rise as commercial centre, 17-18, 114; incorporation of, 18, 20; first civic election in, 22, 78; municipal services in, 22, 66; railway as key to growth of, 23-24; CPR route through, 24, 26; real estate boom in, 26, 28, 57, 84; uncontrolled growth of, 26, 30, 178; rise as metropolitan centre, 26, 28, 30, 32, 36, 38, 166, 170, 172; boosterism, 28, 30; rise as wholesale trade centre, 30, 32, 62, 114; as headquarters of Canadian grain trade, 32, 58; rise as financial centre, 32, 36; industrial development in, 36, 114, 116; population growth of, 38, 40, 42, 44, 130, 173; ethnic relations in, 42, 44, 46, 50, 52, 54-55, 126, 128, 130, 132, 173-175; language of instruction in, 50, 52, 128; compulsory education in, 50, 52, 128; ward systems in, 56, 57, 133; industrial land use in, 56-57; commercial land use in, 56-57, 62; influx of immigrants into, 57; Ward 1, 57; Ward 2; 57, 62; Ward 3, 57, 64; Ward 4, 57, 62; Ward 5, 57, 64, 66, 68; Ward 6, 57, 64; Ward 7, 57, 64; Central Core, 58, 62, 64, 66; South End, 62, 66, 68, 70, 74, 76; West End, 62, 66, 68, 70, 74, 76; North End, 64, 66, 68, 76, 102, 104, 132, 174; residential segregation in, 64, 66, 68, 74, 173, 174; public transportation in, 66, 70, 132; and suburban development, 70, 74, 76, 78, 132, 173; municipal politics in, 78, 80, 84, 86, 88, 98-100, 102, 104-106, 142-144, 146, 181-182, 184, 186, 188, 190; 1884 election, 84, 86; community and cultural life in, 88, 98, 152, 156, 190, 194; women's rights in, 100; Municipal Act amendment, 100; social problems in, 102, 104; moral reform movement in, 104, 106; recovery from World War I, 114, 116; decline as metropolitan centre of West, 116, 122; unemployment in, 116, 122, 126; and the Depression, 122, 126, 139, 142, 156; development of park facilities for, 138-139; 1919 election, 143, 144; 1922 election, 143-144; voting patterns in, 146, 152, 188, 190; decline of rural puritanism in, 152; post-World War II optimism in, 163; and

national economy, 166, 170, 172; relations with provincial government, 170, 172; as cosmopolitan centre, 174-175; post-World War II construction in, 176; and 1950 flood, 176, 178; and urban sprawl, 178-179; urban planning in, 178-179, 186; public housing in, 179-180; building boom in (1960-1970), 180; hydro-electric power issue in, 181-182; decline of partisan politics in, 182, 184; and metropolitan government, 184, 186. *See also* Greater Winnipeg; Metropolitan Winnipeg
Winnipeg Act of Incorporation, 20
Winnipeg Arena, 178
Winnipeg Art Gallery, 190, 194
Winnipeg Art League, 88
Winnipeg Arts and Crafts Society, 88
Winnipeg Baseball Stadium, 178
Winnipeg Blue Bombers, 194
Winnipeg Board of Arbitration, 32
Winnipeg Board of Control, 102
Winnipeg Board of Trade, 80, 84, 105, 116, 144; and CPR route, 26; and end of CPR monopoly, 30, 32; and freight concessions, 32; methods of attracting immigrants, 40, 42; role of in municipal politics, 84, 86
Winnipeg Canoe Club, 98
Winnipeg Chamber of Commerce, 144
Winnipeg Citizen's Election Committee *see* Citizen's Election Committee
Winnipeg Citizen's Railway Committee, 26
Winnipeg City Council, 126; structure of first, 22; and CPR main line proposals, 26; methods of attracting immigrants, 40, 42; and appointment

of Town Planning Commission, 179; and the Urban Renewal and Rehabilitation Board, 180; and hydro-electric power issue, 181-182; and Winnipeg Election Committee, 182; and Metropolitan Winnipeg, 186
Winnipeg City Hall, 58, 62, 80
Winnipeg City Hydro, 181
Winnipeg Convention Centre Complex, 180
Winnipeg Cricket Association, 98
Winnipeg Development and Industrial Bureau, 36, 88; and immigration, 42
Winnipeg Electric and Street Railway Company, 38, 70, 176; and 1922 municipal election, 143-144; and reorganization of hydro-electric industry, 181-182
Winnipeg Free Press, on prostitution, 105; political support of, 106; on public power monopoly, 181
Winnipeg General Hospital, 22, 62, 80, 84, 178
Winnipeg General Strike, 52, 109-111, 114, 126, 128; effect of on municipal politics, 142-144, 146
Winnipeg Grain Exchange Building, 58
Winnipeg Grain and Produce Exchange, 32
Winnipeg Little Theatre, 156
Winnipeg Ministerial Association, 38, 104
Winnipeg Musicians' Association, 156
Winnipeg Operatic and Dramatic Society, 88
Winnipeg Parks Board, 138
Winnipeg Police Commission, 105
Winnipeg Property Owners' Association, 86
Winnipeg Real Estate Exchange, 88
Winnipeg Rowing Club, 98

Winnipeg Saturday Post, on labour strikes, 38
Winnipeg School Board, 46, 50
Winnipeg Sewage Disposal System, 144
Winnipeg Stadium, 178
Winnipeg Stock Exchange, 36
Winnipeg Studio Club, 88
Winnipeg Swimming Club, 98
Winnipeg Symphony Orchestra, 156, 194
Winnipeg Telegram, on Slavic immigrants, 46; political support of, 105; on "aliens", 128
Winnipeg Theatre, 62
Winnipeg Times, on municipal management, 84
Winnipeg Tourist and Convention Bureau, 116
Winnipeg Trades and Labor Council, 38, 52, 99, 105, 110
Winnipeg Tribune, on Ukrainian teachers' journal, 50; on anti-alien sentiments, 128; and relief assistance during Depression, 156; on Winnipeg Electric Company, 181; on public power monopoly, 181
Winnipeg Women's Art Association, 88
Winnipeg Women's Labour League, 143
Winnipeg Women's Musical Club, 88
Wiseman, Adele, 194
Wolseley, G. J., 23
Women's Christian Temperance Union, 46, 105
Woodsworth, J.S. 52, 54, 146
World War I, 76, 132; effects of, 109, 110
World War II, 132, 156

Young, George, 16

Zionist Society, 54